Mary Price

85

LUKE FILDES, R.A.

A Victorian Painter

Luke Fildes, a self-portrait
1918

LUKE FILDES, R.A.

A Victorian Painter

By L. V. Fildes

London
MICHAEL JOSEPH

First published in Great Britain by
MICHAEL JOSEPH LTD
26 Bloomsbury Street
*London, W.C.*1
1968
© 1968 *by L. V. Fildes*

Printed in Great Britain by
Billing & Sons Limited, Guildford and London

TO
my Brothers and Sisters,
who have reminded me of things
I had forgotten, and told me others I
had not known

CONTENTS

ILLUSTRATIONS

AUTHOR'S NOTE

This book was written seven or eight years ago. Circumstances have prevented my undertaking any general revision of it. I think I ought, however, to state that the Tate Gallery's comments on page 122, about my father's picture, *The Doctor*, no longer apply, having subsequently been replaced, in the Official Guide, by a more appreciative reference to the picture.

THE ARGUMENT

A friend of mine who filled the dual role of latter-day painter and respecter of tradition was remarking upon the little that he and his contemporaries knew of the late Victorians. Men who had come on the scene during the Edwardian and the neo-Georgian eras had been plentifully publicized, "But," he added, "we don't know enough about the Golden Age of the 'Eighties and 'Nineties. You," turning to me, "must remember those times! Why don't you write something about your father and his friends, how they lived and what was their approach to Art?"

I had thought of attempting something of the kind soon after my father's death, and had put the idea aside. At the time it looked like a full-dress affair in the form of a "Life", and materials for a full-dress Life were lacking.

There was another reason why I had not gone on with the idea. The Press, not content to salute with one accord my father on his death for the "high position he held in the world of art", "the last of the great painters of the Victorian Era", "the Grand Old Man of the Royal Academy", and more in the same vein, had taken the occasion to tilt at the school of criticism that in recent years had been inveighing against pictures which "told a story". "Luke Fildes", one obituary summed up, "stood for something in art which it has become a fashion to sneer at—the story picture." People who "affected to despise" his picture *The Doctor* were called "critical exquisites"; disparagement of a picture for having a dramatic appeal was characterized as "paltry criticism". And so on. Of course, the critics who were themselves being criticized had something to say in reply, and they had their opportunity within a twelve month after my father's death when a number of his works were shown at a Memorial Exhibition at the Royal Academy. Thus my father's memory was being mixed up in a sort of controversy, and I had neither the wish nor the qualification to take part in it.

xiii

But all that had been over thirty years ago. The controversy over pictures which "tell a story" had worked itself out, and my painter friend's suggestion did not require any controversial subject to be raised. It would not do, though, to keep only to a period within my own memory, my father was high in his profession by the time I was born. Besides, without the modest beginning and the contrast of ultimate achievement I should be missing the savour of a Success Story.

There will often be a second figure in and out of the story, my mother's brother, Henry Woods. He was my father's closest friend and confidant in the art world for more than sixty years. Indeed, my first thought was to make the book "Two Victorian Painters". My Uncle Harry, though a popular and devoted member of the Royal Academy for forty years, did not achieve eminence with the Public as did my father. Nevertheless he painted Venice—where he made his home for the greater part of his working life—with a charm, an understanding, a fidelity in representing the Venetian scene, which many painters in the long line of Venice addicts have failed to catch.

Being so closely related to a pair of Royal Academicians I can hardly escape being prejudiced, I confess, to a bias towards the traditional. This does not really matter, as "odious comparison" between Victorian Painting and Modern Art are not part of my purpose. I had better complete my confession, however. I had a third Royal Academician for my god-father and a fourth for my father-in-law. To complete the tally, my mother was an R.A. Exhibitor. All this I set down in a spirit of boastfulness— I know of no one else with such a record, for though I share with my brothers and sisters items one, two and five, I have items three and four all to myself.

And now, as I reach the threshold of my opening chapter, I feel a waft of Victorianism in the air. It may come from that habitat of Victorian Fame—the Lecture Theatre at the "V. and A."—where, not so very long ago, I heard a lecturer describing my father and Frank Holl, R.A., as "the two Social-Realists" among painters of the Victorian Scene.

I

A COUNTRY STUDENT COMES TO TOWN
1843-1863

My father was born on the 18th of October, 1843.

Nature auspiciously contrived that the event should be on the Day of St Luke, the Patron Saint of Painters. A puritan tradition of biblical names in the family caused the boy to be given the name of Samuel as well as that of his Patron Saint, and it was as "S. L. Fildes" that he was to make his reputation as a black-and-white artist before turning to painting and climbing the heights as simply Luke Fildes.

His parents were in a small way. His father, James Fildes, had some minor employment with the Port Authority at Liverpool after service in the Merchant Marine. They lived at No. 22 Standish Street, a street which has since been rebuilt, and there my father had his home for the first ten years of his life. His memories of that childhood had become indistinct by the time he reached manhood, for at the age of eleven he was taken away from home by his grandmother to Chester for reasons he never comprehended and was adopted by her.

This grandmother, Mary Fildes, was a remarkable person. As a young married woman, in the years following the Napoleonic Wars, she had taken part in the Reform Movement which was being organized amongst the mill-hands of Lancashire by William Cobbett and Henry Hunt —the famous "Orator" Hunt. The climax to that activity of hers had come on the stricken field of Peterloo, so called out of irony when men's minds were still running on the recent glories of Waterloo. History books tell of how one August afternoon in 1819 "a vast but orderly concourse of working men and women" assembled on St Peter's Field outside Manchester where, on the orders of the magistrates, they were charged by troops of Yeomanry. A number of the "orderly concourse" were killed and several hundred seriously wounded.

Mary Fildes was one of the seriously wounded. She had driven to the place of assembly on the box-seat of the carriage which brought "Orator" Hunt, and she had mounted with him on the platform from which he was to address the concourse. She was holding aloft a pole with a Cap of Liberty on top, as may be seen in a contemporary print. In the confusion of the subsequent massacre she was tumbled off the platform and, to quote an account based upon the evidence of eye-witnesses: "Mrs. Fildes, hanging suspended by a nail in the platform which had caught her white dress, was slashed across her exposed body by one of the brave cavalry."

The years went by and Mary Fildes became more than a local celebrity. She was in with the Chartists of the 'Forties. But at last she exchanged the tensions of Manchester for the relaxation of Chester, and settled down as the proprietress of the 'Shrewsbury Arms' in Frodsham Street. From there, in the first year of the Crimean War, she descended upon my father's parents in Liverpool and, as I have told, took her grandson away and adopted him.

So far, the copying and colouring of illustrations out of books—as any child might do—would seem to have been all the interest the boy had in art, but after the move to Chester a more lively interest began to show itself. At the school where his grandmother was sending him as a day-boy, drawing was one of the subjects taught as an "extra". His grandmother, however, did not let him take it, but so interested was he in the other boys' drawing that he used to stay behind after school hours to watch them and then, in imitation, make drawings by himself in the evenings at his grandmother's.

One day he saw an advertisement of evening art-classes at the local Mechanics' Institute. He obtained his grand-

mother's permission to attend them. Three months later
the master in charge said: "You ought to be educated for an
artist."

By that time my father was fourteen years old. The notion
of his becoming an artist by no means pleased his grandmother, whose ideas about his future were "something
more substantial". It was not in order that he should be an
artist that she had consented to his attending the evening
classes. She suspected artists were a set of vagabonds. A
struggle of wills started between the opinionated and obsti-
nate grandmother and the grandson who was finding that
he had a will no less strong of his own. The grandmother
gave way, as she did on every succeeding round of the
struggle between two strong characters, without any lessen-
ing of their affection. For him she was always "The Indulgent One".

When my father decided that he wanted to be an artist
he had never seen a masterpiece. Instinct soon told him,
though, that the art-classes at Chester were not the road he
ought to be following. The master in charge lacked artistic
sense and imagination, on top of which he had promoted my
father to be a pupil-teacher, and there he was—at the age
of fifteen!—teaching perspective and anatomy to the serious
interference of his own studies. A letter from his father
could have brought him only cold comfort: "I am glad to
hear you have begun your teaching, which I trust may
lead to a means of earning a competency for you through
life."

Just when he was feeling the full frustration of having
to teach when he wanted still to be learning, he had the good
luck to become acquainted with a water-colour painter
named Alfred Sumner, who lived in Chester. Sumner began
giving him lessons. He made him work from nature. He
was the first artist my father had met; they went for walks
in the country, Sumner holding forth on Art, talking "shop"
and doing his pupil a power of good.

This opening of my father's eyes to something of what an
artist was, unsettled him still more and, when not yet quite
seventeen, he decided on his own initiative to move to the
School of Art in Warrington, well known in the North

Country for the excellence of its teaching under J. Christmas Thompson.

His schooling in every subject but art now perforce came to an end; there was no time for anything else. When, therefore, in after years he passed, wherever he went, as being a man of cultivation and distinction, it was the result of much self-improvement at all sorts of odd moments, fortified by that happy communing with agreeable thoughts and things which sits so easily upon members of the artist brotherhood.

One of the pupils at the Warrington School when young Fildes arrived there, was a boy named Henry Woods. Two-and-a-half years the younger, Woods had been at the school three years already. He was something of a prodigy and he boasted at having won a Department of Science and Art bronze medal at Warrington a year younger than my father had at Chester. The two became each other's greatest friend and artistic confidant for life.

Henry Woods was the eldest of a family of nine brothers and sisters whose parents lived in Warrington. Half way down the scale was a small child, Fanny. Years were to go by before the new friend met Fanny Woods, fell in love with, and married, her.

Fildes had come to his new school filled with high hopes, but the little that remains of the work he did in those Warrington days is dreary copying of engravings and lithographs. And he was still a pupil teacher!

Plans, however, were taking shape up in London which were to open a way for him and many another budding art student the length and breadth of the country. The new Museum of Fine and Applied Art—the South Kensington Museum—was rising on the site where the "V. and A." now stands; alongside it was to be the National Art Training School, as the Royal College of Art at that time was called. There were to be scholarships at the National Art Training School for which students from the provincial art schools could compete. And, as a send-off to all those cultural enterprises, there was to be a new International Exhibition with more emphasis this time upon the Fine Arts than the Great Exhibition of 1851.

When the 1862 Exhibition opened, Fildes obtained leave from Christmas Thompson, at the Warrington School —and from his grandmother!—and went up to London for a week.

He saw in that week more pictures than he had ever seen before, but whatever impression they made on him it was not a wish to become a painter. It took him eight more years to come to that decision.

But London itself was quite another story. He succumbed to London. In later years he would recall the impact London had made on him, and the appearance of the South Kensington Museum area, as he first knew it. The Exhibition Building stood on the site where the Natural History Museum now stands, flanked by the newly built Queen's Gate and Exhibition Road. Behind the Exhibition, sloping up towards Kensington Gore—there was no Royal Albert Hall in 1862—stretched the gardens of the Royal Horticultural Society, Cromwell Road, westwards, stopped at Gloucester Road. Between the villages of Old Brompton and Earl's Court all was open ground given up to orchards and market gardens. No Inner Circle Railway had begun burrowing through Kensington. On the other side of Exhibition Road there was much building of the new South Kensington Museum in progress—the old parts one sees now of the "V and A."—and of the School of Art at the back.

The one immediate result of his week in London was that Fildes went back to Warrington and surprised Thompson be telling him that he had made up his mind to leave the School of Art.

"What are you going to do?" Thompson asked him.

"I don't know, but I'm going to London," his pupil replied.

"Why don't you try for one of the new scholarships at South Kensington?" Thompson asked. "If you get it, you will have a definite object in view—you will have a right to your education."

This was good advice and Fildes took it. It was too late to try for one of the First Year Scholarships, but if he stayed on at Warrington he could try for one in the Second Year.

What his grandmother thought is unknown, but inasmuch as the Scholarship would be worth £50, and a young man would be hard put to it to keep himself in London on that sum even in the sixties—and this young man was growing into a good-looking one with a touch of the dandy about his clothes—the Indulgent One must have promised to help things out.

He was successful in the examination, and on the 7th of October, 1863, almost three years to a day after his first arrival there, he left the Warrington School of Art, taking with him a copy of Mrs. Jameson's *Sacred and Legendary Art*, in two volumes, which his fellow students had presented to him "as a token of their affection and esteem". He was within a fortnight of becoming twenty years old.

And so he came to London, as many a young man from the country had done before him, and in London he made his home for the rest of his life.

❦ II ❦

A VICTORIAN APPROACH TO ART
1863-1866

Men who were fellow students at South Kensington used to remember him as the most industrious of them all. "The way Fildes used to work when we were all students together" became a legend. He was remembered, too, as a good-looking young man, well turned-out, old for his years for having had no proper childhood, and likely to become a personality.

But he was still unhappy in his work. The sense of frustration which had dogged him at Chester and Warrington was with him still; the trouble now was the realization that he did not want to be an industrial designer, and it was for the training of industrial designers that "South Kensington" had been set up. However, the authorities were not indisposed to have some leaven of Fine Art in the schools, and several young painters and sculptors who began to make a name in the next few years were scholarship holders at South Kensington about the same time as my father.

The turning-point for him was his seeing some illustrations by Millais in *Cornhill* and *Once a Week*. Millais had just been elected a Royal Academician at the age of thirty-four and was one of the adornments of current English Art. With these drawings he was making one of his excursions from painting into "black-and-white". The decade of the sixties, with the five years on either side, was a great period of English book illustration. Novels, magazines, publications of all kinds had to be illustrated and the services of "black-

7

and-white" artists were in great demand by the engravers who supplied the publishers with wood-blocks. Such was the prestige of being one of the "Illustrators of the Sixties" that men of mark as painters, Millais for example, took an occasional hand at it with the men who were "black-and-white" specialists.

When Fildes told the authorities at South Kensington that he wanted to go in for book illustrating, Burchett, the Principal of the College, was not unnaturally disappointed. He had marked Fildes down as a promising designer of ecclesiastical mosaics. But he gave his pupil every encouragement and recommended him for a renewal of his scholarship for another year. Book illustrating being outside South Kensington's orbit, Fildes had to look elsewhere to supplement his studies. There were the Academy Schools (the Royal Academy was then housed in the same building as the National Gallery in Trafalgar Square). At the Academy Schools tuition was free. Fildes submitted an extremely academic and competently executed drawing of a *Discobolus* as evidence that he was up to the required standard and was admitted a Probationer. A Studentship in the Painting School followed six months later, in January 1866, but he never made full use of the Academy Schools because, being now the poorer by £50 a year through the ending of his South Kensington Scholarship, he had to begin earning some money. He was now twenty-two years of age.

He obtained an introduction to one of the leading wood-engravers, William Luson Thomas. Their meeting was to have a considerable influence on both their lives, and it had for its immediate result Fildes' transformation from being admitted an Academy student into being a full-blown black-and-white artist, all in the space of four months. This is how it came about. As previously mentioned, wood-blocks for book and magazine illustrations were supplied to publishers by wood-engravers, and a draughtsman, unless his work was so well known to the public that publishers would stipulate in a particular case that he it should be who would make the drawings, depended for work upon whatever connection he was able to build up with one or more of the wood-engraving firms. Nor was that the end of the draughtsman's and the wood-engraver's interdependence. However well a draughtsman might make his drawing on the wood-block, if the cutting of the wood-block were not skilfully done by the engraver, the printed illustration would bear but little resemblance to the draughtsman's work. The engraver, for his part, would be hard put to produce a good block unless the draughtsman's work had certain features of engraveability, of which a definiteness of line came first. All these necessary features were evident in the examples of his work which Fildes brought to show William Thomas. The latter immediately offered him the job of redrawing parts of other men's drawings which lacked the quality of engraveability. Hack-work, but a beginning; it would give him experience in the feel of the wood-block and an entry into the art-industry of book illustrating. Art-industry is the right word: it stresses the inescapable truth that where a community wants Art to be produced in its midst, the artist must have something more substantial to work for than Art for Art's sake.

It was a time when a young artist on the threshold of his career had fewer ideological torments than, it would seem, he has nowadays. The notion that beliefs dating back to, say, the era of Apelles must now be scrapped had not been thought of. A young artist knew that the broad highway of tradition was able to lead him to as many adventures as his most fanciful and reforming moods might crave for. He had not to worry about any hesitation on the public's part to be interested in contemporary art, for art was not thought to be the concern only of the Discerning Few. Large sections of the public had leisure and money for cultivating an interest in what artists were doing, and that precisely was what they did with much of their leisure and money. As matters were to turn out, the closing decades of the Victorian era, when the artists of my father's generation were making their reputations, would see the visual arts reaching a state of effulgence in this country. That was a fact which remains a fact notwithstanding that subsequent fashion has rated Victorian Art as of little account.

And so everything was set fair for my father when he began his career, albeit as a kind of stooge on hack-work.

❧ III ❧

"BLACK-AND-WHITE"
1866-1872

The hack-work did not last long. Cassell, Petter and Gaplin were bringing out a new illustrated edition of *Foxe's Book of Martyrs* in monthly parts, William Thomas was supplying the illustrations for it. Sir John Gilbert, George du Maurier, J. D. Watson, Boyd Houghton and William Small were the best known of the illustrators engaged by him, and he offered his young friend Fildes two illustrations to do. They appeared in May and July 1866.

Fildes began to be known. He was given work by other engravers, notably Swain. For the next two years his work appeared in such periodicals as *Once a Week*, *Good Words*, *The Quiver*, *The Sunday at Home*, *Cassell's Illustrated Readings* and *Cassell's Magazine*. The drawings were mostly "fancy" accompaniments to selected "gems" of prose or verse. He would himself have preferred illustrating the everyday life around him, and in the expectation of doing so one day, he carried in his pocket a notebook for jotting down a word or two which would fasten in his memory likely subjects he was seeing on his walks through the London streets.

His release from "fancy" subjects came the following year. Victor Hugo's *L'Homme qui Rit* was being translated under the title of *By Order of the King* and was to be serialized in *The Gentleman's Magazine*. Fildes was commissioned to do the illustrations. Publication began in May 1869 and continued until the following March. Some of those Victor

Hugo illustrations are quite remarkable. Victor Hugo himself, writing to Joseph Hatton, the editor of *The Gentleman's Magazine*, said "Plusieurs de vos estampes sont on ne peut mieux réussies." Hatton replied, "I rejoice to learn that you are pleased with the illustrations by Mr. Fildes", and warming to his subject went on, "The same pencil which strove so successfully to realize the gaunt form of the kindly philosopher, the terrible image of Gwynplaine and the sublime loveliness of Dea is now engaged, for the first time, in giving pictorial life to the poetic creations of Charles Dickens." (The reason for the mention of Dickens becomes apparent shortly.)

Thus Fildes' release from "fanciful" subjects came about; but even when engaged upon fanciful subjects he had been developing a sense of the dramatic which had the knack of projecting itself across the footlights. A taste for theatre-going may have helped. By that time Henry Woods had followed him up by winning a scholarship at South Kensington and been installed in London. The two friends had immediately set up lodgings together at a Miss Byron's in Cadogan Street, Chelsea. They became inseparable. Theatre-going in a pit on a Saturday night after a week of hard work was their relaxation. Woods admired Buckstone and Toole, Fildes admired an actor then recently come to London named Henry Irving.

One drawing out of many "fanciful subjects" calls for special mention. This is a drawing called *Hours of Idleness* which appeared in *Once a Week* in June 1869, and its particular interest lies in the circumstance that at last Fildes had been invited to his friend's home in Warrington. Woods on his visits to his parents was always talking about the wonderful friend, Fildes, he had in London, and to such a length did this go that eventually his sister Fanny, by that time some seventeen years old and a very pretty girl with a mass of Titian-red hair, had opined with the concurrence of her younger sister Annie, that she did not believe any such person existed. "He's only another Mrs. Harris. If there's such a person as your Mr. Fildes, why don't we ever see him?"

After this challenge, their brother Harry brought his friend Fildes with him on his next visit home.

No. 1 Fennel Street was a straggling house dating from early in the eighteenth century. It had a cobblestoned stable yard, disused as such, and out-buildings of which one was a hay-loft with a swing in it. Whether the idyll which I was to hear from my mother in years to come, happened on this first visit or on some later occasion matters not. The important thing is that it did happen sometime or other, and this is how my mother told it me:

"The first time Dada kissed me" (he was "Dada" when we children were young) "I was so excited that I dashed out to the hay-loft, and I swung and I swung and I swung until I hit my head against the ceiling."

The two sisters were allowed to come to London on a visit to their brother, and they were taken by him and his friend for a picnic up the River Thames. And so we get the drawing *Hours of Idleness*, for it shows two young women and two young men idling time away in a boat which drifts along a back-water. When my father came to paint his first picture *Fair, Quite and Sweet Rest*, that drawing was the study for it.

One evening in that summer of 1869, William Thomas asked Fildes if he would draw something for him more important than he had ever drawn before, and he could have the choosing of his own subject. Fildes went back to Hunter Street, off Brunswick Square, where he and Woods were by that time lodging and tumbled into an easy chair to think. Obviously from Thomas's manner something was afoot. He started looking through his pocket-book and his eye was caught by the word "Casuals". It brought back a memory of a winter's night outside a police-station: a queue of outcasts miserably huddled in driving sleet, waiting for tickets of admission to a night's shelter in the Casual Ward. Here was his subject. Before he went to bed he finished sketching out the design, and this design grew into *Houseless and Hungry*, to be recognized as one of the masterpieces of English book-illustration of the sixties.

By the 6th of September, William Thomas was writing: "And now for the grand secret—the drawing you have made, and others I have, is for a new weekly journal, to be a high-priced paper, the very best we can get together by the combination of the best writers, artists, engravers and printers. I have you in my eye for many good drawings, and only hope you will be able to do them. . . . In the meantime, please keep this entirely private. I have paid you the compliment of selecting you first to speak about this matter."

That was *The Graphic* in embryo, which for many years was to reign as the monarch of the illustrated weeklies; a stand-by for many artists and a feature of contemporary art at home and abroad. And then the mode for artists and engravers in illustrated journalism would go out and *The Graphic* lose all individuality and separate life. The name is not completely dead; it survives as part of *The Sphere*—"*The Sphere* with which is incorporated *The Graphic*".

"Virtue meets its own reward", Thomas was next writing. "The pains and trouble you have bestowed in your drawing of the Casuals has not been thrown away. Yesterday and today I saw Sir F. Grant, Watts, Elmore, Faed, Leslie, Yeames, Frith and others" (the President of the Royal Academy and notable Academicians)" and all expressed their great pleasure with what they saw. . . . Tell Woods I was sorry I did not have a chat with him the other day. I hope he is getting on with a drawing for me."

It was on the 4th of December 1869 that the first number of *The Graphic* appeared with *Houseless and Hungry* in the place of honour. Among the thousands of people who saw it was John Millais. Millais had been asked by Charles Dickens to recommend him an artist to do the illustrations for his next novel, *The Mystery of Edwin Drood*. Several versions exist of what happened that morning when Millais saw *The Graphic*. This one will do as well as any. Millais (and perhaps Frith was with him) jumped into a hansom and drove to Hyde Park Place where Dickens lived. Catching sight of Dickens on his doorstep, Millais leaned out of the hansom, waving *The Graphic* and calling out:

"I've got him!"

"Got whom?"

"The fellow for *Edwin Drood*."

Houseless and Hungry told Dickens much that he wished to know, but not whether the artist could draw pretty girls, and there were going to be two of them in the book. Dickens's publishers, Chapman and Hall, were asked to seek out the

artist at once and make enquiries. Examples of Fildes'
ability to draw a pretty girl were submitted, and Dickens
was soon writing him:

> Office of "All the Year Round"
> Wednesday, Jan. 16th 1870.

Dear Sir,

   I beg to thank you for the highly meritorious and
interesting specimens of your art that you have had the
kindness to send me. I return them herewith, after having
examined them with the greatest pleasure.

   I am naturally curious to see your drawing from "David
Copperfield" in order that I may compare it with my own
idea. In the meanwhile I can honestly assure you that I
entertain the greatest admiration for your remarkable
powers.

> Faithfully yours,
> (Signed) Charles Dickens.

and then the paean of triumph to Woods, out of town:

> 17th Jan. 1870.

Dear Harry,
   At last!
   Congratulate me! I am to do Dickens's Story. Just got
the letter settling the matter. Going to see Dickens on
Saturday.

   Now for what I can do. This is the tide! Am I to be on
the flood? My heart fails me a little for it is the turning
point in my career. I shall be judged by this. But I shall
try! . . .

> Ever yours,
> S. L. Fildes.

Dickens took to my father from the start. He was constantly inviting him to parties at Hyde Park Place and
introducing "my new illustrator" into his circle of friends.
There was little time to lose. The first monthly instalment of
the book was due to appear in April and was already in print.
Two illustrations had to be done for it. Two would have to
be done for every subsequent monthly number. There were
to be twelve numbers in all.

A new method had recently been invented which enabled a drawing made by an artist on paper to be photographed on to the wood-block. Thus an artist's original drawing need no longer be destroyed in the process of engraving. Fildes used this new method for the *Drood* drawings, and was one of the first, if not the actual first, to use it. He was able, therefore, to keep his *Drood* drawings and at a later date to sell them to a buyer in America.

Dickens, for all his friendliness towards his new illustrator, was not easy to work for. The scenes he wished to have illustrated were those into which he had put the utmost of his descriptive powers. Fildes demurred. Those were the very scenes, he contended, which least required graphic illustration; an illustrator's usefulness could best be put to commenting on, and emphasizing perhaps, the less outstanding passages in the text, and what chance had an illustrator who was expected to compete in his particular medium when the scene had been described so powerfully in words?

It is strange that this problem should never have arisen between Dickens and any of his previous illustrators, but it would seem that it had not. Somewhat reluctantly he agreed to Fildes choosing his own subjects, though the final approval of a drawing lay with the author.

Nor at first was Dickens in the least communicative about the course the story was to take. No hint of the plot must on any account leak out. One day Fildes, reading the proofs of the next Number, saw that Dickens was thinking of Jasper as wearing a voluminous cravat whereas he had been shown hitherto in the illustrations as wearing a small tie. He asked Dickens whether the difference mattered. Dickens looked nonplussed and thought for a while.

"Can you keep a secret?" he asked.

"I hope so," Fildes replied.

"Well, you see, Jasper must have a large cravat. It is what he uses to strangle Edwin Drood with!"

The first number was out in April, and on the 16th Dickens was writing W. P. Frith:

"You please me with what you say about my new illustrator of whom I have great hopes."

In early June Fildes was to go on a visit to Gad's Hill to discuss the illustrations for the July, August and September numbers which Dickens had finished writing, and Dickens was proposing taking him round the "Cloisterham" country. In particular they were to visit Maidstone Jail so that the artist could see the condemned cell. The concluding illustration in the book, the twenty-fourth, was to be John Jasper in the cell waiting to be hanged for the murder of Edwin Drood. Dickens had told his illustrator that this concluding illustration must outvie Cruickshank's famous one of "Fagin in the condemned cell" in *Oliver Twist*.

That visit to Gad's Hill did not take place. On the morning of the day he was to have left London my father opened his paper and read the news of Dickens's sudden death.

In the few months of friendship Fildes had with Charles Dickens he came to know also the Dickens family, and soon they asked him down to stay at Gad's Hill. It was during that delayed visit that he had the idea of *The Empty Chair*—the drawing he made of the Library at Gad's Hill with Charles Dickens's desk and chair as he had left them. The drawing was published in the following Christmas number of *The Graphic*, and such still was the national grief at Dickens's death that thousands of the prints were put in frames and hung on the walls of the homes of England. Some of them can be seen to this day. A water colour which Fildes did of the same subject was exhibited in the Academy of 1871. It is now in a collection in Philadelphia. His last work in memory of Dickens was a water colour of the grave in Poet's Corner, executed for *The Life of Dickens* which John Forster wrote.

At the time Dickens died there were three numbers of *Edwin Drood* awaiting publication. These, making up the first half of the book, were published in due course with six illustrations Fildes did after Dickens's death. As years went by the mystery of the story bred a literature of its own, and speculations would break out in the Press as to what the second half of the book would have been. Fildes, as the supposed confidant of Dickens, would be appealed to for his views. His correspondents ranged from Augustin Daly, the impressario of New York, to Lord Curzon of Kedleston.

For his part, my father was satisfied with the little he had been told by Charles Dickens—John Jasper strangled Edwin Drood and would finish up in a condemned cell—so what need was there for further argument?

A commission to do the illustrations for Charles Lever's *Lord Kilgobbin*, which opened in *Cornhill* in October and ran for a year and a half, was a compensation for the loss of the last twelve illustrations for *Edwin Drood*. These were followed by the illustrations for Miss Thackeray's *Willows*, also in *Cornhill*. He had been doing drawings, too, for *The Graphic*, in particular stories by Wilkie Collins and Charles Reade in the Christmas numbers of 1871 and 1872. He was staying at the lock-keeper's cottage at Hurley when Charles Allston Collins, Dickens's son-in-law and Wilkie Collins' brother, brought him back to town to meet Wilkie Collins at dinner ("morning costume just as you happen to be"). Incidentally, of the leading novelists of the time, Anthony Trollope was about the only one whom my father did not illustrate. It is a point I make because some experts have professed to recognize as his, and to say so in print, some very poor illustrations in the first edition of *The Way we Live Now*.

But black-and-white work was ceasing to be his chief interest. By the solid standards of the Victorians—the prices he could charge—Fildes had reached the front rank of book illustrators, and at that point he did not mean to stop. Significantly he had, early in 1871, some eight months after Dickens died, taken a studio. He had not felt the need of a studio so long as he was only a black-and-white artist. He was, as he neared the age of twenty-eight, turning to be a painter, and but for a few short returns in later years, his career as a black-and-white artist was at an end.

Fildes' career as a black-and-white artist must be almost unknown to the public today. An idea of it could be had only by looking through many books and magazines of the later sixties and early seventies—it was not a long career—and nobody without a special interest in the subject is likely to do that. All the public has ready access to is *Edwin Drood*, which is still in print and readily obtainable. As a matter of personal taste, I prefer his post-Drood period. Nevertheless, the *Drood* drawings have a special place in his children's interest for having more reminders in them of our Mother, our Aunt Annie and our Uncle Henry Woods, and of a diversity of old friends in the form of pieces of furniture we have known all our lives.

A large quantity of sketches and studies for the finished drawings of his black-and-white period exist. Sometimes there are a dozen or more studies for one finished drawing. They are drawn from life and generally in a larger scale than the finished drawing, and as a whole have a *bravura* and a beauty of draughtsmanship which the illustrations in their final form sometimes lack. Here is a question. Illustrators of the sixties not infrequently complained of the way their work was treated by engravers, but my father was eminently "engraveable" and is not known to have had complaints on that score. Were then, the final drawings sometimes less good than the sketches and studies? It is possible. Most of them would have been on wood-blocks no larger than a few inches square, a cramping limitation for one who, as a painter, would work in life-size.

Luke Fildes as a student of 20

Luke Fildes on holiday in his 83rd year

Salmon fishing in North Wales, from *Once a Week*, October 1868

Houseless and Hungry, from *The Graphic*, December 1869

IV

THE CASUALS

1872-1874

The studio Fildes had taken was at No. 22 King Henry's Road, off Haverstock Hill. The house was four-storeyed, with a studio and a small flat on each floor. It looked, when I saw it last, much as it must have been those many years ago. Fildes took one floor, Henry Woods another, Edward Humphery and Laslett J. Pott the other two. Humphery was an occasional Academy Exhibitor with some private means of his own; Laslett Pott, already well known as a painter of "historical" subjects, was an Academy Exhibitor of some years' standing. They made up an agreeable little colony.

After his career in black-and-white, Fildes had nothing to learn about the delineation of character and the grouping of figures against a background, and moreover was not without some experience of painting in water colour, but he had everything to learn about oil painting. On the principle that doing a thing is the best way of learning how to do it, he determined to begin straight away by painting a full-size picture. But first he must decide on a subject.

He had two in mind: his *Graphic* success of *Houseless and Hungry*, and his drawing to which I have already alluded, *Hours of Idleness*. Both, be it noted, were "illustrations" Most of the world's paintings had always been illustrations of events in literature or real life. He had become acquainted with Millais at the house of Charles Allston Collins. Whom better than Millais to consult? Millais, all worldly wise, plumped for *Hours of Idleness*, The other subject could wait.

"You want to begin by selling your first picture," was Millais's advice. "Why, this *Hours of Idleness* may even get hung in the Academy!"

In his relief at being freed from the confines of a page in a magazine, Fildes took an eight-foot canvas for this subject of no great import—two young men and two young women drifting idly in a boat in a back-water. Much of the painting of the background was done out-of-doors in that summer of 1871 on the Thames at Hurley Lock, where he was staying at the lock-keeper's cottage, a discovery of Frederick Walker's five years before when painting his *Bathers*.

Hours of Idleness became *Fair, Quiet and Sweet Rest*, and when the time arrived to paint the figures in their Watteau-esque costumes, Fanny Woods and her sister, Annie, the original inspirations of the drawing in *Once a Week*, sat for the two young women in the picture, and their brother Harry sat for the young man who lounges in the bows of the boat.

Millais had counselled well. The picture was bought before the Academy "sending-in" day for £600 by McLean, the well-known dealer, who was rewarded for his backing of an unknown painter by a quick resale at a good profit. Mary Fildes, on hearing that her grandson had sold his first picture for £600, simply didn't believe it. "No picture is worth that much", was her definite opinion.

Millais' prediction that the picture might be hung in the Academy was not only realized but was improved upon. It was given a centre "on the line" in one of the early rooms. The artist has not been born who thought his works were invariably shown in exhibitions to the best advantage, but in all the years, more than fifty, that my father exhibited at the Royal Academy, he seldom thought he was badly hung. In return for this good treatment by that Body he was ever a most loyal supporter of its Exhibitions. I believe he never sent a picture to any rival gallery.

The critics were, on the whole, kindly disposed towards the new painter. As an example of the interest which public and Press took in contemporary art in those days, *The Times* gave thirty-eight lines to *Fair, Quiet and Sweet Rest*, nor was that by any means an exceptional amount of space. In those days, notices of the Academy Summer Exhibition might extend over ten issues of a newspaper. Amongst the things written of Fildes' first picture were, "Technically the execution of the work is masterly"; "It is full of sunlight." On the other hand, a third opined: "The young painter must be warned against too much dash and daring", from which remark one may infer that the technique was thought in some quarters to lack the "finish" then looked for. But it was an encouraging beginning.

Fildes was becoming established in the Higher Bohemianism. A note from Stacy Marks, a recent A.R.A., accepts his invitation to an evening party. George Augustus Sala, the leading journalist of his time, accepts for the same party!

I detest suppers—they interfere so much with steady drinking—thus your programme jumps with my humour entirely. I am glad also to receive your note as I specially wanted your autograph in order to sell it, or rather barter it, to a lady who offers me a *carte-de-visite* in exchange. Thus we shall be satisfied all round; and we are all going to heaven and Vandyke is of the Company.

Very faithfully yours,
George Aug: Sala.

P.S. A wonderous sketch that of yours of a drunken chaplain in the Xmas No. of Graphic. It would have made the very Ordinary to drink punch with Jonathan Wild.

J. L. Toole sends a box for the Gaiety, and there is a dinner "to meet du Maurier" in a hotel under the Piazza at Covent Garden—"six o'clock, morning dress, rump-steak and onions style of thing".

And now a successor for next year's Academy had to be thought about. Fildes set aside *Houseless and Hungry* for the time being, and chose a variation of *Fair, Quiet and Sweet Rest*: this time one young man and one young woman (for whom again Fanny Woods sat) in a boat in a backwater. This seeming lack of originality can be explained by two circumstances: the artist already had a buyer for this particular subject, and the time was drawing near when Fanny Woods and he would marry. The latter of these circumstances makes it odd that Charles Allston Collins and his wife—Charles Dickens' daughter Kitty—should have suggested *Simpletons* as the title of the new picture, and even more odd is it that Fildes accepted the suggestion.

Simpletons did not make any particular mark in the 1873 Academy. However, it had its admirers and Fildes had commissions for a year or two to make replicas in water colour of it. The picture had been painted for Lord Ronald Gower, a well-known *dilettante* of the period, and even a practising sculptor. The Academy Exhibition had not been open long when rumours began to reach Fildes that the picture was for sale. As Ronald Gower was not a dealer, and had owned the picture for only a few weeks, the painter thought some explanation was called for. Friends took up the matter with Ronald Gower, and a letter was brought forth.

Stafford House,
15th of May 1873.

Dear Mr. Fildes,
     I have written to Mr. Cosens to tell him that the sole reason of my thinking of parting with the picture is that my future house will be too small for a picture of its size.
Yours sincerely,
Ronald Gower.

But this explanation was not borne out by rumours which were reaching the ears of the painter and his friends that the owner of the picture was speaking slightingly of it. In August, Ronald Gower wrote again from Stafford House:

Dear Mr. Fildes,
     Thanks for your note. . . . I enclose part of a letter I got yesterday. I can't think how Mr. O'Connor heard the rumour—not through me at any rate—you know my only reason for thinking of parting with it—want of space.
Faithfully yours,
Ronald Gower.

John O'Connor was a well-known scene-painter for the theatre and an exhibitor of landscapes at the Royal Academy,

John O'Connor eventually negotiated for a new purchaser to give Ronald Gower the price he had paid my father, and there, for the moment, the matter lay. But it was far from being ended. Victorians did nothing by halves. Particularly was this so with their disagreements. Feelings between my father and Lord Ronald Gower had been more strained than the tone of the correspondence would suggest, and there was a sequel to be narrated in its proper place.

The year 1873 had begun with an event which *The Times* called "a remarkable instance of speedy production joined to a high degree of artistic merit". *The Graphic* had been given permission to publish an engraving from a photograph of the Emperor Napoleon III as he lay on his death-bed at Chislehurst. The utmost speed was necessary if the engraving were to appear in the next number. Fildes, though having given up black-and-white work, was persuaded by Thomas to do the drawing on the wood-block—to have done it on paper and transferred it to the wood-block photographically would have taken too much time. He received the photograph of the dead Emperor on a Monday evening at 7 o'clock, immediately began drawing on the block and, working all through the night, finished by 10 o'clock on Tuesday morning. The block was then divided into thirty pieces. One piece was given to each of thirty engravers. The engravers completed their work by 10 o'clock on Wednesday morning. By 10 o'clock on Thursday morning, the thirty pieces had been reassembled, the joints between them smoothed out, and four electrotypes in copper made for the printers from the reassembled block. The art of commercial wood-engraving was at such a high pitch that *The Times* was able to report that, though engraved in small pieces by thirty different hands, the finished illustration was "remarkably broad, bold and harmonious" as can be seen from any copy of the print today.

All his life through, my father was most exact in money matters. He did not keep formal accounts, but was fond of jotting down figures on scraps of paper. One scrap shows that for the year ended 30th April 1873 his earnings—including £50 for the drawing of the dead Emperor and £400 for the painting of *Simpletons*—came to £553 15s. 0d. against an all-over expenditure of £425 3s. 3d. Money then, it must be appreciated, was worth several times more than it is today.

Another scrap of paper records the financial side of a week's tour in Scotland which he and Henry Woods made in the following June. They started from Warrington, and with stops at Ballachulish, Fort William, Oban, Dalmally, Inverary and Glasgow arrived back at their starting-point, at a cost for the pair of them, of £13 12s. 10d., without any evidence that they skimped themselves. Fildes, who was earning more than Woods, did not charge his travelling companion for his railway fares!

Later that year, in September, he was writing to his grandmother:

> I am hard at work in London, and have been all the summer, on my big picture for next year's Royal Academy. I am anxious about its success. I want it to be one very much, as so much depends on it. It is a very important work, and like all things that are pretentious, if they are not very successful they have a corresponding failure. But I hope for the best. It promises well now, and I have six more months to do all I know on it.
>
> The owner of my first one is anxious to have this one also. They are both the same size, 8 feet. It is at the Vienna Exhibition and you will be delighted to know that they have awarded me one of the highest class medals for it. The owner of the picture is immensely pleased at it, and if he buys the one I am now doing he intends sending them both to the Great American Exhibition to be held in 1875. He says "to get me more honours".

The "owner of my first one" was a North Country industrialist, Thomas Taylor. He did buy the "big picture for next year's Royal Academy" and he paid Fildes £1,250 for it, a large sum in those days for an unknown painter and worth, I suppose, more than £5,000 in money of today.

The "big picture" was *Applicants for admission to a Casual Ward*, the *Houseless and Hungry* drawing of *The Graphic* so redesigned as to have become almost a new composition. None of the twenty-one figures was a professional model. They were all characters out of real life whom the artist had

discovered in his nightly wanderings round the London
streets, most of them so sunk in utter misery that they were
suspicious of his approach, and he had difficulty in getting
them to his studio. This difficulty, however, did not occur
with the big old Boozer in the middle of the queue, for whom
a pint mug of porter at his feet, replenished at intervals by
the pot-boy from the nearest pub, was an ample inducement.
The big old Boozer had always to be put in quarantine by
being made to stand on sheets of brown paper sprinkled with
Keating's Powder.

The labourer next to the big old Boozer in the queue,
who holds the child in his arms, used to bring that child
with him every time he came to the studio. One day he was
resting behind a screen and my father, happening to look
round it, discovered him nursing the child with the utmost
tenderness. My father told him not to move, and taking
paper and pencil made a study of the two of them just as they
were. Out of that would come *The Widower* three years later.

Fildes' career was being watched by nobody more closely
than George Augustus Sala. He it was who advised him to
drop the "S.L." and become "Luke". *The Casuals* was the
first picture my father signed as "Luke Fildes". Just before
the Academy "sending-in" day, Sala wrote in his neat
copperplate script.

> 68, Thistle Grove,
> Brompton, S.W.
> Thursday, March 26, 74.

Dear Mr. Fildes,
    I should rejoice to come to see your picture, but I can't
stir just now [here is interposed a drawing of the writer
immobilized by a gouty foot swathed in bandages]. I
hope to be able to get out by the opening of the Academy,
and to do justice to your good work.
>   Always yours,
>   George Augustus Sala.

Like Byron, Fildes "awoke one morning and found
himself famous". The appearance of *The Casuals* on the
walls of the Academy gave rise to one of those legendary
occurrences in the history of that Body when a barricade has

had to be erected round a picture and the police called in to help regulate the crowds. There was, as far as I know, but one dissident note in the Press—a peevish dismissal of the picture by the *Manchester Courier* on the ground that it was "disgusting". The *Daily Telegraph* gave more than a full column to *The Casuals* alone. It was variously hailed as "a great picture", "a truly wondrous performance", Fildes was "Hogarth's successor", a foreign critic saw him as "opening a new path in Art as Gustave Courbet had done in 1851 with his *Stone Breakers*". The critics were at pains to point out that there was nothing of sentimentality in *The Casuals*. "There is no exaggeration here"—"There is not a figure which is not faithful and true in sentiment."

As for the picture's technique, it is interesting to find among the Press notices a second instance of the bogey of "Unfinish" popping up. One anonymous critic smugly observed that "the execution may betray an approach to flippancy which one would rather not see in the work of so young a painter", and Francis Turner Palgrave in a signed article in *The Academy*, after very properly disclaiming as a literary critic any expert knowledge of painting, ventured to ask "whether greater completeness and refinement of finish might not have placed the whole upon an even higher level?" The interest of this lies in the thought that when the history of Victorian Art comes finally to be written, my father may have to be treated as an innovator!

The Casuals has hung for many years in the Royal Holloway College at Egham, where it has been open to view by the public. I doubt if it is known to the present generation. The fate of being unknown to the present generation is one which has overcome many a masterpiece of the Victorian era. Like the writers of that era the painters indulged in Moralism, of which *The Casuals* is an outstanding example. Moralism was not yet thought to be a defect in a picture; nor was sentiment.

Meanwhile, the happy balance between the moralist and the aesthetic approaches to art which my father, for his part, was always to maintain, was foreshadowed in this letter he received from Sala after the opening of the Academy Exhibition of 1874: It was addressed to:

"Luke Fildes (stick to the Luke: wasn't he the painting Apostle?) Esquire" and it ran as follows:

For God's sake don't let your triumph in this picture lead you to cultivate *exclusively* this class of subjects. You are to remember that Hood wrote the "Plea of the Midsummer Fairies" as well as "Eugene Aram" and the "Bridge of Sighs", and unless I am a Dutchman the *real* bent of your genius will be to cultivate the beautiful in form and in spirit. So good-bye Mr. Fildes, till we meet again in print (I am going to pitch in to that *dog* of yours, gnawing a bone: he is not wanted: You have written up "Hunger" plainly enough on your canvas) and good luck to you.

Always faithfully yours,
G. A. Sala.

V

MARRIAGE AND DOMESTICITIES

1874-1875

Since the episode of the swing in the hayloft at Fennel Street, there has not been much mention of Fanny Woods, Henry Woods' pretty sister with a mass of Titian-red hair. She had other attributes besides—she was something of a song-stress, and her mother, a pillar in the life of the parish church, saw to it that Fanny was a regular member of the choir. She had, too, a natural gift for drawing and painting, like her brother. In after years her art became subordinated to her husband's and her children's welfare, but in her girlhood it was: "Now run along home, Fanny, and make some more drawings", as the stock of Shepherds and Shepherdesses (a sure selling line on her mother's stall at church bazaars) showed signs of giving out. And Fanny would come back with a fresh supply, and if she had not been too pressed for time the Shepherds and Shepherdesses would be coloured into the bargain.

One key to her personality was her delicious gift of ex-tracting humour out of the most ordinary situations. She revelled in that gift. As a child a star turn of hers was to gum a piece of fur on her upper lip and give imitations of Sims-Reeves after the eminent tenor's visits to Warrington on his provincial tours—*Come into the Garden, Maud, She Wandered down the Mountainside*, and all the rest.

Now, as she was approaching her twenty-third birthday, she and Luke Fildes had fixed their wedding-day for the middle of July in this year 1874, and one would have expected that as soon as the Academy opened at the beginning of May, and he had savoured the triumph of *The Casuals*, the prospective bridegroom would have set about the preparations for the ceremony. But that is not what happened. Instead he went off with Marcus and Laura Stone for a Continental tour which would last the best part of six weeks.

Marcus Stone, though not more than three years older than Fildes had been exhibiting at the Academy ten years longer. He had begun painting considerably younger than Fildes had done. There was a spice of rivalry between them in that Stone had illustrated Dickens's *Our Mutual Friend* but been passed over in Fildes' favour for *Edwin Drood*. On top of that, Stone was apprehensive of Fildes being elected an Associate of the Royal Academy before him. In the circumstances it must be counted to their credit that they were on sufficiently good terms to go holidaying together, though why particularly at such a moment in Fildes' life? Over the years they will be saying unsympathetic things about each other: but it will not mean that they are not friends—they were Victorians. Like many of their contemporaries they were immoderate when they disagreed. And they both had artistic temperaments.

The three travellers crossed to Paris on the 20th of May. Paris was hardly yet herself again after the Siege of the Franco-Prussian War. Next morning they visited the *Salon* which they found disappointing. By easy stages with rests at Troyes, Basle and Lucerne, they came to Berne. From Berne, Fildes wrote to Woods thanking him for various newspaper cuttings about the Academy Exhibition.

Stone is very delighted with the Daily Telegraph notice you enclosed. . . . You would be astonished were you here to see the extraordinary effect it had on him. His spirits quite visibly rose and he seemed altogether a different man. Much pleasanter and less cynical. It has really done him a great deal of good and it after all is what he ought to have had long ago. I mean this generous appreciation of his existence as a painter.

The next letter to Woods was from Domodossola a week

later. A wild idea to walk over the Theodule Pass from Zermatt into Italy had been abandoned because, as he explained in another letter to Woods, the snow was too heavy for Mrs. Stone to go through. How the idea could ever have entered their heads is beyond comprehension, snow, or no snow; there was an ascent to be made of 6,000 feet, a glacier to be crossed, a similar descent the other side, and all for three travellers who were complete novices, and two of them—Marcus and Laura Stone—without any athletic aptitude of any sort.

This letter to Woods told how they did pass into Italy: "We started this morning from Brieg at 6.30 in our own carriage and three horses, to cross Napoleon's Great Pass of the Simplon, and we climbed and climbed for six and a half mortal hours to get to the top, dined and descended into Italy with four horses and arrived here (Domodossola) at 6.30 p.m. exactly—42 miles. . . . This place is ridiculously like one of the old Italian country towns as represented on the stage . . . the buildings are painted all over like scenes with sham doorways, sashes, windows and shutters, and one expects to see them move about as canvas ones would . . . a tiny little *place* not a bit bigger than they could do in Covent Garden. . . . This morning in Switzerland I left the fruit trees in full blossom; this evening, coming along this valley in Italy, the cherries are full ripe—the cherries are sold in the streets. . . . I have made up my mind that you and I must do this together."

Three weeks after leaving London, they arrived in Venice. The most described, the most depicted of all cities of the world, the aspiration of every artist happy in its unconsciousness of any need to be vulgarized as yet, was in the middle of a *sirocco* at its worst. For the first four days the heat was so intense that my father wrote to tell Woods "I couldn't look at a thing though the great Titians, Veroneses and Tintorettos abounded". But things soon mended and he was expatiating on Venice as a paradise for painters. "You can go out for a walk or a row, and spot at least half a dozen pictures, beautiful ones, in an hour and every time you go out. The shipping is splendid, too, such colour. You can have a gondola which is bigger than a punt and splendid to

paint from as it is so beautifully fitted up, for a day and a man
for 5 Lire—4/2d of our money—and 6d. for himself."

Woods had kept plying Fildes with newspaper notices
about *The Casuals*, to which he replied:

Venice, June 19th, 1874

My dear Harry,

I got a letter from Fanny this evening, she tells me
you are in Warrington. . . .

I don't know that I should say so but I don't like
shewing any of the notices to Stone. . . . I fancy somehow
that he is very gloomy and to speak plainly he seems the
very reversed of pleased; for instance, you know the copy
of the *Courrier de l'Europe* I took away with me thinking
Stone would translate it to me. I showed it to him, and he
read or skimmed it over, laid it down and never said a
word about it though he knew at the time I did not know
a word of its contents and still thinks so. . . . So I never
speak a word to him about my notices and truly speaking
I really don't think I am doing him an injustice by saying
what I do say now. He doesn't like it and he can't
conceal it. . . . Stunning place this for painting. I wish you
could come sometimes.

The tour ran its course, and Fildes returned to marry
his bride at St Saviour's, Hampstead, on the morning of the
15th of July. It was the quietest wedding imaginable; only
Henry Woods, a pew-opener and the verger were the
congregation. They were a good-looking couple—my father
was neither tall nor short—some five feet ten inches. He
held himself well, was well built and had he been born into a
walk of life which led through a public school, he might
well have been a type who was "good at games". Like many
of his generation, he adopted the fashion which the Army
had brought back from the Crimea and never shaved. His
hair was dark chestnut with a wave in it. I have already
said he was somewhat a dandy in his dress. My mother, for
her part, was a most comely young person by all accounts.
She, too, was neither tall not short. The strawberry and
cream complexion of a Lancashire lass set off the splendour
of her Titian hair, and there was a look in her expression of

expecting that something pleasant was going to happen any moment.

After spending three days at the old Clarendon Hotel in Oxford the newly-wedded couple started to row down the river "in one of Salter's boats." As a joint diary they began to keep records. "We had with us 2 portmanteaux, a case of wine and preserved soups, 2 leather bags, rugs and cloaks and macintoshes." Those still were pioneer days on the River Thames!

Stopping by day for picnics and for bathing, and by night at the 'Nag's Head' at Abingdon, 'White Hart' at Benson, 'Swan' at Streatley and 'French Horn' at Sonning, they came to Hurley, and at Hurley they rested for several days. On two of them "Luke made a sketch of the mill" and "Luke made a sketch close to the mill" the diary records.

The next three months were mostly spent at Goring with Henry Woods there much of the time, and out of the stay came my father's interest in the six or seven miles of country which take in the two Stokes, Aston Tirrold and Blewbury. It came to be known as the "Fildes country", for in it were the scenes of his next three "big pictures".

But there was no question of another "big picture" yet. His exhibit for next year's Academy was to be a single figure of his wife as a Milkmaid. It was to be painted entirely out of doors, with a large expanse of sky and a cornfield in the distance. This picture of *The Milkmaid* was one of the very few into which Fildes introduced an effect of landscape; and yet he was given at different times to out-door sketching all his life.

Early in September my mother noted in the diary, "Luke made a great many improvements in study for milk girl". Towards the end of the month there was: "Sat for Luke seven hours out of doors for head", and a few days later there were six more hours of sitting! The prolonging of summer that year must have been propitious for "sittings out of doors": on September the 25th was, "We dined at 6 and afterwards went on the river for a row. Beautiful moonlight night."

The Casuals had been one of the successes of the Autumn Exhibition at Liverpool that year. Royalty in the person of the Duke of Edinburgh was paying a visit to Liverpool and Fildes was bidden to the Mayor's Banquet celebrating the occasion. The festivities included a concert at the Philharmonic Hall at which Adelina Patti sang. My mother had gone with my father up north. They stayed at Fennel Street, made trips into Liverpool and spent a day with Mary Fildes at Chester.

Back at Goring there was much to be done in the way of packing up. King Henry's Road was becoming too small and as Marcus and Laura Stone were to be in Paris for the winter, Luke and Fanny Fildes had decided to join them there.

They were met by Marcus at the station on their arrival and soon were settled in "really delightful rooms at No. 3 Boulevard St. Michel, close to Notre Dame on the Surrey side of the river", as Fildes wrote to Woods.

Fildes had brought with him the canvas of *The Milkmaid*, intending to finish in a studio in Paris the picture he had begun in a meadow in Oxfordshire. His task was the more formidable for his having to share Marcus' studio, and because Parisian models did not look at all like English milkmaids.

Those and other troubles were recounted in letters to Woods. The Boulevard St Michel was two and a half miles from the studio. "When I consider that I will go out early and not return before 5 o'clock, this would be too long to leave Fanny alone." So they were moving to the Rue de Luxembourg "only 3 or 4 doors from the Rue de Rivoli and almost opposite to the Place de la Concorde, a beautiful situation. . . . It will be often decidedly irksome to be so close to the Stones. They do so love to take possession of us, but I shall very plainly give them to understand that we wish to have our own way and not be bothered, but on the other hand it will certainly be more pleasant to Fanny to have someone to go about with in the day, . . . We go into our new place tomorrow. Humphery is here with us now waiting for us to breakfast with him, so I must shut up."

"We have been at very great expense so far but now that we are settled we can live decidedly cheaper and better than in London", he was writing a week later to Woods. "I hope you are getting on well with your picture, take great pains with it, particularly the actions of your figures. I get to my studio every morning before 9. I make my own breakfast, buy my lunch on my way to work, and leave at 4. I am a most exemplary being, trotting in and out of shops. We have to do everything for ourselves in the culinary way. We always dine out, and it is very jolly."

Meanwhile the two wives were going everywhere together and their friendship ripened. Laura Stone, the elder in years and married state, took to giving good advice to her friend who was so proud of her Titian-red hair that she went about with it down her back. Laura Stone had to protest.

"Fanny! If you won't wear a hat and put your hair up, I shan't go out with you any more. You are making yourself *conspicuous*!".

My mother hired a piano, and a master used to come and give her singing-lessons. It was nine years afterwards that I remember myself, five years old, standing by her side whilst she sang to her own accompaniment what I came to know in time were arias out of Italian operas. And then for some reason she gave up her singing, and I have never known whether she sang well or not. In later life, on hearing some aria out of Bellini or Donizetti, she might remark, quietly as if to herself, "*I* used to sing that!" But in Paris that winter she was working hard at singing.

The succession of models for *The Milkmaid* were finally summed up by my father as "undersized dirty drabs", and on the 6th of January in the New Year, 1875, my mother wrote in the diary: "I sat for Luke." And that is the last entry in the diary which they had begun to keep on their wedding day.

And so it came about that *The Milkmaid* was finished from my mother as it had been begun. The picture was in the Academy of 1875 as *Betty*. My father did not think of it as one of his successes, although it was well enough liked to be chosen by *The Illustrated London News* for reproduction in colour as a Christmas supplement.

It might be expected that their stay in Paris that winter would have led to my parents becoming acquainted with some, at least, of the French painters. It was a busy time in

Parisian Art circles; the first Exhibition of Impressionists had been taking place. But there is no evidence of anything of that kind having happened. They and the Stones seemed to have been self-sufficing. Nor (to anticipate a subject I shall come to later) is there any evidence of my father having been much of an admirer of contemporary French painting at that or any other time.

Though in no more than his fourth year of exhibiting as a painter at the Royal Academy, and with no talk yet of his being made a member of that body, Fildes on his return from Paris set about a project very much in keeping with the complete confidence he had in his own future. He would build a house; and he would put into it all the money he had. The house would be designed by Norman Shaw, the most fashionable "domestic" architect of the day, and would be one of the first of the stately mansions which the leaders of the profession were beginning to have built for themselves and the site had to be worthy of the house.

There was a country lane which led up from the Kensington High Road to the stables of Holland House. Holland House was a most remarkable place—a famous example of Jacobean architecture which with its formal gardens and surrounding parklands were still a precious piece of rurality in the midst of London's engulfing spread. The country lane gave access also to Little Holland House—the dower-house of the Hollands—and also to a farm. The dower house and the farm buildings were being pulled down and a new road, to be called Melbury Road, was to be made taking in part of the country lane. Building-leases were being granted to tenants who were prepared to put up stately mansions. Fildes heard of these projects from his friend, Val Prinsep, whose parents, the Thoby Prinseps, had rented Little Holland House for many years, and Val Prinsep had been brought up there. Val Prinsep had commissioned the Pre-Raphaelite architect, Philip Webb, to design him a house and studio in Holland Park Road, a turning off the country lane; Leighton was living next door; Watts was building a house in the new Melbury Road; the ubiquitous Marcus was in treaty for a plot. Fildes decided that it was there, in Melbury Road, that his own house must be.

On the 3rd of May 1875 Norman Shaw wrote him: "I do most heartily congratulate you on having got that bit—and I feel quite certain you will *never* regret it. What is £20 or £25 a year in comparison to such a delicious site—*absolutely nothing*."

The "delicious site" was the one in the angle of Melbury Road with the view to Kensington High Road on the south and to Addison Road on the west, and having the park of Holland House on the two other sides.

Not long after the signing of the lease, Mary Fildes, by that time full of years, paid a visit to Manchester to have a look at some property she owned there. She was taken ill and she summoned her grandson to her bedside for the last time. Her final benefaction to him was to leave him all she had. His inheritance was enough to pay for the building of the house in Melbury Road. Had Mary Fildes lived to see it she would surely have wondered what her grandson wanted with so fine a home.

❧ VI ❧

THE WIDOWER
1875-1877

Sala had been promised a sketch of *Betty*, and that summer of 1875 he sent Fildes two reminders. Also he wanted Fildes to see "a very rare and complete collection of the wonderful acquatint etchings of Goya which I brought home with me from Spain the other day. For the number and beauty of the impressions I think I can beat the British Museum Print Room!" Sala had recently moved to Gower Street. Fildes must call and see the new drawing-room where the sketch of *Betty* would hang. "If you don't find *me* at home, you will be sure to find Mrs. Sala scrubbing the stairs or nailing down the Kamptulicon."

Fildes' name was now entered on the list of Outsiders to be considered for Associateship of the Academy. This step was taken by Henry T. Wells, an Academician of standing and an influence in Academy politics. He wrote on August 2nd 1875:

My dear Mr. Fildes,

When I inscribed your name on the list of Candidates for the Associateship I felt that the satisfaction was all mine in having the fortune to connect my name in however simple way with your career, and I was eager to take the first step that must be preliminary to bringing you into our ranks. I sincerely hope the day is near when the Academy will open its doors more widely, for it is sad to think of the arrears we have to deal with. It seems almost hopeless longing to expect a state of things permitting us to welcome a fellow craftsman at the moment of a great success, when he crowns continuously good work with an achievement of really high order, a state of things that would allow the Academy to anticipate and justify the public *éclat* rather than follow in its wake. . . . I hope that the intercourse thus begun may strengthen and last long.

Believe me, dear Mr. Fildes,

Yours very truly,

Henry T. Wells.

The intercourse thus begun did, indeed, strengthen and last long. Wells' wife, herself an accomplished artist, had died in the 'sixties leaving him with two daughters, who had become Mrs. Ernest Charrington and Mrs Arthur Street. They and my mother were much of an age, and a time would come when little Charringtons and Streets and little Fildeses, would be playmates together.

Another "big picture" was due, and Fildes was at work on it in the country most of the summer of 1875. It was *The Widower*, the idea of which had come to him from seeing the labourer nursing the child when *The Casuals* was being painted. Now, a cottage background and other figures had to be found to form the widower's environment.

By the following spring rumours had got around that Fildes had a successor to *The Casuals*, and an even more eminent talent-spotter than Wells appeared.

7, Pembridge Villas,

Bayswater.

March 14. 76.

My dear Mr. Fildes,

If I don't hear from you to the contrary I will conclude that Sunday morning between 11 and 12 will be agreeable to you for me to call. I shall be very pleased to see a picture of which I have heard so often and so favourably.

With kind regards from all here I am

faithfully yours,

W. P. Frith.

And a week later:

March 21, 76.

My dear Mr. Fildes,
It has always been my opinion that no really strong man was ever spoilt, in fact it is the test of strength that it will stand any amount of praise and success. You are about to be put to the proof, and I as one of your friends, have no fear of the result.

It was not because I feared the effect of my praise that I did not say half as much for your picture as I thought of it, but because I—unaffectedly—don't think so very much of my own commendation—or rather of the value of it. I now reiterate my congratulations on your present success and your future prospects, and am always, dear Mr. Fildes,

faithfully yours,
W. P. Frith.

Which was followed by:

Sunday.

Dear Mr. Fildes,
Will you allow me to take Lady Shelley to see your picture next Wednesday afternoon about three o'clock? Mr. Frith has just given us such a wonderful account of it. He says he has never been more struck with a picture. . . .

Very truly yours,
Isabelle Frith.

There was now a wail from Norman Shaw:

March 23rd 1876.

My dear Fildes,
Oh dear! Oh dear! bad news for you I am sorry to say. The ground on the site of your house turns out to be . . . a lot of *soft* slushy clay, and what with a lot of extra digging and laying concrete there is going to be an extra £120 to pay.

Building prospects looked better a month later.

April 19, 1876.

My dear Fildes,

The whole of the concrete is in . . . the brickwork is well advanced all over and will I hope be level with the ground in 10 days or less. Then we shall fly along—ask Stone about his—he was far more rebellious than you are, and now his roof is half on . . . you shall have your house done by about Christmas—will that do?

Ever yours sincerely,
R. Norman Shaw.

When the Academy opened, the Press was as appreciative of *The Widower* as it had been of *The Casuals* two years previously. Here are samples:

"The picture which will probably be regarded as the most affecting in the exhibition is *The Widower* by Mr. Fildes. In this work no realism is spared." "The two men, who above all their fellows give emphasis to this collection, represent two opposite schools of Art the one classic and academic, the other domestic and realistic. Their names are Frederick Leighton, the Academician, and the other L. Fildes, the Academician that is to be." "One of the pictures of the year, and in many respects its best picture. . . . In whatever manner the painter wishes to be read, his beautiful picture may be hailed as a manly, conscientious and soulful piece of work, unstrained, undefaced by maudlin sentiment, but exquisitely touching." "Technically, the treatment is broad, vigorous and true, just a little too rough, perhaps, in its touches but soundly and faithfully expressive of all that colour, light and shade that nature demands." "The picture which will touch all hearts and gather crowds round it for the rest of the season is *The Widower* by L. Fildes. . . . Realistic art is often decried by certain *dilettanti*, but in the hands of the true artist it can be sublimed, as here, into the region of sacred poetry. The man who could view the picture without emotion would not be a desirable person to know." "The exhibition which contains Mr. Leighton's *Daphnephoria*, Mr. Poynter's *Atlanta*, Mr Fildes's

Widower and Mr. Millais's landscape *Over the Hills and Far Away*, has some right to be remembered in virtue of these works."

By way of contrast *The Times*, whilst granting that *The Widower* was "certain to be the most talked of, and in that sense, most popular picture of the year", warned the artist that his subject "was not happily chosen". "The painter, we submit, is under a mistake who brings big dirty boots, squalling and scrambling children, parental and sisterly love, into such contact. . . . It is a great pity that painters do not bear more in mind the fact that their pictures are meant to adorn English living-rooms, and that intense painfulness, overstrained expression, and great vehemence of momentary action or short lived attitude are all qualities that make pictures unpleasant to live with."

And yet the proof of the pudding was in the eating; my father never lacked a private buyer for a work of Social Realism. The problem has long since solved itself through his Social Realist pictures gradually passing into the possession of public galleries. *The Widower* has for many years been in the National Gallery at Sydney. A much reduced version which my father painted many years afterwards, is now in the Walker Art Gallery in Liverpool.

As soon as the 1876 Academy had opened, my parents were off to Venice. It was my mother's first visit there. Sala had received his *Betty*, and this letter followed them:

My dear Luke Fildes,
Unless I grievously err, I have not yet written to thank you for the beautiful picture of *Betty*. There has been a reason for my delay. As you may have heard I have been for many months *very ill*. . . . I have been doing the Academy slowly and painfully—for I am not the man I was—and tried to say what I thought about your *Widower*. It touched me very deeply indeed. . . . You bold young geniuses lash in your colour so audaciously that we weak-eyed fogies are puzzled, sometimes, to know whether there is any drawing underneath the paint at all. Well, you may say, Rembrandt painted with his thumb and

Goya (I have a complete set of his etchings which I should like you to see) painted the *Dos de Mayo* with a fork.

Always yours,

George Augustus Sala.

My parents were a few weeks only in Venice though my father was able to pass the time very profitably. They spent most of the summer in his Thames villages again whilst he made studies for his next "big picture", which for various reasons would not be finished for three years, however. It was a commission from Holbrook Gaskell, one of the North Country industrialists who were leading patrons of the Arts. He had left my father to choose his own subject.

Fildes had come back from Venice with the conviction that to settle there would be the making of Henry Woods. His brother-in-law had been unable to find himself as a painter of English subjects. So off to Venice Woods had gone to explore its possibilities, and at the end of September my father was writing to him there from Streatley. The studies he had been making for the "big picture" would, he said be "put away for this season and allow me to take up the work I am to finish this year. I have quite decided not to try and do a large picture for the next R.A. I should only spoil it by such haste."

In their usual style my parents would seem to have remained on the river until well into October and then at the end of the month, back in King Henry's Road, my father was writing Woods, who was still in Venice: "Since my return I have sold three more small pictures to McLean for £150 and the Venetian Canal picture to Virtue for £250. These, with the two large Venetian subjects to McLean for £1,050, are the extent of my trading so far. I have made but indifferent studies, but I think they will do, for the single-figure subject for the R.A., which I hope to get at pretty soon. If I am successful with that and sell two others I have finished almost at Streatley, I shall have made my income for this year, and I shall want it all."

He went on, in the same letter, to discuss what adornments Woods could buy for the house in Melbury Road, but not to spend much, because everybody was afraid of war breaking out between Turkey and Russia "which will stop picture buying. . . . It is already being felt at the 'Dudley' . . . Fanny's two pictures are hung there and well, but she has heard nothing about them." And he added that she was preparing for the advent of their first child which might arrive in about a month.

In November he was writing Woods: "Fanny is first rate. It is within the bounds of possibility that you may be an uncle before you arrive in England. . . . The house is getting on famously and looks stunning. The staircases may be in by your arrival. It is a long way the most striking and most superior house of the whole lot. I consider it knocks Stone's to fits, though of course he wouldn't have that by what I hear he says of his, but my opinion is the universal one."

Philip, my parents' first child, was born shortly before Christmas. His birth heralded a year in which happiness, disappointment and tragedy would come in turn.

The first disappointment was the little attention which *Playmates*, my father's only contribution, attracted in the Academy Exhibition of 1877.

"You must look on this", Norman Shaw wrote, "as an off year. When your life comes to be written, your biographer, after recounting your triumph in 1874 and 1876 will say that owing to domestic circumstances you were prevented from producing a great work in 1877, but that in 1878 you wreathed your brows with victory and achieved a success etc. etc. It will come all right enough."

Ever since *The Widower*, people had been expecting Fildes to be the next Associate elected. However, that was not how matters worked out. Ouless, Peter Graham, J. B. Burgess and Marcus Stone were all elected in 1877, but not Fildes.

Having done no black-and-white for several years, he must have been set thinking about it by this letter from Christ Church, Oxford:

July 2/77.

Dear Sir,

As I am writing this on a matter of business, and as I am unknown to you, even by name, I had better begin by stating that I am the writer of two little books (possibly unknown to you, called *Alice's Adventures in Wonderland*, and *Through the Looking-Glass*) which were illustrated by Mr. Tenniel, whom I do not doubt you know well by reputation, if not personally. And my motive for addressing this to you is that I have seen (and admired more than I can easily express) your pictures in *Edwin Drood*.

My position is this: that I have some half-defined ideas, and a small amount of material, for another tale; but I have been for a long time discouraged from going on with it, by the apparent hopelessness of finding an artist worthy to succeed Mr. Tenniel, whose help is no longer to be had. May I then venture to trouble you with a few questions?

(1) Is it likely that you would be willing, at some future time, to illustrate a book of the same general character as *Alice's Adventures*? (If you do not know the book, I will send you a copy to look at.)

(2) If so, would you now undertake a small commission for me—to draw 2 or 3 pictures for a short tale? (This tale would perhaps be embodied in the book, if it is ever written.)

(3) It would be well to have some rough idea of what you would expect to have to charge for drawings of the same amount of finish as those of Mr. Tenniel.

With apologies for thus troubling you, I remain
faithfully yours,
(Rev.) C. L. Dodgson.

Such a book as I am hoping to write would require pictures of (1) children, (2) perhaps fairies, (3) Grotesques like the "Queen of Hearts" in "Alice". It is true that neither children nor Grotesques occur in *Edwin Drood*, but I fancy I see in those pictures almost unlimited power of drawing, and wonderful variety (quite avoiding the painful family likeness that spoils so many of Cruickshank's pictures) and I am inclined to believe that the artist of those pictures can draw anything he likes!

My father, of whose reply there is no copy, would not seem to have said—as he might—that he did not want to draw

Fairies and Grotesques. Instead, he would seem from Lewis
Carrol's next letter, to have temporized:

July 14/77
Dear Sir,
I beg to thank you for your letter and specially for a
few hopeful (or at least not entirely discouraging) expressions in it—such as "I have not positively decided to do
no more wood-drawing".
Twelve months hence (or whenever your present work
is done) will probably find me as artistless as I am now.
So, if you should then be thinking of again drawing on
wood, I hope you will give me the "first refusal".
I fear you go on the theory of having only one "iron
in the fire" at once—*My* theory is that you can hardly
have too many. The work of my life is Mathematics—
but I try light literature as well, and give a good deal of
time to photography, and even trespass on *your* territory
occasionally, in sketching my little friends at the sea-side
—and various other "irons" as well, so that there is
always *something* to turn to, in harmony with the inclina-
tion of the moment. I fancy a man with only *one* line of
work must do a good deal of his work "Against the grain",
and I think Ruskin is right in saying that all such work
is bad work.
Believe me faithfully yours,
C. L. Dodgson.

Twelve months later my father was to take up black-and-
white again for a spell, but not for Lewis Carrol. I have no
knowledge of any further exchanges between him and the
author of "Alice" after that delightful opening in the
summer of 1877. My father may not have liked Ruskin
being quoted at him!
My parents spent the whole of that summer at Streatley
once more, and of course Philip was with them. The house
in Melbury Road was nearly ready. Much interior decoration and furnishings remained to be done, but the house was
habitable. They could wait no longer, and in they went. "I
am surprised to learn that you are installed in the house!"
wrote Norman Shaw in mid-October.

My father's conception of No. 11 Melbury Road as a fitting background for his career was, as I said earlier, a fine example of self-confidence. He was still an Academy Outsider, but he foresaw the time when visitors in their hundreds would be trooping on Show Sundays to see his year's work, and therefore, the central feature of the house must be a Triumphal Staircase leading by easy grades up to his studio. ("One of the finest rooms in London!" as King Edward VII was to remark years afterwards, the first time he came to sit for his State Portrait.) And then there was a Dining Room, Drawing Room, Morning Room (the "Balcony" Room, as it came to be called), a "Boudoir", Bedrooms and Nursery and Kitchen quarters.

The garden was as much a part of the background as the house itself. It had been part of the garden of Little Holland House, of which I have already spoken, and the old trees remained—towering elms, a noble acacia, oak, sycamore, and the finest white-blossoming may-tree, as tall as the house, that ever was seen. A many-buttressed wall of great age was the eastern boundary, and on the other side of it was the country lane I have already mentioned as leading up to the stables of Holland House. On the far side of the lane there were more towering elms and a bank which was a mass of wild-flowers in spring and summer. Every day at milking time, with mooings and tinkling of bells, cows came along the lane and through the gates by the side entrance of No. 11 and into Melbury Road, and then down to Tunks and Tisdall's Dairy in the High Road, Kensington. Squirrels, owls and peacocks from Holland House used to visit the garden—and such as I have been describing them, the rural surroundings of the house would long remain. It was in the autumn of 1877, as I have said, that my parents moved in. My parents had not long been settled when Philip fell ill. He died on Christmas morning.

The character and bearing of their doctor throughout the time of their anxiety made a deep impression on my parents. Dr. Murray became the symbol of professional devotion, the memory which would one day inspire the painting of *The Doctor*.

❧ VII ❧

THE RETURN OF THE PENITENT
1878-1879

After the affair with Lord Ronald Gower over *Simpletons*, John O'Connor and other friends had put my father up for the Beefsteak Club, but on his name coming up for ballot he had been blackballed! Suspicion for the machination of that gaffe had fastened upon Ronald Gower; who was a member. A year or two went by, and then my father received this note from John O'Connor:

> My dear Fildes,
>   Will you be surprised to hear I have put you up today for the Club? Hare and Kendal have seconded you, and the Enemy will not appear in the matter. . . . I did not intend to let you know until it was over but I thought it best to do so in case you have any objection. . . .

As a matter of fact, with the "Savage" and the "Arts", Fildes had all the clubs he needed, but if the "Beefsteak" would rectify its gaffe, he did not wish to stand in its way. The next he heard was Carlo Pellegrini, the eminent cartoonist "Ape" of *Vanity Fair*, writing:

> Beefsteak Club,
> 12th March 1878.
>
> My dear Fildes,
>   Last night you were elected member *unanimously* !!!!
>   Yours ever,
>   Carlo Pellegrini.

47

Fildes took up his membership, paid his first year's dues, and after an interval sent in his resignation.

Club life in those days loomed large in artistic circles. A diary kept by Henry Woods gives occasional glimpses of it. One could dine at the Savage at five o'clock, go to see the play at the Globe Theatre and look in on Toole in his dressing-room, and be back at the Savage where "they were still keeping it up". Or if not Toole at the Globe there might be a note from the Lyceum:

My dear Mr. Fildes,
      Come and see me tomorrow after the play,
                                       very faithfully yours,
                                              Henry Irving.

The evening of all evenings was Saturday at the Arts Club—the old "Arts" in the north-west corner of Hanover Square. My father was for years a "regular" on those Saturdays, and the painter Perugini was another. Carlo Perugini had married the widow of Charles Allston Collins, Kate Dickens as had been, and when the two husbands foregathered on a Saturday evening at the "Arts", Kitty Perugini and my mother, who despite a difference in age were intimate friends, took it turn and turn about to dine at each other's home, so that when Fildes and "Peru" left the Club, they would go to whichever home it was that evening and be reunited with their wives.

My father had nothing ready for the Academy of 1878— the "big" picture he had begun for Holbrook Gaskell two years previously had been slow in developing, but my mother had sent in two pictures both of which were hung. This gesture of hers to keep the family name in the Academy Catalogue caught the fancy of Norman Shaw, by that time an Academician. "It must have been great fun", he wrote, "to see Mrs. Fildes 'varnishing' and you at home! Pray present our compliments—2 on the walls and 3900, or thereabouts, in the cellars is I think, a Triumph".

Enquiries were coming in again to know whether he would undertake black-and-white work.

June 21 1878.

My dear Luke,

I am anxious to know whether you have thought over the Christmas subject I suggested to you, whether you are disposed to undertake it, and at what price.

Sincerely yours,

Edmund Yates.

Founder, owner and editor of *The World*, Edmund Yates was a *persona* in journalism. The outcome of this enquiry was a "powerful" two-page drawing which appeared in *The World* Christmas number of 1878. It was my father's first black-and-white work for several years.

An enquiry from Macmillans if he would illustrate the next story by the author of *That Lass o' Lowries* led to nothing, but he did agree to illustrate *Men's Wives* for the large-paper edition of Thackeray which Smith Elder were bringing out. "I may mention", George Smith had written "that Mr. Millais has promised to make some drawings for *Barry Lyndon*."

"I do not know", Fildes wrote back, "whether my terms are unusually high or not for doing drawings of this size and style. They very probably are . . . but I must ask you somewhat in proportion to what I should get with the same amount of work as my painting. I am slow at wood-drawing and rather quick at painting . . . and painting is more agreeable to me than wood-drawing, even though illustrating Thackeray!" His charge was thirty guineas a drawing. They were in pen-and-ink on paper, and did not have to be destroyed by engraving. They have survived and are some of the best he ever did.

Throughout the summer of 1878, the "big picture" which he had begun two summers previously was still giving him trouble. Its subject had come to him when he was sketching in one of his Thames-side villages and a pale-faced girl had walked down the road and crossed over to the other side, obviously wishing to escape attention.

"Who is that?" my father asked an elderly dame who was watching him at work.

"That's Mary Brown, sir. She's just come out of Reading Jail!"

"What was she there for?"

"Well, sir, you see she had a baby and—well—it died. This is her first day out!"

That much of a hint, and the sight of a house standing empty at the end of the village, had set my father's imagination running—a girl who, after falling into trouble, had come back to her old home and, finding it deserted, was crouching on the door-step whilst the villagers looked on and passed comments to one another. And he was going to attempt a new departure for his background; an evening glow in the sky, a light upon church-tower and cottages down the road, an essay in landscape. But it was all going very slowly.

Meanwhile Woods, having made friends with the cosmopolitan artist set in Venice—Ludwig Passini, Pettenkofen, van Haanen, Eugene de Blass, Wolkoff, Ruben and Thoren, and encouraged by having had some Venetian subjects hung in the Academy, was proposing to return to Venice and see whether he had not better follow his brother-in-law's advice and make Venice his scene of future action. On the way he would stop in Paris and visit the *Grande Exposition*. *The Casuals* had been lent to the British Fine Art Section, and he would report to Fildes how it looked.

> Hotel Romain, rue du Dauphin,
> Paris.
> August 24th 1878.

Dear Luke,

Your picture looks first rate. . . . I noticed yesterday that there was a considerable number of people looking at it. . . . The Exhibition takes one's breath at first, but you soon get the run of the pictures, and my eyes, what a feast: Jules Breton, everybody one likes. . . . I hope you will lose no time in coming for the pictures, and I hope it will not cause you to be put out with yours, or to make any alteration in painting or otherwise on returning. I think it will make you feel happy and contented with what you

In the Court, from *Edwin Drood*
1870

Municipal Art Gallery, Warrington

Fair, Quiet and Sweet Rest
1872

Applicants for Admission to a Casual Ward

1874

The Widower

1876

have there, and rouse you up a bit in finishing your
picture at home. . . .

With love to you both,
yours affectionately,
Harry.

The following day:

Dear Luke,
    I am going off tonight. . . . When I get to Venice I will
give you a hint or two about seeing the Exhibition, for
economising time. . . . I am really sick of Japanese
things, Indian war-spears, armour etc. [And then he gave
particulars of the hotel he had been at near "the Church
of St. Roch in the Rue St. Honore" where a sitting-room
and bedroom for two people could be had on the first
floor at 15 frs a day, on the second at 13 frs. and on the
third 10 frs., the exchange then being 25 frs. to the
pound.] But I find to get enough to eat in the Restaurants
is very expensive; the fixed price dinners in the Palais
Royal are simply a swindle.

On arriving in Venice:

Hotel Nazionale,
Venice.
August 28th 1878.

Dear Luke,
    I arrived here yesterday morning. I was simply
stewed all the way. It was over 88 deg. in the optician's
shop on the Riva today. . . . I was rather knocked up
yesterday, and in the afternoon went to bathe at the Lido.
On the steamer I found Thoren the Austrian I knew
before and Van Haanen. I was very much pleased to
find the latter here; he is a very good fellow, just the fellow
you would like. When I mentioned your name, he said
"Ah! Mr. Fildes is a very great artist" and was full of
enquiries; he had seen one of your big pictures. I was
very glad to hear a clever fellow like that come out at
the mere mention of your name. The Austrian remembered your picture in Vienna!"

c

My father replied:

> Melbury Road,
> 16th September, 1878.
>
> Dear Harry,
> Fanny and I intend leaving for Paris tomorrow morning and we go to the Hotel St. Roman. . . . I have been pretty steady at the picture and I consider I have improved it very much. I will go on with it now regularly until it is finished. I am glad to hear you are likely to be satisfied with your visit to Venice. I should not begin anything very big. You are sure to be safe if you keep to the moderate size. . . .

And then:

> Melbury Road,
> Kensington.
> 8th October, 1878.
>
> Dear Harry,
> We enjoyed ourselves very much at the Exposition and had a good look at it. . . . It is a show that ought not to be missed by an artist. I am sorry I could not agree with you about my picture looking well. It was put in so dark a room that it was quite impossible to judge of whatever merits it does possess. I have the same objection to the whole English Section (Fine Art), the place is so badly lighted. . . . I believe my visit has done me much good and I hope my picture will be the better for it. I am working at it, but it gets on very slowly. Fanny and I go to Streatley, I think on Monday next, so that I may make some final studies. . . . There is nothing of any importance happening with the exception of the death of Sir Francis Grant. . . . Of course there will be a great fight for the Presidency. Leighton of course is the only one fit, but there are many doubts of his election because of that, perhaps.

Woods wrote back:

Casa Zabeo,
1089 S. Gervasio e Protasio
Venice.
Oct. 19th 1878.

Dear Luke,

I was very glad to get your letter, and that you had
been to Paris. . . . Notwithstanding the clumsy pigheaded-
ness that darkened the English Galleries I maintain that
your picture looked well. . . . Passini told the American
Consul here that the English Gallery was the most
interesting in the Exhibition. I am next door to the Church
close by S. Trovaso . . . quite in the thick of the studios.
. . . I met Mark Twain and have had a walk with him in
the evening. He came to see me with Graham; he is a
nice quiet sort of fellow. He was making extensive notes,
here, he showed me his note-book, full of jottings of
things that attracted his attention. . . .

Van Haanen is painting a fluffy red-haired girl in a
pale green bodice; you would make a hit with her. He is
designing a subject picture, he goes to work exactly as
you do, the full size at once, altering every day, painting
over and over thinly whilst designing . . . aiming first to
get the effect in colour. . . . Being a figure painter he says
it is best to avoid the picturesque backgrounds that you
find here as it is an impossibility to work a figure composition to them. You have said the same thing. . . . I find
Passini's backgrounds very simple. It is very difficult for
me to avoid sitting down to them.

So difficult indeed did Woods find it to avoid picturesque
backgrounds that he gave up the attempt. In time he evolved
a speciality of town-scapes in which the background mattered
more than the figures. Some of his town-scapes could have
been even more charming with no figures at all! But then
he might not have sold them!

All this time, notwithstanding the outstanding successes
of *The Casuals* and *The Widower* at the Academy, Fildes was
still an Outsider. This, however, did not inhibit him from
approaching the Council upon an errand of mercy. Hablot
K. Browne—"Phiz"—had fallen on evil days through illness.

That such a distress should come to the illustrator of Dickens' middle period offended Fildes' sense of fitness, as the last of Dickens' illustrators. He approached the most influential of his acquaintances on the Academy Council, Henry T. Wells.

Wells wrote back:

Thorpe Lodge
January 14th 1879.

My dear Fildes,

It may or may not have been a coincidence, but we had this evening a letter from Frith urging H. K. Browne's claims for the Turner Fund. I feel very confident of a good result at our next meeting. I had an excellent opportunity for reading your letter to the Council, and if I am not mistaken its effect on my colleagues was as favourable as on myself.

Yours very truly,
Henry T. Wells.

As the result of these representations "Phiz" got his pension. And it was purely a coincidence that eight days after the letter from Wells, Fildes was elected an A.R.A.

On Academy Election nights there was a custom at the Arts Club for the health of the new Elect to be drunk in punch. My father had not been at the Club that night; he had stayed quietly at home. The news came to him through the classic agency of a self-appointed messenger in the person of one of the models from the Life School at the Academy, who was tipped a sovereign for his pains. How the news of my father's election came to the Arts Club appears from a note he received from Edward Humphery. It was Marcus Stone who brought the news and, commented Humphery, "I am not quite certain that he was altogether satisfied, which may appear strange".

Out of all the letters my father received congratulating him on his election I have not found one more perceptive than the one he had from that delightful member of the artist community, Mrs. Louise Jopling.

How glad you must be that you kept your big picture back. It will be a splendid one to commence with as

Associate. . . . Please give my best love to your wife, and with many good shakes of the hand believe me, dear Mr. Fildes, your sincerely,

Louise Jopling.

Another congratulation came all the way from the battle front in Afghanistan:

Gen Tytler's Headquarters,
Basamul,
Feb. 20th 1879.

My dear Fildes,
I have just received a newspaper in this part of the world . . . it announces that you have been elected an A.R.A. . . . I hope that long before there is another Afghan War you will become a Royal Academician.

Yours sincerely,
Frederick Villiers.

And as though some occult influences were guiding the thoughts of eminent War Correspondents in my father's direction, there came this letter from another of them:

Sunday Evening

My dear Fildes,
I have had several long thinks about the title of your picture which has very deeply impressed me.

The Prodigal is not nice. . . . I can recall no instance of its being applied to an erring woman, and it is further indissolubly linked to the association of forgiveness, and even welcome, on return to repentance. . . . At length what seems to me the right think came suddenly to me— the single word—"Outcast"—I don't of course know how you may like it, but to me it seems to cover the whole ground. I hope to see you soon at the Club. Meanwhile believe me yours very truly.

Archibald Forbes.

Fildes had been very undecided what to call the picture. The title, *The Return of the Penitent*, it finally was given was the suggestion of Holbrook Gaskell, who had commissioned the picture, though it did not entirely meet my father's views. On its appearance in the 1879 Academy the picture was rapturously received by the press. "One of the most celebrated pictures of the present year, both now and in after times." "This noble work, painted with great breadth and power", "The pastoral beauty of the scene and the brilliancy of the atmospheric effect". "One doubts if any other single picture exhibits quite such a range, catches so much of the charm of serene landscape, so much of the beauty of the face and figure, so much of truth to character." And Tom Taylor in *The Times*—who had disliked *The Widower* as something to live with, weighed in with an article in which he said; "I should, myself, rank this picture very far above anything its painter has yet exhibited. I have heard it called Stagy. I fear that any painter who aims at telling a story dramatically must be prepared for this charge."

Story telling, or not, the picture remains as much an object for admiration now as it was eighty years ago. Unfortunately, where it hangs in the City Hall at Cardiff it can be seen only by artificial light, and by that much loses its "charm of serene landscape". The more is the pity as it was my father's one big adventure into that medium.

He was taken up with landscape at that time. Henry Woods's diary tells of Sketching Club days in the country when my father, Marcus Stone, Perugini, O'Connor, Woods himself, Gordon Thomson, Keeley Hallsewelle, Haynes Williams, Laslet Pott and others were present, and there was an "Inn and Gardens by the river for a simple joint etc. pastry and cheese dinner" at 5s. which the artists thought somewhat expensive! That particular rural spot was Greenhithe down the Thames.

A few weeks after the opening of that year's Academy my uncle's diary records on the 13th of June: "A son was born at Melbury Road tonight at 6.30. I was there. Everything passed off very well. I dined with Dr. Murray at Luke's."

The son was myself. My parents chose as my godfather the friend Val Prinsep I have already mentioned. Val Prinsep had been elected an A.R.A. the same evening as my father. Though never in the front rank of painters, he was a person of consequence in the world of art and in its contacts with Society. He figures in those memoirs of the time in which Watts, Ruskin, Rossetti, Burne-Jones and William Morris appear. Family connection with the old East India Company had led to a commission for his going to India and painting the Ceremony at Delhi when Queen Victoria was proclaimed Empress of India. He had written a book, *Imperial India* about it. He wrote, too, a play which was staged at the St. James's, and one of the last "3-decker" novels ever to be published must have been his *Virginie*, a tale of the French Revolution, of which he gave me a presentation copy. He was a generous godfather who tipped me many a sovereign.

However, what impressed me most as a small boy about my godfather was his immense size and physical strength. When Du Maurier's *Trilby* began coming out in *Harpers*, Taffy was commonly said to be a portrait of Val Prinsep. Be that as it may, my god-father and Taffy had a taste in common for feats of strength. There is a tradition in the family that Val Prinsep walked into No. 11 Melbury Road one day and bent a poker round his neck. That he did such a thing in my father's studio is credible, but that he did it in my mother's drawing-room is an embellishment I must reject.

By the late summer my uncle was back in Venice. The artist colony received a new recruit. My uncle wrote:

> I have introduced Whistler to a Russian named Wolkoff. They are very happy together and I am very glad. I could do with Whistler very well, but for his confounded conceit and ever-lasting seeking for notoriety. I cannot stand it. He has started two "moonlights" entirely from memory. They are, I must admit, remarkably true as far as they go. When I have time I will go to see him paint something; what I have seen of it here is so curious. His etchings will be very good I think.

Whistler had come to Venice primarily to restore his fortunes by doing a number of etchings which had been commissioned from him by the Fine Art Society in Bond Street, and he stayed a year during which time my uncle saw a great deal of him. Some months earlier Whistler had scored a sensational success by toppling Ruskin off his pedestal as the arbiter of taste in the Art of Painting. He had brought an action for libel against Ruskin—and won it—because Ruskin had written of him as "a coxcombe who flung a pot of paint in the public's face". Though winning his action Whistler had been awarded no more damages than one farthing and he had, moreover, been obliged to bear his own costs. Bankruptcy, the selling up of the "White House" in Chelsea and all its treasures, and retreat abroad had been the unhappy sequel.

The story of the libel action has often been told, and I allude to it solely because it has a bearing upon the subject of Victorian Art versus French Impressionism which I shall come to later. A British jury found itself in the unenviable situation of having to decide a question on which philosophers, art-critics and practising artists had never reached a conclusion over the centuries: What is Art? That Ruskin had overstepped himself was obvious to his legal advisers, and their problem was how to minimize the damages. W. P. Frith, a very reluctant and ill-at-ease Burne-Jones, and Tom Taylor, of *The Times*, as expert witnesses for the Defence, committed themselves to the proposition that Whistler could not have suffered damage to his artistic reputation, for the simple reason that he had no artistic reputation to be damaged. The works he produced were not, according to them, "works of art"; works of art had to be "finished", and Whistler's works were only sketches. Those opinions, so far as damages mattered, won the day in the minds of the honest, but bemused, members of the jury.

Woods' assessment of Whistler's "moonlights" as remarkably true "as far as they go" is therefore, understandable. They did not go beyond the stage of sketches.

"Whistler is getting on very well with the etchings, but some little pastel drawings he has made are very excellent and interesting", was my uncle's next report.

Christmas of 1879 drew near. Woods wrote: "Whistler and I were at a dinner-party at Mother Harris's (his way of referring to the wife of the American consul) the other evening to meet rather swells—I hope you are all well, and the baby; this should be the jolliest Christmas you have had."

❧ VIII ❧

VENETIAN INTERLUDE
1880-1881

Rather more than a hundred years ago a movement of
Idealism swept over this country and hardly was any class
of the community untouched by it. On its artistic side the
movement has been associated with the Pre-Raphaelites, but
it went wider than that. Pre-Raphaelites, Classicists,
Medievalists, Aestheticists, Social -Realists, portrait painters, landscape painters were all of them finding patrons in
the new class of rich industrialists and merchants whose
imaginations the movement had caught. Nor did the movement stop at wealthy patrons. People whose means, though
not equal to buying originals, were equal to buying repro-
ductions, found what they wanted in the new trade in
engravings of contemporary paintings, and more modest
requirements were met by the galaxy of illustrated books and
periodicals then coming on the market.

The dynamic of it all was the closeness of understanding
between artist and public. Now, with the start of the 1880's
Victorian painting was entering upon its fullest effulgence.
Even to a very small child like myself the world of the
1880's seemed full of brilliance. Artists in those days were
very important people. They and their doings were constantly in the public eye. In *Punch*, that mirror most accura-
tely held up to Nature, picture galleries and artists' studios
were so often represented as the scene of social happenings
that they must have been places with which readers were
assumed to be familiar, and hostesses—from Du Maurier's

duchesses down to Mesdames Leo Hunter and Ponsonby de Tomkyns—apparently relied upon the presence of some popular member of the Academy to make a success of their parties.

On their side, the artists justified their place in the community by producing what the public wanted in great variety, with a deep sensibility and an abundance of technical skill.

There was a stroke of ill-luck, therefore, in Fildes having nothing for the Academy of 1880—the second year, as it happened, out of the last three. Writing in January to Woods in Venice he was lamenting "the most awfully dark and hopeless winter that has ever been known in London. . . . Ever since last September painting in London has been a most hopeless occupation, two or at most three hours a day a week is the usual thing. . . . I have done no painting whatever since I wrote last. . . . I am going on with wood-drawing, but this is frightfully slow. This year will be a most disastrous one in a financial point of view."

My father was apt to let his sense of the dramatic impinge upon his private affairs. This was a trait with which Woods was familiar, and in a bantering mood he began his reply with "I was basking in a warm sun on the Zattere when the postman handed me your letter". He had no intention of being as sympathetic over the dark weather in London as doubtless he was expected to be. Indeed, he remarked that dark weather at that time of year was the "sort of thing which influences all our Academy Exhibitions, and yet the Exhibitions manage to take place!"

Nor were my father's financial forebodings to be taken literally. Dark weather apart, he had put aside his painting in order to carry out the biggest commission for black-and-white he had ever received. This was thirty large illustrations in *The Graphic* for Amelia B. Edwardes' serial of *Lord Brackenbury*. Amelia B. Edwardes, was a well-known writer in her time, good enough to be serialized alongside such writeres as Wilkie Collins and Charles Reade. To illustrate a story of hers was a not unworthy occupation for an A.R.A.

With the sale to *The Graphic* of the publication rights of those drawings, the sale of the drawings themselves to

Holbrook Gaskell and the sale of the Thackeray drawings he had done for Smith Elder the previous year, my father was little worse off than if he had another "big picture" ready. And think of the minute cost of living—later in the year my parents took me and my nurse to a farm in the country for six weeks, and the total cost of board and lodging for the four of us was under £30!

I have not seen the finished *Brackenbury* drawings, and have no idea where they now may be. But the sketches for them are in my possession. They are in a new technique of wash instead of line—a painter's, not a draughtsman's technique. The engravings as they appear in *The Graphic* from February 1880 onwards, are intensely dramatic and full of an interest in landscape to which, as I have said, my father seldom gave scope in his pictures.

That closing stage of my father's "black-and-white" career was attended by a typical note of Victorian asperity. I have already mentioned his having done a drawing, *Found dead on the Embankment*, for a Christmas Number of *The World* when Edmund Yates was on "my dear Luke" terms with him. Afterwards he designed, on commission from Yates, a cover for a new magazine Yates was bringing out, called *Time*. In May of 1880 he sent Yates an account for £30, with a covering note in which he said, somewhat unguardedly as the sequel shows, that Yates might think it a good deal to charge for the work.

My dear Fildes, [no longer "My dear Luke",] [Yates wrote back,] I enclose cheque for £30, I agree with you it is a large price for the drawing. It must be agreeable to you to be able to earn money so easily.

Faithfully yours,
Edmund Yates.

The concluding remark could have been taken as an attempt, albeit a poor one, at jocularity. My father took it as a personal insult. His reply is missing, but its nature can be inferred from Yates' next letter:

The Temple,
Goring,
Oxfordshire.
Saturday, June 5th 1880.

My dear Fildes,

You have not read my note in the spirit in which it
was written. Nothing could be further from my intention
than to suggest anything dishonourable in your conduct
in charging me £30 for the frontispiece of *Time*. You
yourself in your note forwarding the charge expressed
an opinion that I should probably "think it is a good deal of
money for the work", and in my reply I merely agreed
with you. I should have said nothing more on the subject,
but since you have re-opened it I may tell you that my
principal feeling at the charge was surprise. Surprise
that you should have treated me, an intimate friend, on
the same terms that you treated Mr. Agnew, Mr. Smith
the publisher, or the proprietors of illustrated news-
papers.

I can only illustrate my meaning by saying that if I
had been in the Tom Taylor line and you had asked me
to write a few pages descriptive, say, of the "Casuals" or
"The Return of the Penitent", I should not have dreamed
of taking any money from you for my work. Of course I
did not expect you to draw my frontispiece gratis, but I
thought, with the relations between us, that the price was
high.

Faithfully yours
Edmund Yates.

From its present condition, this reply from Yates must
have been torn into shreds by my father, and then on second
thoughts carefully retrieved and stuck together again. There
is a draft of my father's rejoinder:

My dear Yates,

The mere agreement with me that the charge for the
drawing appeared high would certainly not be sufficient
to annoy me. It was the additional sentence that "It must
be very agreeable to you to make money so easily", with

abundant suggestiveness, that induced me to read your note in a different spirit than it was written.

It forced me to, what you call, "re-open" the subject. But in assuring me that you had no intention of imputing anything dishonourable to me you yet, in your second letter, take away with one hand what you give with the other. . . . I think it due to me to say that I receive for every drawing I am now doing for the Graphic £20 from a buyer *apart from the high price I receive from the Graphic.* . . . In sending you the original drawing of "The Embankment"—the *first* I have *given* to the proprietor of a paper or publisher—I sent you what I could have got £30 at least for; I trust some day you will get £40 or £50 for it. Drawings of that size of mine have sold by auction for £44 some years ago.

Having thus informed Yates of the prices his drawings could command, my father went on—or the draft of his letter so indicates—to offer to reduce this charge of £30 to the derisory figure of £15.

No more letters from Yates exist amongst my father's papers, and the inference can be drawn that an estrangement ensued.

My father's connections with Venice were not yet as close as they became later, but he was always interested in what was happening there. A letter from Woods about that time described a Ball at the Prefettura—"Madame Blaas was the prettiest woman there. There were an enormous quantity of Austrians. Everything was very English in the whole conduct of the affair. The waltzes were played too fast, and too much jumping. The Naval and Military were in strong force. I felt rather conspicuous not having some Brummagem ware on my breast."

"Bettina (one of my landladies)", Woods wrote in another letter, "gave me a very good hint the other day. She came into the studio, saying 'Ah! those beautiful cabbages; I see them always when I come in' 'But I want you to see the people first', I said. 'Then I should paint that girl in stronger colour', she said, and I have, and now I have got the picture in hand. This sounds like a blooming idiotic anecdote, but excuse it; it got me out of my difficulty."

Another letter tells of opera at the Fenice and the Goldoni (2 *lire* for a stall and 4 *lire* for a box level with the stage— when the *lire* was 25 to £1), and circus at the Malibran— "so you see Venice is pretty lively. Whistler shines at Mrs. Harris's Monday evenings. I believe if the papers were to take no notice of him for a time he would collapse altogether. We breakfast together on Sundays generally. Some of his etchings are very fine indeed *as far as they go*, also some of the pastel drawings. He says everybody will be going in for pastel things now. I said it was no new thing, and called his attention to a box of the articles with paper etc., which I had got before he saw Venice, and reserved to myself the right of doing some if I liked."

During the year of his exile in Venice, Whistler became as friendly with my uncle as he ever became with anybody, but that did not prevent him working off on my uncle his favourite trick of putting people out of countenance. A band of young American art-students used to follow Whistler about wherever he went, and this was sometimes a cause of annoyance to the older members of the artist colony, agreeable young fellows though the students may have been. My uncle, thinking he would drop Whistler a hint about it, looked in on him in his studio one day. He found him hard at work at his easel, and he stood by his side for a time, watching him paint, being interested in how Whistler got his effects. Eventually he broached the subject of his visit. Whistler heard him through without pausing in his work or offering any comment, then remarked, "Waal, 'Arry, I needn't tell the boys. They've heard what you said, *there they are*!" and with a sweep of his arm he pointed to four or five of the acolytes sitting on a bench which a screen had prevented my uncle noticing on his entering the room.

Woods was back in London for most of that summer of 1880, and No. 11 Melbury Road took on something of a military base. He had for some years been a keen Volunteer in the Artists' Rifles and was now prevailed upon to take a commission. The Corps did its "skirmishing" and "sham fights" on Wimbledon Common, to which Melbury Road was nearer than King Henry's Road where my uncle still had his studio and flat. So he kept his uniform and equipment at Melbury Road. Anybody less of a military man in appearance than my Uncle became in time I cannot conceive, but he must have been a smart looking rifleman in the eighties because he and Hamo Thornycroft, his sculptor friend and a neighbour of my father's in Melbury Road, who were alike as two peas, were always posted conspicuously at the foot of the stairs when the "Artists" mounted the Guard of Honour at the Royal Academy on Banquet night. The Prince of Wales became used to seeing the pair of them and would pause to remark upon their soldierly bearing.

A yet more unlikely member of the Artists' Corps, to many people's minds, was none other than the President of the Royal Academy, Sir Frederick Leighton, himself. He not only commanded the battalion, but commanded it well. Whistler forgot to enumerate that accomplishment of Leighton's when framing his famous "tribute". The tribute has appeared in print so often that I tell it once more solely because my uncle's version of it is better than any other:

"Leighton? That man's doing a fine job as your President. Stands well with Royalty. Distinguished appearance. Makes a first-class speech. Good linguist. No mean musician"— (pause for reflection)—"*Paints a little; Sculpts a little.*"

The time came for the Volunteer's return to Venice (inevitably his absences from England soon obliged him to resign from being a Volunteer any longer).

At the end of August he was writing about Whistler's doings in Venice while he had been away:

Whistler, I hear, has been borrowing money from everybody, and from some who can ill afford to spare it. He shared a studio for five or six months with a young fellow named Jobbins. Jobbins never could work there with him in it. He (Whistler) invited people there as to his own place, and has never paid a penny of rent. He used all the colours he could lay his hands upon; he uses a large flat brush which he calls "Matthew", and this brush is the terror of about a dozen young Americans he is with now. Matthew takes up a whole tube of cobalt at a lick;

of course the colour is somebody else's property. . . . He
is an epidemic, an old-man-of-the-sea. These young
chaps were quite flattered at first when he joined them.
It made me roar when I heard of his goings on amongst
them, he evidently pays for nothing. There is no mistake
that he is the cheekiest scoundrel out—a regular Ally
Sloper. I am giving him a wide berth. It's really awful.
There will be *Grande Festa* if he ever goes away.

Whistler's treatment of the "young fellow named Jobbins"
had something at the back of it. Whistler had with him in
Venice his favourite model of many years, who was also his
mistress, and one day a discussion took place amongst some
of the Artist colony as to how much, or how little, recognition should be given to Whistler's domestic establishment.
One of them, W. H. Jobbins, said that really Whistler was
going a bit too far. He, for one, did not think he would
know the fellow! The sequel has appeared in print, and
again I tell it because my Uncle's version is much the best
I know. Entirely forgetting that he had ever uttered such
sentiments about Whistler's mode of life, or even harboured
them, Jobbins happened to be passing Whistler's lodgings
a week or two later, and on the spur of the moment rang
the street-door bell. Whistler, who lived on the top floor,
came out of his apartment, looked over the banister to see
who his visitor was, and noting it was Jobbins, called back
in to the apartment, in ringing nasal tones: "Maud, Maud.
Come here and look! It's little Jobbins. It isn't *true*, Maud;
he *isn't* going to cut us!"

Fildes' only reaction to these tales of Whistler's goings-
on was: "I am not surprised." My father disliked Whistler
as a man and could not bring himself to take him seriously
as an artist. In this he missed something which my easier-
going uncle managed to enjoy.

There was now talk in the artist colony in Venice about
a brilliant young American who lived in Paris named John
Sargent. He might be coming to Venice on a visit. Whistler
did not look favourably upon the prospect of his compatriot's
arrival. He was saying so to my uncle shortly before they
both were going to a Reception in one of the Palaces to

which all artistic and fashionable Venice had been invited. Summing up his views on the possible rivalry of the two Americans, Woods remarked:

"Well, one sergeant doesn't make a battalion any more than one whistler makes an orchestra."

A ruminative look came into Whistler's eye.

"Are you going to say that anywhere, 'Arry, before the Reception tonight?"

"Most unlikely, Why?"

"Do you mind, 'Arry, if I say it tonight?"

"Not at all. You may have the whole thing."

"I only want the bit about the sergeant and the battalion. I don't want the other bit."

Whistler was on the point of returning to London. He was worried about the Arts Club from which he had been expelled. He asked my uncle what he should do. My uncle advised him to humbly pray to be reinstated. The following day my uncle entered in his diary: "Went to Florian's. Saw Whistler. He paid me the 60 *lire* he borrowed some time ago. He goes away next Tuesday morning. Confidence, I believe, is restored to him in the Bond St. Art Gallery, and they have sent him money."

Three weeks later is the entry: "Sat with Sargent for a while at Florian's." Sargent asked him to his studio and he was very much struck with Sargent's work. "His colour is black, but very strong painting."

In September the *Brackenbury* drawings in *The Graphic* came to an end. With another touch of the dramatic Fildes wrote to Woods that the drawings had caused "a complete stoppage of all my other work. . . . What I shall do afterwards I have not decided. . . ." Three weeks later, on the 18th of October, he was writing, "I am anxious to do an important picture this year but I have almost come to the conclusion it is out of the question, and such being the case I am thinking most seriously of going to Venice for a few months. I may be able to do *something* there, if only pot-boilers. . . . I can't drop on any subject that I care about. Everything I think of has some strong objection to it. . . . It is utterly useless for me to try to do a picturesque and physically beautiful subject in a dark London winter. I am too conscientious to "fake up" the picturesque . . . and I can't drop on a good story that I can paint *now*".

Shortly before Christmas my father wrote my uncle to find a studio for two months "with a good light, of course, or it will be out of the frying pan into the fire". The letter went on:

> I saw Whistler last night at the Club, and he gives me a fearful account of the disagreeabilities of a winter in Venice . . . I have not seen Whistler's etchings yet, but I hear on all sides that they are absurd fakes. We have an election on at the R.A. One honorary foreign Academician and two Associates on the 20th of Jan., and three more Associates on the 28th of Jan. I scarcely know who'll get in. Dicksee, of course, but who the others are to be it is hard to think. Possibly Bodley, architect, and some men talk of Thornycroft as sculptor. The other two places may go to the many who are trying. Who they are I don't care a damn excepting yourself, but I don't think you have any chance this time, though there are many who are *most* favourably inclined to you. You see both Stone and I, who would have stood by you, will be away".

The two months my father was now about to spend in Venice were the real beginning of his "Venetian Period", which lasted off and on for the next ten years. The suggestion has been made by art critics, though I know nothing of any statement by my father to the same effect, that his election to the Academy had made him grow critical of his technique as a painter, and that his seeking the light and colour of Venice was his method of improvement. Whether that was so or not—and I shall have to return to this subject later—when he arrived in Venice on the 10th of January, 1881, it was with the immediate intention of having something to send to the Academy for that year's Summer Exhibition.

On that first evening Fildes and Woods went to Florian's after dining at Dreher's, the favourite resort of the artist colony, and Sargent came in and joined them. It was the first time my father and Sargent had met. They were constantly meeting during the next two months. Once only does my uncle's diary give a hint of what they talked about when he records another evening on which my father and he were at Florian's, and "Sargent joined us and we talked about French Art". Sargent, fresh from Paris, familiar with the work of the Impressionists, should have been worth reporting at length. Another topic likely to have been discussed is Carolus-Duran, one of the leading portrait-painters in France and Sargent's master. My father had seen and admired portraits by Carolus-Duran in the *Salon*, and when a few years later he himself became a portrait painter he admitted, when painting my mother, to having been influenced by Carolus-Duran's work—the only case in which he did admit to any French influence.

Wolkoff, Ruben, Thoren and Van Haanen, of my father's friends on previous visits, were in Venice. Even in that luminous city the winter light fails for a painter by mid-afternoon, and one could knock off work with an easy conscience. Friends in the artist colony were always to be found dining at Dreher's, and there was the Opera every night at which a box cost a few *lire*.

By the middle of March, Fildes had done what he wanted and the artist colony assembled at the station to see him off. Woods followed a week later, taking with him two pictures —*At the foot of the Rialto* and *The Gondolier's Courtship* which marked him out for early election to the Academy. He stayed at Melbury Road on that visit to England, and he had hardly unpacked his pictures on the afternoon of his arrival before Mr. Schwabe, a prominent collector of the time, called and bought them both. Mr. Schwabe eventually left his collection to his native city of Hamburg. It included one of my father's more important Venetian pictures, and it survived the bombing of the Second War.

Mr. Schwabe might be likened to an old Hanseatic merchant prince. Because he took an interest in small children he still lives in the memory of one of them after all these years. On the way home from walks in Kensington Gardens a detour would be made to the Schwabe mansion in Kensington Palace Gardens—"Millionaire's Row"— where the largest musical-box I have seen would be set in

motion, and a toy singing-bird in a gilt cage perform. The
concert would conclude with a dish of German sweet-
meats being handed round.

The news that Woods had two uncommonly good
pictures down at Fildes' house, brought members of the
Academy along to see them. He was still hard at work,
putting the finishing touches to them on the day they had
to go into the Academy. Val Prinsep, followed by the
President himself, Leighton, were just in time to see them
carried downstairs to the waiting van, and my father and
uncle were just in time to dress and get to Schwabe's for
dinner, where several of the senior members of the Academy
were expected to be.

Playing Mecaenas at one's table to one's artist friends was
as much a part of being an art-patron as buying their works.
A giving of dinners about the dates of the Academy's
Sending-in Days would herald the opening of the London
Season, which synchronized with Private View Day at the
Academy. Not to have tickets for the Private View was a
social flop, and hosts and hostesses were grateful to any
member of the Academy who could spare them tickets.

My father had three pictures in the Academy of 1881:
a single-figure which he had brought back from his recent
visit to Venice, and two English single figures. They were
only minor works. But a spell had been cast, and he was
bent upon getting back to Venice. No sooner had the
Academy opened than we all—my parents, my uncle,
myself and my nurse—set off.

Arriving in Venice, where Van Haanen was at the station
to meet them, my parents went straight to a hotel and then
found an apartment opposite the church of San Sebastiano,
a "whole furnished floor of seven or eight rooms for 300 *lire*
a month with attendance as to making beds and cleaning
up". In English currency, £12.

There seems to have been no question yet awhile of my
father painting the large type of Venetian pictures he would
be doing in three years' time. The next "big" picture he
had in mind was to be another English subject, and he was
now engaged in Venice on nothing more important than
half-length figures and heads which, though not to be

classed as pot-boilers (his own expression), served very usefully as such.

The day's work began early and by mid-afternoon my father and my uncle were ready to take the steamer out to the Lido. The Lido was then a very sparsely built upon and thinly populated spot, with no sign of a building on the Adriatic side of it except the *Stabilimento* for sea-bathing. Waiting on the sands at the *Stabilimento* would be my mother, myself and my nanny, who had spent most of the day there, picnicking. My father and my uncle would usually be accompanied by Thoren, or Ruben or Count Thun or others of the circle. It was then the turn of my mother to come into her own, sitting there under her parasol in the midst of a circle of sun-bathing courtiers over whose prostrate forms I clambered.

Before the summer grew too hot we returned to England. We had been home only a day or two when my father had a visit from Edmund Gosse who at that time of his career was the representative of *Scribner's Magazine* in Europe. *Scribner's* were proposing to reproduce some of my father's *Drood* sketches. This led later to *Scribner's* wishing to publish some sketches illustrating an old Berkshire village, and to Edmund Gosse's saying: "I think I will myself write the accompanying article."

Meanwhile a long-standing promise to Stacy Marks and Keeley Halsewell, to row from Oxford to London had to be fulfilled, but "though it was very enjoyable and pleasant", as my father wrote my uncle, "I wanted to get settled somewhere in the country to begin my R.A. picture".

He decided at last upon Aston Tirrold, and it was here that he was to paint *The Village Wedding*—one of the most successful of his "big" pictures.

"I have made a rough design for the picture", he wrote to Woods, "I really think it will come well—there are lots of opportunities for good character painting in it. . . . I have seen Stone several times; he is in a state of great elation, having at the last election for R.A. got six votes and afterwards, on the ballot, he got ten. . . . He is quite as bad as ever finding fault with the world generally, being under the impression that you and I and himself are the only perfect beings at present existing—all of which is extremely pleasant and agreeable to hear. He seems to want very much to join us in the village where we go, but I scarcely know how the thing will work".

Ten days later my father was writing:

> The Chequers,
> Aston Tirrold,
> near Wallingford, Berks.
> August 24th, 1881.

My dear Harry,

The lot of us came here on Monday. . . . You know this old village—we walked through it that Sunday going to Blewbury. At this little inn—the only place I could find for miles round—we are very comfortable. . . .

I left London with the idea of painting this "Village Wedding" quite in modern costume, but I really think it will be utterly beyond me to do so. It is so ugly and *nasty* I cannot bring myself to do it. I don't mean the people in their every day clothes—they are just passable—but I mean those in their wedding attire,—all Reading and Wallingford slop goods degrading in every aspect. . . .

It is very pleasant in many respects here. We have the run of a lot of large orchards belonging to the Inn, and they are nice pleasant people. (He an old Indian Mutiny man and she a good cook.) They have never had anyone staying with them before. . . . I have got a splendid large barn for a studio and we have a pony and carriage for four which I tool about the lanes. Lots of fruit and excellent living, and three young pups for Val to play with, pretty flower garden separating the road from the house, and a private sitting-room—in fact all is well in the midst of the most beautiful scenery and villages with rustics who dress pictorially worse than the denizens of Scotland Road and Vauxhall Road in Liverpool! And I think when I say *that* I have exhausted my contempt for them as an artist. It's like eating stones and sawdust after my fare in Venice! . . .

The Stones are in London and have been all the summer. They made a kind of a proposal to accompany us to the country, but Marcus cooled down rapidly on learning there was no club, or society, or the something he seeks for in this world. I am glad of it, for he is such a wailing prophet of evil and disaster. He won't work himself, and finds fault with everyone else's. . . .

Remember me to Van Haanen, Ruben and all friends, also Fanny. . . . We send our love to you.

Affectionately yours,
Luke Fildes.

Four days later he was writing: "I have designed my picture, if I will keep to it—and it promises to be much the most *agreeable* picture I have yet done. . . . I, of course, can't take so big a canvas out of doors to paint the real thing, nor can I get much of the real thing to sit."

Woods suggested that a way to get round the ugliness of rustic costume would be to antedate the period, to which my father replied at some length: "The picture won't have a scrap of what is considered my 'forte', viz. Sentiment. This may be unwise, but if I hate anything, I hate *manufactured* sentiment, so I am going in for just what I think likely to happen and paint an episode in a quiet little village somewhere in my own head, the quiet little village life with the coarseness and ugliness of immediately modern times pressed out of it, and yet not put back far enough for people to say I am not painting my own time. I am certainly doing so. I am painting what I remember when a youngster among the people I used to know. I notice what you say about going back to old costume but I am sure you will agree with me on reflection that what I might, and should, I admit, gain in the picturesque I should certainly lose in naturalness. When my picture is finished I believe it will convey the impression that it is a genuine record of something experienced by the artist; whereas all costume pictures convey to me that the painter has been more influenced by what he has seen in other pictures. . . . But you agree with me, I know, quite thoroughly in this question. The chief anxiety I had was the same you feel, that the utter ugliness of the best of the people's dress under such circumstances would be too dreadful to paint large. It would be all very well in a *Graphic* drawing, but a large picture, No! Well, I am beginning to think it can be done, and if it *can* be done it will be enormously better in my eyes to do it so!"

He was still at Aston Tirrold a month later. Writing to my uncle towards the end of October he said: "It has not been altogether the pleasantest thing in the world to do to paint out of doors now. . . . I got into the country certainly too late for the important picture I am doing, but with all these disadvantages which, after all, arise every year with me in some form or other in England, I have good hopes of the success of this picture. I think I am decidedly further advanced than I have ever been at this period, and though I have quite 30 or 35 figures, or pieces of figures, certainly that number of heads, to get through, I don't feel afraid of the time to finish as I used to do. . . . I have taken great trouble these last eight weeks arranging and re-arranging the composition and getting my sizes and action correct though roughly done, and hitting the tones as seen in nature. I have done all this actually on the canvas which is 9' by 6' (the picture when finished will be 8' by 5' 3") and it is no joke lugging that kind of thing about." For lack of suitable models in the country my father was intending to finish the figures in London, and he ended that part of his letter: "If we have any light in London the next 5 months I ought to get finished in good time."

During the stay in the country he had made several short visits to Melbury Road in order to hasten progress on the work of enlarging one of the windows in the studio, and he had seen something of Marcus Stone. "I tackled him", he wrote to my uncle, "on the picture he is now painting— one of the old sort—the eternal girl in large hat and white dress with the same old lover in a red coat in a garden— with every tone wrong and not a blade of grass done from nature, nor from a study from nature. The result is that the two last times I have called he has excused himself from showing his picture to me . . . at which I am pleased, for I do not care to see pictures if I am not to speak candidly about them."

Back in London at the end of October, Fildes continued to make progress with *The Village Wedding*. Writing to my uncle at Christmas, my mother said: "Luke's picture is getting on very well. I like it much better than his "Penitent", and I think it will be a greater success . . . it is very unlike any of his other works."

※ IX ※

THE VILLAGE WEDDING

1882-1883

It was Henry Tanworth Wells, it may be remembered, who had sponsored Fildes' election as an Associate. Wells' standing in the Academy was due less to his prolific contributions to its Exhibitions for more than fifty years than to the part he played in its politics. He was an enthusiastic planner and reformer, and a moulder of his colleagues' destinies. A time was to come when he marked down my father, though abortively in the long run, for the holding of high office in the Academy. Whether or not those plans were taking shape as early as 1882, the year was only two days old when a typical Wellsian prod came my father's way. As a newcomer to the Academy, my father had been given the job of Secretary of the Academy Club, an inner symposium of the members, and had been writing to them for their annual subscriptions. He received this letter from Wells:

> Thorpe Lodge, Campden Hill, W.
> January 2nd, 1882.

My dear Fildes,

I have the sign of your commencing secretarial duties in a most praiseworthy manner and in response to your appeal I beg, "Dear Sir", to enclose my cheque. . . .

> Yours very truly,
> Henry T. Wells.

I began this letter by congratulating you upon the official character of your letter. Just a parting word, may

76

I venture to suggest that another year it might be useful to give the address to which the heavy payments are to be sent? You see, my dear Fildes, nature will assert herself and you give proof of your artist (i.e. unbusinesslike) temperament in spite of your best intentions.

There was subtlety in the prod. Wells was perfectly aware that "my dear Fildes", so far from being unbusinesslike, would have been justified in thinking himself somewhat a man of affairs. To pretend the opposite was the Wellsian technique. The allusion to an artist temperament had, however, a point; the artistic temperament used to come out in my father's gestures of self-dramatization. There was a case of this a few days after Wells' letter. Excusing himself to Woods for not having written lately, my father put the blame on his new secretarial duties: "I have had all the correspondence connected with the Royal Academy Club and the accounts to attend to at night, etc. etc."

But other things too, had delayed correspondence— there was the painting of *The Village Wedding*. "I have been having two or three models every day, and Sundays too", he wrote. "I am getting on very well with the picture and I expect it will be one of my successes. McLean offered me £1,600 for it three weeks ago which I declined on the spot."

There was to be an election of an A.R.A. and Fildes wrote in his next letter to Woods that he was not at all sanguine about the latter's chance. But this was one of the occasions on which my uncle's instinct was surer than my father's. He thought he had a chance, and in order to while away the anxieties of Election Day, he recruited another member of the Artist Colony in Venice to join him in a sport of his inventions—walking to Padua from Fusina at the mouth of the River Brenta. It was a sport as beneficial to the soul as to the body, inasmuch as it was along that road that Palladio had built summer villas for the Venetian aristocracy of the *Cinquecento*, which were still standing. But on this occasion there was no stopping to look at Palladian villas. Such was the energy Woods put into the distraction of his anxieties that he and his companion knocked one hour off the record for the walk previously standing to the credit of himself and Thoren. Back in Venice that night Woods called at Florian's to see if there was a telegram from my father. "There was nothing", he entered in his diary. "I was very tired tonight."

However, at half-past two in the morning, there came a ringing and a banging on the street door, and a telegram was handed in. Frightened out of her wits, Woods' landlady roused him. He opened the telegram and turning to her, with a gesture of his hand upon his breast, allayed her alarm: "*Sono professor; niente altro Buona notte* " "I didn't get a wink of sleep afterwards", he wrote my father next day. "I thought of the extra week before 'sending-in'; the Dinner; the six Private View tickets; attentions to make one part with same; the three Varnishing Days, lunch and smoking included; and all the other lumps of fat an A.R.A. is blessed with. Having enjoyed all these, I tried to learn an Italian verb and lighted up a German pipe (a present from Passini). No wonder I had no appetite for breakfast."

It was in the following month, February, that my memories of my parents begin. I was two years and eight months old, and I was perched on my father's shoulder as he carried me down from my nursery to my mother's bedroom. My father must have told me that I had a little brother, because my mind was full of what a little brother might be. I soon saw what a little brother was at the sight of my mother in bed, with a bundle nestling in the crook of her arm.

In time the family would increase: a daughter Kitty, two more sons, Geoffrey and Denis, and a second daughter, Dorothy. We have been a happy family together. How far any of us, his children, can be said to have influenced our father's artistic career is problematical, and hardly enters into my story.

The choice of a godfather for my brother Paul brought Gordon Thomson into the family. As young members of the circle round William Luson Thomas, he and my father had been friends for years. He had been one of the first of my father's bachelor friends whom my mother knew. When we children began to grow up, we took him to ourselves with

a greater ease in some respects than our own father. A name
had to be invented for him. We arrived at "Gording".
Gording must have been well into his seventies when,
five and twenty years later, he used to come on walking
tours with my brother Paul and myself in the Black Forest
and the Salzkammergut.

Gording had been one of those civil servants who contrived to combine a secondary career, as writer or artist,
with their primary career in Whitehall. His was a particularly
happy instance in that his department had been closed down,
and at a comparatively young age he had found himself the
recipient of a pension for life from the State with complete
freedom to devote all his time to black-and-white draughtsmanship, his secondary career up to then. His speciality was
the comic; he was on the staff of *Fun*, *Punch's* chief com-
petitor.

As we grew older, we children suspected that Gording,
who remained a bachelor all his life, had a tender place in
his heart for our mother. If one of us hazarded this notion
in her presence, she would shrug it off but look by no means
displeased. He was to her never anything but "Gordon".
The code of the Victorians—and even of the Edwardians—
inhibited "Fanny" on his side. He called her "Lady Fanny",
a formula of compromise which Marcus Stone also used.

Every spring Gordon Thomson would lampoon the
leading Academy pictures in *Fun*. Having guyed *The
Penitent* three years previously, he was now lying in wait for
The Village Wedding. It speaks well for the firmness of their
friendship that despite the seriousness with which my father
always thought of his own work, lampoons by Thomson
never upset my father's equanimity; it was clever of Thomson
to coin the phrase *une édition de luxe* for one of my father's
pictures.

The Village Wedding, however, was not yet ready for
lampooning. Writing my uncle at the end of February, my
father had said: "The picture overwhelms me. I have such
a devil of a lot to do ... I am not sure I can complete it. ...
It would be a very good picture if I had time." In the end
he did not have time, and the only picture he showed in the
Academy of 1882 was a single figure *Nina*, from his previous

summer in Venice. But 1882 was not a lean year financially. McLean bought five other contemporaries of *Nina* at an average of £200 each, and in July Agnews bought another Venetian subject for £650. None of these, other than *Nina*, am I able to identify.

Woods came to London that year, putting up at Melbury Road, to pay his "duty calls" on his new colleague in the Academy, and for the opening of the Summer Exhibition. Incidentally, these spring-time visits to London became a settled feature in his life, to be interrupted only by the First World War. He sold his two pictures well: *Bargaining for an Old Master* to Holbrook Gaskell for £750 and *A Venetian Fanseller* to Agnews for £450. These sales set him up for the year. On his way back to Venice in May, he broke his journey in Paris and wrote: "I am sending you catalogue of the *Salon* and a small Exhibition they call "International". England is represented by Millais's *Raleigh* and portraits of Mesdames Peru and Jopling . . . Alfred Stevens, Baudry and Knaus have pictures worth running over to see. The whole Exhibition is in one room. At the Salon, there is any amount of nudity, blood and filth, but there are some good pictures, far less than I have seen before. I was immensely struck with Sargent's picture. I believe there is a deal of talk about it."

He also went to an exhibition of Courbet's work at the *Beaux-Arts*. "His landscapes interested me a good deal. I saw the *Stonebreakers*, but I don't understand why it is a great picture."

My uncle's principal exhibit in that year's Academy, *Bargaining for an Old Master*, had given him great trouble in the placing of seven foreground figures against a very elaborate background which in accordance with his usual method he had painted *in situ* before putting in the figures. On his return to Venice, he was consulting my father about this method of procedure—"I am going to commence this time differently. I shall work my composition of figures first."

"From what you tell me of your picture", my father replied, "I am sure it is a capital subject—much more direct in purpose than anything you have done before in *beginning* a picture. I am quite sure having a leading idea to start with will greatly simplify your work—above all people you are one who requires a distinct motive and subject in your picture, to keep you in some sort of bounds. Be careful now about introducing any incidents but those that *bear particularly* on the matter in hand, and the same remarks apply to your treatment of the accessories and background. I should like to see a sketch if it is only a scribble."

What better advice to anybody setting out to paint a figure-subject? But, alas, it was the same old difficulty: Woods, pre-eminent in topography, did not shine as a figure painter. The outcome of this exchange of views was that by the time my uncle brought the picture to London the following spring, he had concentrated so much on the figures that he had neglected his background and, to ward off my father's criticisms, he had to sit down, then and there, and repaint the whole background from sketches.

There had been talk about the need for my uncle to find better quarters than the couple of rooms and studio he had been occupying in the Casa Raffaelli; the more so as my father was planning to spend more time in Venice and my mother no doubt would be with him. By the beginning of August 1882, Woods was reporting that he had taken a lease of the whole of the first floor of a building on the Grand Canal, facing South and approached, on the land side, from the *Campo San Maurizio*. The place was well known to all of them, its having been the American Consulate where Mrs. Harris had entertained my uncle and Whistler. "I shall be able to put the lot of you up. . . . I am looking out for furniture," he wrote.

No. 2727 San Maurizio was from now on to be his home for more than thirty years, and the stopping place of my parents. For a studio he found a pavilion in a garden which once had belonged to a *Palazzo Vendramin*, in that garden-like quarter of *San Sebastiano* which has ever remained little known to tourists because of its remoteness. The pavilion was to be adapted to its new purpose and a glass studio was to be built as an annexe in the garden. "So there will be some inducement", my uncle wrote, "to get through your picture and spend some time here next winter under comfortable

circumstances". Then he turned to more mundane subjects:
he had done a two miles swim from *Fusina* on the mainland
to the island of *San Giorgio in Alga*. "I think I could have
gone on to Venice but it was getting dark." My father's
reaction to this exploit was to ignore it and to comment upon
a more serious topic: "I hope you will be very particular
about the drainage question, for I remember well a most
terrible odour which I encountered every time I went to
Mrs. Harris's, on the staircase immediately on entering
from the *Calle*."

All that summer my father was struggling in London with
The Village Wedding and spending his week-ends at Lowestoft, where my mother was with Paul and myself and—in
true Victorian fashion—a nurse and an under-nurse to look
after the two of us. William Lomas, a family friend, was in
Lowestoft at the time and he painted a pleasant study—
which I now have—of my mother reclining on a sand-dune
with a novel and a sunshade and the cold-looking North
Sea as background. It has a look about it, with its greys,
of a Boudin, and Lomas, all Gallic, has signed it "Souvenir
de Lowestoft".

What the difficulties were which kept *The Village Wedding*
so long in being completed I have no idea. Most of it had
been painted the previous autumn at Aston Tirrold. It is,
truly enough, a most elaborate composition of a large number of figures, but the picture in its finished form shows
no signs of any difficulty of composition. Edward R. Russell,
the first Lord Russell of Liverpool, had seen it in my father's
studio earlier in the year and he had written an appreciation
of it for the *Liverpool Daily Post:*

> Mr. Fildes has got a character for lugubrious subjects.
> . . . The truth is, if one were to express the artist's own
> feelings, that he is not animated by a taste either for the
> sombre or for the gay, but by a yearning . . . *to paint the*
> *people*. The sorrows and sadness of the people first touched
> his sympathies, but he knows well enough that the people
> have joys. . . . When the world sees the new picture,
> which is bright, highly coloured, vivaciously composed
> picture of a rustic wedding party returning from church

The Return of the Penitent
1879

The Village Wedding
1883

Mrs Luke Fildes
1887

through a snugly thatched and pleasantly wooded Berkshire village—it will be acknowledged that Mr. Fildes is a master of sunlight as well as of shade, of festivity as well as of wretchedness, and a master of reality in each. . . . In this amusing and lively scene, with which everybody must sympathise at a glance, . . . while central figures of the rural bride and bridegroom deservedly fix the attention, the canvas is delightfully crowded with children, with women, with old men, and with the wedding *personnel* of mother, sisters and soldier brother, each person doing exactly what is natural and all together making up a picture of infinite variety and interest. I will only add two words: one in recognition of the well chosen and realized facial expression of the newly united pair, which is delightfully faithful to life; and the other a tribute of admiration to the realistic painting of all the dress in the picture. . . . Mr. Fildes not only knows how everything gets to set in wear and, on the other hand, how everything new looks before it has set. . . . It is a pleasure to foreshadow what is likely to be one of the painter's choicest and most popular successes.

One wonders after that what the painter could do to add to his picture. But he was still hard at it months later.

By October Woods had completed his move and had set up an establishment. It consisted of Antonio—a veteran of the stricken field of Solferino—as gondolier-cum-major-domo, and a cook-housekeeper named Anna. Antonio looked after my parents for many years on their visits to Venice; as for Anna, there was a succession of them, all with the same name. The studio was not yet ready and my Uncle came to London for a few weeks. He travelled by the newly-opened St Gotthard route. He was full of his experiences in the great floods on the Venetian mainland where he had been staying with his friend, the painter de Blaas, near Vicenza, and the countryside had been so deep under water that Verona had petitioned Venice for the loan of gondolas.

Woods returned to Venice before the end of the year. On Christmas Day he was dining on board s.s. *Tanjore* in the port of Venice. *Tanjore*, commanded by his friend, Captain

D

Briscoe, was one of the P. and O. fleet which plied between Venice and the East, a favourite route to India in those days. So often was *Tanjore* at Venice that Mrs. Briscoe lived there, and the Captain and his wife were popular members of the foreign colony. My uncle used to tell a story about Briscoe. Earlier in that year, 1882, the Mediterranean Fleet had bombarded the forts at Alexandria in the course of the campaign to suppress Arabi Pasha's revolt, and during the operation *Tanjore* had been caught between the fire of the two opposing forces. Only by Briscoe's seamanship was *Tanjore* extricated from a predicament. But it so happened that in the course of the operation one of Her Majesty's ships, the frigate *Condor*, under the command of a young naval officer named Lord Charles Beresford, had carried out some manoeuvre which had elicited the signal from the flagship: "Well done, *Condor*." The signal had run the length and breadth of the Empire; Lord Charles Beresford had become a national hero. But a few months later a rumour began to circulate in the coffee rooms and wine shops of Venice, where *Tanjore* and her captain were well known, that the signal flown by Admiral Seymour had been "Well done, *Tanjore*". Wishing to get at the truth of the matter, the next time some units of the Fleet came into Venice, my uncle questioned a young naval officer about it. "Yes, there was a signal flown for *Tanjore*" was the reply. "I believe it was, 'To hell out of that or I'll blow you sky high'."

The close of the old year in Venice and the opening of the new—1883—were marked by a presentation of *tableaux vivants* at the Bronsons, who were well known members of the Anglo-American colony. My uncle acted as producer, and he wrote my father: "The frame was large enough for two figures. We had perhaps the most beautiful women in Venice to pose ... Countess Mocenigo of San Stae (you have not seen her, a beautiful girl) in Watteau costume, perhaps the best of the evening. The house was packed, titles two a penny. Princes were very cheap. I nearly shed tears at the Princess Metternich's affability at the finish." And a second showing of *tableaux* had been given in the presence of Don Carlos, the Spanish Pretender.

To my uncle's playfulness of that nature my father would

not bounce back the ball. On that occasion his choice of reply fell upon the apparent unsaleability of *The Village Wedding*. "It improves every day, for I am now putting the top coat on. I have had no sign of a buyer yet. It's true nobody has seen it." In a second letter: "I have not felt inclined to write you . . . with the hope that I should have been able to send you the good news of the sale of my picture in which I have been working so long and hard, but I have now I think given that prospect up. . . . I am afraid it is a fact that no one will consider the question of buying so large a picture—my only chance seems to be now its making a success in the R.A. . . . This is pretty hard, after all my sacrifices of time and money. The picture seems to be an enormous favourite, but no one comes to buy. Agnew would not even come and see it. He says he daren't entertain the idea of buying a big picture these times. I did expect to have arranged with the Fine Art people but tonight our negotiations have fallen through—Well! It will be a lesson for me. I have fully made up my mind not to paint any more large pictures unless they are commissions. I cannot stand the risk and anxiety I have had over this one. I shall now go in for what everybody else does, viz: the safe business. I have done my share of the big things. I have worked desperately hard and I think the picture is an artistic success, and I feel disappointed at the total absence of encouragement."

If those laments were intended to strike a spark of pity they failed.

"I knew", my uncle wrote back, "you could not have sold it as yet, or you would have told me, but I have not the slightest doubt about your getting through this superfluous formality (artistically speaking) before it leaves your house for the R.A."

I suspect my father's qualms to have been less than he was making out. Within a few days, Agnew, on second thoughts, had come to the studio and bought *The Village Wedding* for 2,500 guineas, the highest price my father had ever received for a picture. Thomas Agnew and Sons published an engraving of it which sold all over the Empire. "Many a Colonist", one paper opined, "can trace likeness to friends in the Old Land amongst those assembled so picturesquely."

I remember *The Village Wedding* in my father's studio, or rather what to me was the principal figure in it, the Trooper in the Life Guards, who gives an arm to the bride's mother and sister. He used to come down to Melbury Road from the new Cavalry Barracks in Knightsbridge and was glad to have a shilling for the morning's work and his bus fare. The two girls in the forefront, one of whom throws an old shoe at the bridal pair, were my mother's parlourmaid and head-housemaid and great would be (so I gathered in later years) the flutterings "below stairs" on the mornings when the gallant Life-Guardsman was due to come for a sitting.

"Show Sunday" fell that year on the 8th of April. My mother had instituted a system by which the parlourmaid, stationed on the landing outside the studio door, dropped a coffee bean into a brass bowl for every visitor who came up the Triumphal Staircase. This year the tally was little short of seven hundred; but a time would come a few years later when my mother regarded any falling short of one thousand as a decline in my father's popularity.

The picture's success in the Academy was all that my father could have hoped. That year, however, he seems to have kept none of the newspaper cuttings except Gordon Thomson's "guying" of the picture in *Fun*. Gordon Thomson took the view of *The Village Wedding* that the principal figure in the wedding procession was a gaffer bringing up the rear who happened to bear a distant resemblance to Gladstone, then passing through a period of unpopularity because of his Administration's weak handling of the situation in Egypt. Gording turned the picture into a political cartoon. He seized upon this figure of the old gaffer and metamorphosed the shoe which my mother's parlourmaid was aiming at the bridal pair into a shower of brickbats descending upon the Prime Minister's head.

On the opening of the Academy that year there had been some criticism in the Press of Frank Holl, the newly elected R.A., for having turned from "subject" pictures to portraiture, and my father, who in a few years' time would himself be turning to portraiture, had written to Holl deprecating the criticism. Holl wrote back:

My dear Fildes,

I am very much obliged to you for your letter of the 30th.

I troubled over the notice in the *Telegraph*, and read it, I must confess, with some contempt for the writer's opinion on the subject of portraiture. Had he said that I was to be blamed for my rendering of the same, one would bear it as we have to bear these things, but as he seems to fancy that portraiture is not a particularly high ambition, then surely he lays himself open to being considered rather ignorant of the subject he writes upon, for I fancy, and I am sure we all do, that the portraits in the Galleries of Europe do not form by any means the least important part.

A month later, early in June, hard upon the heels of my uncle who had been in London for his usual spring-time visit, my parents went to Venice. My father had a commission of two thousand guineas from John Aird, the great Public Works contractor, to paint an important Venetian subject for next year's Academy, and a commission of £850 from another patron to paint a smaller Venetian subject.

By this sudden departure half way through the London season Fildes had left behind him some secretarial duties towards the Royal Academy Club to be performed by a deputy. The deputy was Stacy Marks, who sent my father a full report of the Club's outing at Hampton Court. Frith had been in the Chair. "The dinner was ample in quantity good in quality and very well served—at least that was the general opinion as far as my knowledge went, though Marcus Stone in proposing the Chairman's health said—and persisted in saying when met by cries of 'No!'—that it was 'very bad'. . . . We had an extra guest in a Mr. Selli, Mus.Doc. He had invited the Club to go into the Chapel in the Palace and hear him play on the 'Father Schmidt' organ. . . . I invited him, nothing loath, to dine with us. He knew Frith and so sat on his left, I being on the right. Well, I had to stop the old boy from ordering more expensive wines than those we were drinking—he professed to know, and probably did, which were the best in the cellar—

but he was too artful and scored off me with an extra bottle of champagne at 15 bob, which you will see down in the bill. . . . Happy Fildes! Blessed Woods! To be away from all Soirees, Garden Parties, At Homes, and invitations for a few days in the country—which cut into the London painter's time so sadly. . . ."

In Venice, whilst the two painters were at the studio my mother was going on her social rounds. She was having tea one day with Robert Browning at the Pallazzo Rezzonico. Several admirers from America begged the poet to read something out of his works. It was not a good afternoon for Browning; the further he went on, the more involved, to the company's embarrassment, he became, until "Pen" Browning, his son, went across to him and gently removed the book from his father's hands. "Thank you, Dad", he said, "we have all enjoyed that very much, but you mustn't tire yourself." And Browning sat with a confused expression on his face. My mother felt sorry for him, and she asked him if he knew about the Browning Societies which met at tea-time and used only brown earthenware teapots. This amused him, and the tension was broken.

My mother did not stay long in Venice that year. My father brought her home, deposited the whole family in Lowestoft again, and was back in Venice by the middle of August, where he remained until four days before Christmas when he returned home well satisfied with the work he had done. He wrote on Boxing Day to my uncle: "I have not for three days been able to see any chimney pots. It has been one long fog—not a vestige of sun or light to paint by. And three days later: "Here we are, 3 o'clock Saturday afternoon, and I have had only one meal, that was lunch yesterday, without the gas being lighted, since my arrival. . . . It has been one long dense pall of darkness over the land."

No word of comfort came from Woods. "*Poveretto*," he wrote, "Here I am, a-wallowing in sunshine in the Palazzo Cristallo [his glass-house studio]; there has not been a ghost of a cloud since you left."

Woods was invited for his Christmas dinner that year to the Layards. Sir Henry Layard, after a distinguished public career in the course of which he discovered Nineveh, was

Under-Secretary of State for Foreign Affairs and eventually
Ambassador at Constantinople had, on his retirement,
settled in Venice where he and Lady Layard—one of the
Wimborne Guests—had bought the Cà Cappello on the
Grand Canal. There, for many years they were the leaders
of the then considerable English-speaking colony that
inhabited Venice. Woods became persona gratissima at the
Cà Cappello. He was Lady Layard's mainstay on the
committees of the Sailors' Home, the English Hospital and
the English Church of St. George, and of the latter he was
one of the churchwardens. In a different vein he was the
scene-painter, designer of costumes and stage-manager for
theatricals at the Cà Cappello. All this had a bearing upon
my parents: for it meant that on their visits to Venice they
arrived as a part—as it were—of the community.

❧ X ❧

VENETIAN LIFE AND *THE VENETIANS*

1884-1885

Looked at from Melbury Road, No. 11 has undergone little change. A 'blue plaque' has recently been put up. (Incidentally, the years of my father's birth and of his taking up residence in the house are shown one year later than in fact they were.) A pair of most decorative eighteenth-century wrought iron gates, and the brick piers which Norman Shaw designed for them as a truly worthy entrance into the front garden, were destroyed in a blitz in the Second World War. Otherwise, for anyone passing up or down Melbury Road the house looks very much as Norman Shaw designed it back in the seventies. But thirty years or so ago, after my parents were dead, and the house had been sold, the interior was cut up into flats, which I have not seen and have no heart to see.

I trace back my memories of that interior to the year 1884. Naturally I remember the nurseries best. They were upstairs on the second storey, looking over Melbury Road. So strong was the William Morris influence upon interior decoration and furnishing that my parents, despite their dislike for "aestheticism" had Morris wall-papers in the day and night nurseries. One had a design of frogs going a-wooing and cows jumping over moons—by Walter Crane, I afterwards came to know. And there were black spindly-legged chairs with rush seats, which William Morris' firm in Oxford Street made so popular and were often to be seen in George du Maurier's drawings in *Punch*. And there were, too, the coloured supplements from *The Graphic* Christmas numbers —Millais's *Cherry Ripe* and *Cinderella* which my mother bound round with coloured tape before affixing them with drawing pins to the nursery walls.

When you descended to the lower storeys, everything took on a character of more solidarity. Heavily embossed wall-papers in low-toned gold; distempers of Pompeian red; sage-green wall hangings, burnt-umber woodwork. The well of the main staircase, that triumphal ascent to the Studio, had all four walls hung with seventeenth century Flemish tapestries. For furniture my parents favoured Sheraton with a mingling of Venetian and Flemish black-framed mirrors, Hispano-Mauresque pottery, Venetian brass and copper-ware and touches of Rosetti and Whistler in blue-and-white Nankin and Delft.

Houses like that were a background for entertaining. My father had always been in with the leaders of the stage. The Bancrofts, the Kendals, the Hares, were on dinner-party terms. So were the Gilberts and Sydney Grundy among playwrights. There was an Anglo-American group of painters—Edwin Abbey, G. H. Boughton and Sargent, this last having emigrated from Paris to London. Among writers were Anstey Guthrie ("F. Anstey") and Henry James, but somehow the friendship with him never ripened. The Sambournes lived round the corner in Stafford Terrace on Campden Hill. Linley Sambourne (the *Punch* cartoonist), was a close enough friend of my father's, for my father to stand god-parent to his son.

Week-ends at country houses were becoming frequent. The institution that Stacy Marks had said was a nuisance. There was one when my parents were staying at the Gilberts. The Beerbohm Trees were of the party. Tree and my father were strolling in the garden on the Sunday morning when Tree said: "Let's have a lark with old Gilbert!" In those days "larks" were a great pastime, although my father was not given to them. On that occasion he gave way. Tree plucked some fruit from a mulberry-bush and smeared it over his face—he was a past-master of theatrical make-up—producing an effect of lacerated flesh. He then laid himself full length on the grass, and closed his eyes. My father's role in that school-boyish performance was to run back to the house wringing his hands and vociferating: "Gilbert, Gilbert, come at once. Poor Tree! Poor Tree!" At which Gilbert came hurrying across the lawn to find Beerbohm Tree the victim, apparently, of some dreadful accident. "My God!" he muttered, "my God!" Whereupon Tree opened an eye and gave Gilbert an oily wink.

Gilbert, without further word, turned on his heel and went back to the house, and so oppressive did the atmosphere become that the house-party broke up prematurely. In ninety-nine cases out of a hundred an incident of that kind would have led to years of estrangement—to put it no higher—on Gilbert's part, but never a sign of a rift ever arose between him and my father, and although some of Gilbert's observations upon Beerbohm Tree have become classics of causticity, even their friendship endured.

My father had returned from Venice the previous year well satisfied with the work he had been doing on his main picture, *Venetian Life*, but early in 1884 he was writing to Woods that he had "entirely re-arranged it". ("I have not had the heart to write about it until I once more began to see the picture together again.") It would seem though that the case had been less desperate than he was making out, for when my uncle arrived in London a few weeks later on his usual springtime visit, he entered in his diary: "We had a talk over Luke's picture, which is not so changed as I expected."

On Show Sunday, in 1884, so great was the impression the picture made, that John Aird, who had commissioned it, was completely carried away and bought Woods '*Il mio Traghetto*, which was in my father's studio, on the spot, and still not content he must cross the road to No. 8 and buy Marcus Stone's two pictures.

In painting *Venetian Life* and its companion in that year's Academy, *A Venetian Flower Girl*, my father had made as great a departure from *The Village Wedding* of the previous year as he had made with that picture from anything before. This time he had abandoned himself to a new method, an experiment in pure colour and technique. As for subject, there was nothing more in *Venetian Life* than a group of work-girls resting in the cool of a summer's evening outside the door of a tenement house (a *palazzo* which had come down in the world). But the effect upon public and critics on the opening of the Academy, was immense; "Gorgeousness of colour seldom seen in the work of English painters, masterly drawing, masterly painting." By general consent Fildes, still a junior in the Academy, was again ranked with Leighton and Millais, and now with Orchardson, as the painters of the "pictures of the year".

There was one dissentient voice—that of William Morris, turned critic of painting: "Mr. Luke Fildes' work does, I suppose, lay claim to realistic qualities but can by no means support that claim; his pictures show a contented resting in most commonplace conventionality, except as regards minor pieces of still life, and in the *Venetian Flower Girl*, a rough and I must add repulsive skill of representation of the mass of flowers, which is by reason of slap-dash execution and a peculiar deficiency in sense of colour, turned into a piece of downright ugliness, and consequently has no *raison d'être* whatever". *Plus ça change!* Such is the language that might be used today of an example of excessive Modernism!

William Morris, like Ruskin before him, had a literary directness which had the merit of not leaving his readers in any doubt as to the point he was driving at. In the article from which I have been quoting he went on: "It is no use playing with the question. Those who wish to have art in these passing days must forget three hundred years and go to school with the craftsmen and painters of the 15th and 16th centuries. The alternative is to accept as art the useless cleverness of Mr. Orchardson or Mr. Fildes . . . and I say emphatically that this is not art." A few decades later, when Roger Fry appeared on the scene, the yardstick for evaluating Victorian Painting would be, not the *Quattrocento*, but Post-Impressionism. Which reminds me of an occasion of my father being given a copy of Tolstoy's *What is Art?* He glanced at the title and laid the book aside with the remark that practising artists had not time for speculations of that sort.

In his novel *Trilby* George du Maurier makes Little Billee take Taffy and the Laird to one of the brilliant musical parties at Mechelen Lodge on Campden Hill. In real life, Mechelen Lodge was Moray Lodge, the home of the Arthur Lewises. Mrs. Arthur Lewis before her marriage was Kate Terry, the elder sister of Ellen Terry and, as many people said, the most talented of the Terry family. Musical evenings at Moray Lodge were a gathering of all that was most select in the circle of the fine arts, the stage, literature and music, with an admixture of high society. Calling at Moray Lodge to take leave on his return to Venice that year, my uncle was pressed by Arthur Lewis to stay to dinner, as Irving and Ellen Terry were expected. "I should have liked very much, but it meant unpacking and missing my friends in Paris", he noted in his diary.

The "friends in Paris" were my father, Linley Sambourne and G. H. Boughton, the "regulars" who went every spring to have a look at the *Salon*, and on this occasion were accompanied by Edwin Abbey, Colin Hunter and William Lomas. My uncle, having taken the night boat and joined them, records their joint opinion. Except for Jules Breton, Benjamin Constant and Bouguereau, the *Salon* seemed a "great falling-off", and as for the Independants, "the work was not so bad as the motive for it".

After his success with his two Venetian pictures in the Academy of 1884, my father was all the more set on returning to Venice. He was writing to my uncle, "It is almost impossible to work in London. It plays the devil with one being here in the Season, and as for the letters and other matters to attend to, it is too absurd. . . . I have a great many applications for pictures; five applications for portraits of ladies last week—one of them the new beauty, Lady Kildare—who told me that money was no object if I would paint it, but I have declined all portraits as I have arranged to go out to Venice."

He was, however, delayed by wanting to see my mother in better trim, who had been seedy. Off went the whole family, parents, children and two nurses to the Bath Hotel at Felixstowe. Later, my father deposited us in the house of the landscape painter, Frank Walton, which he had taken for the rest of the summer, at the foot of Holmbury Hill. Our Aunt Annie would keep my mother company. A five-year-old, I remember some of that summer holiday. Wells, R.A., had a house near by, where he was surrounded by his Charrington and Street grandchildren. One grandchild was the most beautiful creature I had ever set eyes upon. She wore a wide sash tied in a large bow in the small of her back and when, a few years later, I began to look at *Punch* I saw her semblance week after week in Du Maurier's drawings.

The family thus disposed of, my father was able to leave for Venice, and after a ten weeks' absence, he came back with another big Venetian picture.

A letter from Edmund Gosse was waiting for him.

During the few years since they first met over a commission for *Scribner's Magazine*, they had improved their acquaintance.

> 29, Delamere Terrace,
> W.
> 12.10.84.

My dear Fildes,

I hope we shall meet before we start for America at the end of next month. My work at Cambridge begins in a few days, and I shall be mostly there in residence until the middle of November, but if you are in England, must somehow make an effort to see you.

I hope my painter and sculptor friends, whose fellowship has been so delightful to me, will not cast me off now that literature has completely divorced me from art. I foresee that I shall write no more art criticism, and I regret nothing in that except the personal intercourse with the artists. Literature is the province of my birth, where I am at home; art has never been more than a very charming annexation, held in a most uncertain tenure.

Believe me, with kindest wishes,

> Ever yours,
> Edmund Gosse.

Woods had been on a flying visit to Melbury Road over Christmas and was now back in Venice. Writing him on the 19th of January of the new year, 1885, Fildes told him "We are all quite well, I am glad to say—our chief suffering is from darkness. It is utterly out of the question being able to paint, so one passes the days designing and pottering about... I amuse myself altering all the figures in my picture. The last one who departed this life is the fair girl on the top step. Suddenly yesterday, in an appropriate gloom, I scraped her out. In faith she *was* bulky; it took me one hour and a half."

The picture he was referring to was *Venetians* which he had been painting in Venice. It was of the same size and character as *Venetian Life* of the year before. Like *Venetian Life*, it had been a commission, but the price had been left open. Now, three months before Sending-in day, my father had the picture on his hands, unsold. The prospective owner felt unable to pay the price my father wanted. On Sending-in day, the picture, though considered a success, was still unsold. Millais, who had been prevented by sudden illness from being at the Varnishing days and had asked my father to perform some service for him, wrote:

5 May, '85.

My dear Fildes,

I have never thanked you for your kind offices on the Varnishing day. I do thank you now most sincerely. I only hope you may never require such assistance yourself. I am happy to say I am getting on all right, and am longing to get into the Studio.

If it is any comfort to you, my two gentlemen Patrons have also thrown me over, so I am the happy possessor of *The Ruling Passion*. If you are still in the same position in regard to your own work, keep your pecker up, and be sure good work in time inevitably finds a purchaser, even in this ignorant country.

My father was to remain "in the same position" for some months yet, an unprecedented experience for him. It was not until the autumn of that year that he sold *Venetians* to the Manchester Corporation, and then at a considerable loss.

The day after Millais' letter, my parents, my uncle and Marcus and Laura Stone—this was the first occasion of women being included in the party—later to be joined by Boughton and Linley Sambourne—were off on the usual springtime visit to Paris for the *Salon*. They put up at the

Hotel Binda, which became a favourite resort of my parents in the Eighties and Nineties.

It must have been on their return from that visit, that my parents brought back with them "The Fairy"! The Fairy was a doll dressed as a ballerina, perched upon a platform which was mounted upon a handle. By imparting a rotary movement with this handle the platform and the ballerina could be made to pirouette to the strains of the waltz from Gounod's *Faust*, emitted by some mechanism inside the toy. Very Parisian! As soon as my parents were inside the hall of No. 11, my father opened a bag and produced "The Fairy". "Come up into the Studio", he said to me. And there, in the Studio, I had the astonishing spectacle of my father waltzing round and round, playing the tune and humming to it, and in that moment I had a revelation of him I have never forgotten.

"The Fairy" was taken into safe keeping by my mother and exalted to being a family mascot. For more than seventy years she has been the central decoration of a succession of Christmas dinner tables, and she carries her years well.

In that spring of 1885 there was building at No. 11. The cause of it was the winter darkness my father so often deplored. A new wing was added to the house, containing a glass studio adjoining "one of the finest rooms in London", and underneath a new day-nursery.

Personally, I regretted those improvements. The site of them was a sunk courtyard paved with red tiles, which had a drain in the middle to catch surface water. Periodically that drain had to be cleared out, and it was one of my joys to plump myself down on hands and knees beside the gardener when he was performing that operation and to inhale the fascinatingly acrid smell of decayed vegetable matter and worms, a pastime for ever after to be denied me. And there was a further cause for regret. Our greatest friends were the Colin Hunter children. Colin Hunter, A.R.A., lived at No. 14—exactly opposite No. 11. Both houses had their nursery windows overlooking Melbury Road and therefore in full view of each other. A system of visual signalling existed which ensured constant communication between the occupants of the two nurseries as to what they were up to. Now all that must cease. The Fildes' nursery would be moving downstairs and be overlooking a garden and a park, in some ways an improvement but lacking a contact with "Little Hunters".

At the end of May a letter very characteristic of its writer came from Venice:

My dear Fildes,

If I have delayed in answering your very friendly letter it has been owing in great part to the enervating influence of the Sirocco and the well known Venetian indolence which comes over one particularly in hot weather, as we have now. I was very sorry to hear that you had been disappointed by the gentleman (if we may give him that title) who ordered your big picture. . . .

Of course I was and still am much annoyed at the rejection of my little picture at the R.A. Whatever may have been the reason for this quite unexpected rebuff, it will at least teach me that one can never judge by appearances, nor count upon the duration of propitious circumstances. Though I try my best to take life and its disappointments philosophically, it must always be painful for anyone to find that he has been treated unjustly.

I am working not very hard, but I have several things in hand. . . . Still I am in the old rotten place . . . as it seems quite impossible to find a better studio or any place to build a glasshouse. . . . There is a great dearth of models; this is a serious drawback, especially to me who does not possess the skill of my favoured friend Professor Cav. de Blaas, who knows the secret of painting "Bon bonnière heads" from any old, ugly beast.

I have been in March at Rome, Florence, Perugia and Assisi, which latter place impressed me very favourably. I look forward with great pleasure to our meeting here in the Autumn and remain with my kind regards to Mrs. Fildes,

Ever yours very sincerely,
C. van Haanen.

On the 7th of June, Fildes was writing Woods about the recent Royal Academy elections. One of them had been

Burne-Jones as an A.R.A., which created some stir at the time:

> Busy with models in the day and having to dine out in the evening, quite prevented me sending you the details of the election.
>
> I have no doubt it was a surprise to you. I mean the Burne-Jones incident, as you will see by the voting there was a dead set for him. I have not the slightest objection to him being in the Royal Academy. I only feel there has been an indecent haste in rushing him in and a very slavish bowing down to him as soon as he graciously consented to allow himself to be elected. My idea about B. Jones is that he is not quite good enough to make such a remarkable demonstration about and it will only make all the Grosvernorites more offensive than before. . . .
>
> The R.A. election took no one by surprise. Stone is not at all strong, and there was no other painter to the fore, so as there was an Architect vacancy of course Waterhouse got it.
>
> I stand no chance at all, nor will I as long as Stone is not elected—people that would vote for me won't because My God! what a slap in the face it would be for Stone! . . . ? I have not many friends in the R.A. or else I cannot understand why, after the important works I have attempted since my election 6½ years ago—*The Penitent, Village Wedding, Venetian Life* and this year's picture, I have not had some better recognition than 7 votes.
>
> I am going on with small pictures for some time and do not intend making that "effort" that people kindly suggest me to do, as if I had never made any, and instead, I'll try, as others do, to make a little more money.
>
> As far as I can make out my plans, I will go to Venice about the third week in August . . . but my visit will not be a long one this year.
>
> Remember me to van Haanen, Thoren, Ruben and all friends.

That letter was crossed by one from Woods of an opposite tenor—"I am very pleased at Burne-Jones' election. I had noticed his name for the first time the other day in the list of candidates; of course, I did not expect his election—still I think it is a good thing."

Had my father really been supposing that he did not stand well with the "Powers" in the Academy—though it was a supposition I cannot believe he seriously entertained— he must have been reassured by an invitation to the "inner circle" he received from Wells a few days later. Millais had just been created a baronet and Wells was having an intimate party in his honour. "My dear Fildes", he wrote, from Thorpe Lodge, "Can you come to a little bachelor dinner here on Saturday next at 7.30 p.m. I hope you can—Millais suggested coming and I am asking Calderon, Armstead and yourself to meet him, knowing that the modest meal will not lose in interest thereby. Morning coat, that is the bargain. So sorry I was not at home when you brought the boys yesterday."

In the 1880's the modish part of Felixstowe consisted of a country lane which began at the Bath Hotel, skirted a short stretch of beach as far as Cobbold's Point, and then turned inland. Bordering on that lane, with views across the sea to the Cork Lightship, were some private houses which stood, as I remember them, in extensive gardens; all, that is, but one of them—Harland House—which, by some turn of fortune, but without destroying the tone of the neighbourhood, had come to letting out lodgings. My father and mother had taken rooms for us children at Harland House that summer of 1885 and they spent most of August there with us.

A gathering of friends took place every morning on the beach—the Streets and the Charringtons, parents and children, Charles Keene of *Punch*, "Old" Harral the woodengraver, Ray Lankester, the Chestons, the Fildes family and sometimes the house-parties of the Ludwig Messels. The Messels lived in a large house they had taken for the summer, a mile or so inland.

I have spoken of the 1880's as a time for "larks" and "dressing-up". The house which the Messels had taken conduced to such diversions. The walls were hung with assegais and Zulu shields and the floors were strewn with shaggy rugs. It was a time, too, of "posed" photography.

I have photographs in which my father is posing as a Zulu, my mother, in a macintosh and hood, as a nun, and everybody in the group looking as solemn as solemn can be, except Ray Lankester who manifestly is quite uninhibited.

When going to Venice later that year my father had intended making only a short visit, but in the end he and my mother stayed nearly three months. For one reason flowers were out of season in Venice, and without them he could not finish his picture—a companion to the *Venetian Flower-Girl* which had upset William Morris. This difficulty would seem not to have been foreseen. Eventually, flowers were obtained from as far away as Serra Valle at the foot of the mountains, and the Edens' garden on the Giudecca did its best.

My uncle was at Serra Valle. It was a village to which he used for many years to move during the full heat of the Venetian summer, and he had returned there to finish some work begun earlier in the year. One day, during his absence, the German Crown Prince Frederick and the Crown Princess turned up at the studio in Venice and had to be received by my father. Vestiges of the Grand Tour still remained to this extent that visitors to Venice made a point of calling at the studios of artists without warning. The easy pace of living encouraged the artists to welcome visits, and a few days after that Royal visit W. S. Gilbert, Mrs. Gilbert and Mrs. Beerbohm Tree walked in.

My parents came back at the end of the year to an impenetrable London fog at a time when Uncle Harry was entering in his diary: "Today has been perhaps the most beautiful I have ever experienced in Venice during the winter. Clear warm sunshine, and scarcely cold in the shade. From the Zattere this morning I could see the local colour on the mainland."

❧ XI ❧

TURNING TO PORTRAITURE
1886-1889

Fildes had been home only a few weeks before he scraped out the whole of the new Flower-Girl's skirt and repainted it ("And in an hour I saw the picture done", he wrote to Woods).

Woods arrived at Melbury Road for his usual spring-time visit, and the first entry in his diary was:

"26 *March*, 1886. Luke had a dinner party tonight. F. Holl, R.A. and Mrs. Holl, H. T. Wells, R.A. and Miss Wells, Abbey (who left later for America via Liverpool), Sargent, Charles Keene (*Punch*), Parsons, and Ouless, R.A."

It was followed by:

"1 *April*, 1886. Christies—There is a most extraordinary collection for sale—Burne-Jones, Rossetti and some early Millais. The Rossettis conclusively prove what a humbug the man was. I never shall forget the reputation he had when I first came to London."

"2 *April*, 1886. I went tonight with Luke and Fanny to the Exhibition of Millais' works at the Grosvenor . . . No living European artist could come up to it."

That last comment, which undoubtedly reflected the opinion of the time, should be contrasted with a story which has appeared in some memoirs and been given currency by other writers. The authoress of those memoirs claimed to

have seen Millais coming away from the Private View at the
Grosvenor Gallery, his head bowed down and tears in his
eyes, and all because of his having seen his Pre-Raphaelite
and later works together and been overcome at realizing how
he had deteriorated. But the story does not make sense.
Nothing he had seen at the Private View could have produced such surprise for Millais; he had hung the Exhibition
himself, had edited the catalogue, and the effect was just as
he wanted it to be. Apart from that, as should be well known,
Millais always maintained that his Pre-Raphaelite period—
all its beauty notwithstanding—was but a stepping-stone to
what he did later.

My father's contributions to the Academy of 1886—
his second *Flower Girl* and another single figure, *The Daughter
of the Lagoons*—were thought to be "a big artistic success".
After the opening, my parents and my uncle paid their
customary visit to Paris and renewed their conviction of the
Salon's inferiority. There was, however, for once in the
Salon, a painting which gave my father an idea. The painting
was a woman's portrait by Carolus-Duran and the idea it
gave my father was to try his hand at something of the kind
and do a portrait of my mother. The decision, so easy and
natural a one for him to take, was to have consequences
which he could scarcely have intended. They revolutionized
the rest of his career.

With the one exception of *The Doctor*, which would come
in five years' time and be the "biggest" of them all, there
would be no more "big" pictures. For forty years, the rest
of his life, he specialised in portraits, with only occasional
and mostly minor excursions into his Venetian style and never
again into Social-Realism.

However, the turn to Portraiture would not mean aban-
doning Realism as such; he had very clear views as to that.
The essential requirement in a portrait was that it should
look like the sitter; if not, why have it painted? A poor
likeness was no excuse for having "revealed" a sitter's inner
character. Indeed, the capability of a portrait—a visual work
of art—to represent something that was not perceptible to
the naked eye was a matter my father regarded with suspicion.

Returning, then, from that trip to Paris in the month of

May, 1886, my parents set about their new collaboration
at once. I remember the excitement of seeing my mother
arrayed in full panoply of evening dress—as I shall be
describing later—in the middle of the morning, and I was
allowed into the studio to watch.

That summer the family spent the holidays at Felixstowe
again, and my father wrote to Woods from there:

I have been down here for two holidays of a week each
and with the usual result of totally unfitting me, apparently,
for returning to work any more. . . . Fanny's portrait
promises first-rate, and so does the smaller picture of
Mrs. Wagg. . . . I think there is no chance of my turning
up in Venice this year. There is no artistic nor pecuniary
reason for me to go this year, and as the cholera seems to
cling to the district, I think it is only prudent to put off my
visit to another year. . . . I have had a little disappointment
about the *Flower Girl*. I hoped that Mr. Schwabe would
have been able to lend me it for a couple of months after
the Exn. A firm of colour printers offered me £200 for
the right to reproduce it in colour, only it was necessary
to have the original for two months, but it turns out that
they were ready in Hamburg for Mr. S's pictures, so he
could not consent to lend it. . . . I suppose you have
read the correspondence and articles this last two weeks
in the "Times" about the R.A. I am confidentially
informed we are all to be done away with. Messrs. Crane,
Clausen and Holman Hunt have appealed to give us
another chance, but I believe they are very firm, and
though they admit they have no personal objection to
some of the Academicians, being personal friends of
theirs, still they will not raise their hands to stem the
torrent of indignation that is sweeping us away. . . .

To which my Uncle replied:

I immediately got the "Times" newspaper, but not the
lot yet. My God! When I think whilst I have been
sweating and trying to work out here, my Academy has
been, and is, in danger still, bombarded with rotten eggs.

An imitator of the newest French fakements, and painter of corns and dirty nails, a purveyor of affected muck for infant snobs, and worst of all, the painter of the *Flight into Egypt*. I wonder who has stirred up all this?

At the end of the year my parents went to stay with the Airds at East Sutton Park, near Staplehurst, for Christmas.

It is a delightful old-fashioned house, [wrote my father in a letter to Venice] built about Eliza's or James's time, with rambling corridors, tapestry chambers, long galleries, immense fireplaces where literally trunks blaze, and full of excellent family portraits, surrounded by a beautiful park, with herds of deer grazing and grouping themselves in approved fashion, and a splendid old church in the grounds. . . . We are in the midst of very heavy snow here. It makes the country look very interesting and beautiful, but quite puts a stop to any moving out of doors. This place is the seat of the Filmer family. . . .

The work goes on fairly satisfactorily. . . . It is true I am not doing any important picture, still the record is satisfactory and at, perhaps, higher prices than I have hitherto got. I had some ten pictures on hand—all sold—averaging £400 each, besides what I have already done this year".

Early in January, 1887, he was writing again, from Melbury Road:

My dear Harry,

Just a line to say on the eve of the Election that from what I hear I have not the slightest chance tonight. I understand the general idea is that it lies between Jones, Stone and Herkomer—Stone for choice—and that I am not in it. . . .

I, though not having the least expectation of being elected, did hope that I should have some decent following to give me some kind of claim to look forward to the next election. . . .

With our love,
Affectionately yours,
Luke.

Fildes did have his "decent following". Nobody was in the running but himself and Stone and Stone scraped home only by the shortest of heads.

8 January, 1887.

My dear Harry,

After my letter of yesterday, the following will astonish you. . . .

Do not fail to write to Stone congratulating him. I am, of course, quite delighted at the unexpected turn things have taken, and really I was relieved to find I had not beaten Stone on the ballot. It would have been something too dreadful for him. . . .

Yours,

Luke

The voting had been Stone 29 votes, Fildes 27.

In less than a week he was again writing to my uncle:

There is another vacancy! through the retirement of Richmond, R.A. last Tuesday. I suppose this will be a chance for me.

And on the 11th February:

I suppose by this you will have received the intimation of the election of an Academician on the 10th March. . . . Of course I am first in the betting now, but I hear that Thornycroft is to be run on the plea that "a sculptor is now due". It may be interesting to you to know that such is Stone's opinion. . . . This vacancy coming so soon I think must be very riling to him; particularly as he was proving on his fingers about the only time we have seen him since the Election that vacancies would in future average about one in five years. . . . I agreed with him that his conclusions appeared to be quite right, but did not mention that I knew of Richmond's retirement. Wells had informed me privately.

On the 10th of March, Fildes was elected by 36 votes to 17 for J. B. Burgess.

On the Sunday following my father's election, my parents were in the studio at Melbury Road having tea, and I was

sprawling on the floor beside them. The door opened and the parlourmaid announced—"Sir John Millais". A personage, of wondrous appearance in my eyes, entered the room. Having greeted my mother, he turned to my father:
"I've come to collect that sovereign you owe me, Fildes."
"Luke, what have you been up to?" exclaimed my mother, and so intent was I on the scene that I remember to this day the note of pleased suspicion in her voice, that he had been up to something rather dashing.
"My dear lady." said Millais, turning to her. "I bet this husband of yours an even sovereign the other night that he would romp home at the election, and he had the cheek to take me. I want my money."
"Luke!" was my mother's delighted cry.
Meanwhile my father, with a shamefaced grin, was delving into a trouser pocket from which he fetched out a sovereign and handed it to Millais.
"Here, nipper, catch hold of that!" said the Great Man, as he spun the sovereign through the air to where I was squatting.
Apart from a bond between Millais and my father as Academy colleagues, with a strong admiration for each other's work, there was a warmth of personal friendship between them into which Millais admitted my mother. The women-folk in Millais' circle all thought of him as a big schoolboy. That sentiment is illustrated by a simple little story told me by my mother. She and Millais found themselves seated together at a fashionable dinner-party, and a few places away from them was the latest society beauty. My mother enquired: "Do you know her?"
"I really don't know," was Millais' reply. "You ask her. *She'll know.*"
Those two words betray the whole of Millais' big boyishness—the football captain's acceptance of the Lower School's worship, the Olympian aloofness of Old Brooke in *Tom Brown's Schooldays.*
The portrait of my mother and one of Mrs. Lockett Agnew were my father's contributions to the Academy that year, 1887. The latter had not found itself and he repainted it completely after the Exhibition as I tell later, but the

portrait of my mother put him, at one bound, into the front rank of contemporary portrait painters. She is standing, three-quarter length, and she wears a black satin evening frock of that stylish style of the mid-eighties. An opera cloak of some orange material, trimmed with brown fur, falls off one shoulder. Her red hair has a background of a red velvet curtain—a daring touch, that. Altogether a lovely work. It is now in the Walker Art Gallery in Liverpool.

My father's first appearance as a portrait painter synchronized exactly with the inception of the last story-picture he was to paint.

11, Melbury Road,
Kensington, W.
4 May, 1887.

My dear Sir,

I have to thank you for your letter of yesterday's date, in which you so kindly mention the generous conditions you are willing to observe in the event of my painting a picture for you. . . .

Since you first spoke to me on this subject a few years ago, I have looked forward to the opportunity of producing something that would worthily represent me and at the same time be a subject that would meet your wishes, you having expressed a desire for an English one.

It is some time now since I painted an English subject of importance—a long time since *The Casual Ward*, *Widower* and *The Return of the Penitent* series, and my strong desire is . . . to do it for reputation's sake . . . at my own time and not to force it to a conclusion because of Exhibition reasons or monetary ones.

The engagements I have will not, I regret, permit me to do more than think it out this year. . . . Meanwhile, without binding you to anything I will work out my idea . . . and the price. I think I shall be able to also give you a clear notion of the subject, treatment and size. . . .

I remain, dear Sir,
Faithfully yours,
Luke Fildes.

The document I have been quoting is endorsed in my father's hand "Copy of letter given to Mr. Henry Tate, 6th May, 1887". This was the genesis of *The Doctor*.

There was a Jubilee Exhibition in Manchester that year, and my uncle went to see it ("There is an excellent show of Burne-Jones, Watts, Orchardson, Mason, Walker, Peter Graham, etc. . . . Luke's *Village Wedding* looks very strong.") This remark by my uncle about *The Village Wedding* was borne out by the result of a sort of Gallup Poll, a competition in which more than 12,000 visitors to the Exhibition took part. *The Village Wedding* headed the poll as the most popular picture in the Exhibition, and its painter headed a second poll as the artist having the largest proportion of his exhibits—in my father's case three out of three—chosen for special notice. He could not, however have been much elated by success in a competition so perverse that Millais did no better in it than the 41st place with his best picture, and no more than eight out of his thirty exhibits deemed worthy of inclusion in the first hundred!

In the latter part of the year, after October and half November spent in Venice, Fildes and Woods paid a visit to Florence and Genoa. In Florence they absorbed the Uffizi and the Pitti Palaces—"I have had the greatest artistic treat of my life", was Woods' entry in his diary, reflecting, I doubt not, Fildes' opinion, too—"This visit will do me a power of good. . . . I am converted to respecting Botticelli. His reputation is in the hands of a party of prigs in England." In Genoa, the attraction for my father was the Vandycks—"the finest he knew and a necessity for a portrait-painter's education".

They parted in Genoa, Fildes for England, Woods for Venice. On his return journey Woods stayed a day in Milan to visit the Brera ("I did not see much in Luini to interest me, but I finally came upon three Vandycks and a Rembrandt that I have gained considerably by seeing. The young golden-haired woman by Rembrandt is perhaps the most perfect artisitic feast I have ever had in my life"). Having committed to his diary those thoughts about the Rembrandt, he wrote off to Fildes: "I congratulate you on having much in common with its quality of work in Fanny's portrait."

The year 1888 opened with a new experience for Fildes—
he came on the Academy Council for the two-year term of
duty which all new Academicians serve. As such, he was
put on the Hanging Committee for the Summer Exhibition,
and he entered upon those duties without fear or favour.
Marcus Stone, now that the race to be Academician had been
run, was tractable. "They have not been pulling well
together on the Hanging Committee", my uncle wrote in
his diary. "Frith, Stocks and Dobson pull one way, and Luke
and Stone another; there have been frequent disagreements.
Frith has remarked to Luke that when he first 'hung', it
was with old Cooper and Webster, and that he never
attempted to differ with them. Luke told him that he failed
in his duty. Now they have got Yeames to help, and they
are chiefly engaged in undoing the work those stupid old
fellows have done."

Leighton, the President, saw there was a new force on the
Hanging Committee. It was to Fildes that he sent a list of
work he considered the Hanging Committee should keep in
mind "in case I may not be able to get down to the R.A.
tomorrow".

On the eve of the opening of the Exhibition there was, as
Woods' diary records, "a big row on the Council and Luke
was at the bottom of that. After the Council had gone through
the annual farce of accepting the hanging of the Exhibition"
—as Woods put it—my father's attention was drawn to the
fact that two portraits had been transposed without the
Hanging Committee's knowledge. Therefore, the rest of the
hangers having gone home, he took upon himself the responsibility of changing the two portraits back to their original
positions. His conduct was impugned on Council. The
President, whilst admitting the "irregularity" of Fildes'
action, said that an act of justice had been done.

My father had only one small work ready for that 1888
Academy—*A School Girl*, his Diploma work. Woods' chief
contribution was *Saluting the Cardinal*. The central figure in
it, entirely fortuitous because of a likeness in the model
who sat for the figure, bore a strong resemblance to the
Cardinal Patriarch of Venice. So strong was the resemblance
that Woods had discouraged one of his Venetian friends, the

Countess Marcello, against bringing the "old fellow"—the
Cardinal Patriarch—to see the picture in his studio. One day
Woods was working from that model in the garden of his
studio, and a good deal of noise had been coming over the
garden wall from some urchins next door. An interval came
for the model to have a rest and he climbed up a ladder,
poked his head and shoulders, clad in Patriarchal vestments,
over the top of the wall and let the urchins know, in choice
Venetian dialect, exactly what he thought of their behaviour
in disturbing the quietude of the *Signor Professore*. They,
believing themselves to be in the presence of none other
than the Cardinal Patriarch himself, dropped to their knees,
crossed themselves and set up a murmur of "Che scandalo!"
at the Patriarch's vocabulary. At that the model, taking them
to be making fun of him, redoubled his objurgations. Cries
from the urchins of invocation of the Holy Mother were
stilled only by my uncle appearing and explaining away the
misunderstanding.

That summer, my father took a house for the family—
"Whitegates" at Frimley. "This is a most charming house",
he wrote to Venice, "in five acres of ground, beautiful
garden and kitchen garden, on the slope of the Chobham
Ridges, all behind being heather and gorse for miles. There
is plenty of room, and Annie and your mother are coming
down to stay with Fanny on Thursday. I am sure they will
all enjoy it."

Some notion of the holiday is given by another letter:

Dear Harry,
We all arrived home last night after a most enjoyable
stay in the country. It has been quite a success in every
way in a most lovely country and yet not too far for me
to go backwards and forwards to town. I usually went
down on the Saturday or Friday and returned to work on
Monday or Tuesday morning. We were just 29 miles
from town and I made the journey four times on the
tricycle—going different ways each time which perhaps
made it 32 or 33 miles, according to the route. . . . It
certainly has set me up splendidly and I never felt better.
It is most enjoyable, and with a little practice as I have

had I should have no hesitation doing my 50 miles a day. I'll have a talk with you about one. I am sure it would suit you first rate. Of course, flat roads are the ideal for cycles, and good ones. Stony and sandy ones are abominations but, unless they are very steep, hilly ones are no obstacle. With the exception of a few gradients. I don't know any about Serra Valle but what you could ride. My idea, though, would be the Padua Road, which I believe is good, also all the Lido.

I can't positively say now what day we'll leave [for Venice]. . . . I have to wait till Fanny gives the word. . . . Mrs. Agnew's portrait a great success, I believe, at Manchester.

Our love,
Yours affectionately,
L. F.

The Manchester Autumn Exhibition, to which my father was referring, had been hung by Wells, who had divided his time between visits to Manchester and a "cure" at Buxton. Wells had kept my father informed and been sending him press-cuttings ("I was glad to have your Mrs. Agnew in her last transformation scene"—the point of this being that my father had entirely repainted it). The Press criticism was that since the portrait appeared at the Academy in 1887, "Mr. Fildes had changed a qualified failure into a very great success . . . the picture must now be acclaimed as one of the finest female portraits of late years. Again— in pose and expression it clearly aims at the frankness, the easy freedom of the most intimate modernity, and it hits the mark. Looking more into detail, we should like to draw attention to the mastery of the flesh painting, which is carried further than one ever saw it taken in a Fildes before."

That October my parents went to Venice again, and on their way out they met my uncle in Milan to look at the Rembrandt he had discovered at the Brera the previous year. They were in Venice only a month. They came home by way of Florence and Genoa, spending nine days on the journey and seeing the things my father and uncle had been seeing the year before.

Fildes had two important works on hand for the 1889 Academy—one, *An al fresco toilet*, which may be said to have closed his Venetian period; the other, a large portrait group of the two Misses Renton, exhibited as *Sisters*. The former became, in course of time, part of the Lady Lever Collection at Port Sunlight, where it now is. It is novel amongst his work as being under life-size. He had begun it in Venice in 1887, and had taken two years over it because, contrary to his usual practice, he had painted the background first! When he came to putting in his figures he had not liked his background and had scraped it all out on his visit to Venice in 1888. The central figure, the young woman whose Titian hair is being dressed, was painted from my mother; and it is exactly as I recall her at that time.

Sisters—his other exhibit—was one of his best portraits. Some critics, claiming that portraits "reveal character and perpetuate influences", professed to see in it more than the painter, with his suspicion of "revealing" portraiture, might himself have claimed.

Fildes' successful début as a hanger at the 1888 Academy had an unlooked-for sequel. Now, in March 1889, Sir Coutts Lindsay, the backer of Greenery-Yallery Grosvenor Gallery—as Gilbert had it in *Patience*—had asked Orchardson and Fildes to hang the forthcoming Exhibition at the Grosvenor, and had announced publicly that they would do so. "Sir Coutts", Fildes wrote to Woods, "told me that he desired to turn over a new leaf and was wishful to put the administration of the hanging entirely into the hands of Orchardson and myself." Considering that Fildes' outlook on art was as far removed from "Grosvenorism" as anything could be, this approach by Coutts Lindsay is of great interest —one may well wonder how far a Grosvenor Gallery hung by Fildes and Orchardson would have travelled from "Greenery-Yallery". In the end, neither of them did hang the Grosvenor. My father was wanted a second year on the Academy Hanging Committee, and Orchardson had to go abroad.

On hearing that my father would be hanging again at the Academy, my uncle wrote "when the younger painters hear that you are again on the Hanging Committee there will be high jinks. I happen to know how your careful attention to their efforts was appreciated last year."

There was an interesting sale at Christie's in March. As part of the Jubilee Celebrations of two years previously, William Thomas had commissioned a group of members of the Academy to paint a *Graphic* Gallery of Shakespearian Heroines. My father had chosen *Jessica* from *The Merchant of Venice*; my uncle had chosen *Portia*. The collection had been exhibited in Bond Street, and it was now coming up at Christies to be sold. The appearance in a sale-room of any recent painting by him is always a bit of an anxiety for an artist; obviously, if the price declines from the one he has been paid for it, the experience is a disagreeable one. As matters turned out at this particular sale, Leighton's *Desdemona* fetched £525, my father's *Jessica* £372 15s. od., my uncle's *Portia* £320 5s. od., and G. D. Leslie, R.A.'s. *Sweet Ann Page* £220 10s. od., and I believe they were the only ones to fetch more than the prices for which Thomas had commissioned them.

And now there was a new experience. At Leighton's urgent request my father agreed to go to Paris and hang the British Section of paintings in the *Grande Exposition* of 1889. He went there at the end of April, just before the opening of the Academy.

The eventual allocation of medals at Paris was a muddle. Writing to Woods, my father said: "I should not have thought of sending had I understood there was to be a competition. . . . I had no confidence in foreign juries. . . . I have written pretty strongly to Leighton about it and told him that I had heard that a second class medal had been awarded to me. I certainly will take the first opportunity of repudiating the judgement and refuse it."

Fildes' lack of confidence in international juries was founded partly on the fact that, as he believed, members of them were chosen more for their knowledge of foreign languages than their knowledge of Art, and partly on the fact that, as again he believed, the members were "mutual admiration societies" who took turn and turn about in awarding medals to one another. Holding those views, justifiably or not, he had early ceased to be interested in

Venetians
1885

City Art Gallery, Manchester

An Al Fresco Toilet
1889

Lady Lever Art Gallery, Port Sunlight

Luke Fildes painting
'The Doctor', drawn by Reginald
Cleaver for *The Graphic*

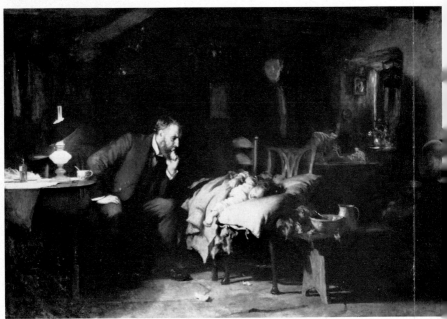

The Tate Gallery

The Doctor
1891

competing at International Exhibitions, and whenever in after years he yielded to pressure to "send something", he was careful to prescribe that the "something" was *hors concours*.

Later that year my father took my mother to Paris to see the *Grande Exposition*, and incidentally the British Section of Painting which he had hung. One adventure on that visit was described in a post-card to Woods:

Dear Harry,
I just drop you a card from the top of the Tower to say Fanny and I are here for a few days. I have been up to the Flagstaff with a private party before the public are admitted. It is very interesting.

Yours,
Luke.

The "Tower", thus summarily disposed of, was the subsequently world-famed Eiffel Tower which was then nearing completion as the principal feature of the *Grande Exposition*.

Fildes, on returning home, had this final comment to make to Woods about the pictures: "We have heard the French and Continental Schools so much extolled, and ours depreciated, that at last one begins to think we are behind hand, but I felt very grateful at my dispassionate visit. My conclusions are that our School is, or will be, in the ascendancy."

❧ XII ❧

THE DOCTOR

1890-1892

One of the popular authoresses of those days was Marie Corelli. My father had a note from her as Show Sunday drew near.

47 Longridge Road,
Earls Court, S.W.
29 March, 1890.

Dear Mr. Fildes,

I venture to ask if you are at home tomorrow to the inroads of your friends and admirers who are eager to see the work of your creative mind? Perhaps you may have heard my name as a writer of many successful books, and for literature's sake you may be inclined to allow me also to penetrate your 'sanctum sanctorum'. . . . I wrote of your exquisite colouring in my book *A Romance of Two Worlds*, which has had, and still keeps, its hold on the public; and if you will allow me to be amongst the spectators of your work tomorrow I shall be proud and very grateful.

Sincerely yours,
Marie Corelli.

The distinguished authoress had made a mistake of a week in the date, and that same day she wrote again:

Dear Mr. Fildes,

Thank you for your kindly note! . . . Easter Sunday will be better than tomorrow, as I can bring with me my half-brother, Mr. Eric Mackay, author of the *Love Letters of a Violinist*—which is such a favourite "missal of love" with fair ladies—and he has lived a good while in Venice, and is quite a worshipper of you! With every acknowledgment of your friendly courtesy.

Believe me,

Very sincerely yours,

Marie Corelli.

With expectations at that emotional pitch Marie Corelli and her brother may have been disappointed to find my father was making but one Venetian contribution to the Academy, and not an important one at that. "As to Mr. Fildes", was the opinion, however, of *The Times*, "he has surpassed himself this year as a painter of ladies' portraits. [They] undoubtedly place him at the head of English portrait painters of this class of subject at the present moment, though we fully admit the power and the uncompromising truth which are shown by Mr. Sargent, the American painter, whom we hope to be allowed to claim as almost a naturalized Englishman. Mr. Fildes is sometimes apt to sin on the side of over-prettiness, as in his Venetian pictures, but in all these three portraits there is, together with a lavish though quite legitimate use of colour, an evident desire to get at the real character of the sitter."

This last remark is interesting in face of his distrust of "revealing" portraiture.

Millais was in the chair at the Academy Club's Greenwich Dinner for the opening of that year's exhibition. A few days later my uncle happened to meet him, and found him in his "big school-boy" mood. "He was still in a state of delight", the diary notes, "at his successful chairmanship. He said: 'I met that American who sat next to you on Monday night'. 'He was delighted with your performance in the Chair', I said: 'Evidently', was Millais' reply, 'because he said to me, 'Sir John, I would cross the Atlantic at any time to hear a speech like you made on Monday'."

The Times announced, on the 21st June, 1890, Henry Tate's foundation of "A National Gallery of British Art". There was a published list of fifty-seven pictures which

Tate had offered as a gift to the nation. In the list the fifty-sixth and the fifty-seventh had no titles, but were described as "now being painted by Luke Fildes R.A., and Sir Frederick Leighton, P.R.A." A fortnight later my father mentioned in a letter to Woods that he had shown a sketch to Tate ("I fancy he was pleased with the idea, and when I told him I should require £3,000 he assented and letters were passed to that effect").

That was *The Doctor*. When, a year later the picture was in the first flush of its triumph, a leader of the medical profession delivered an address to a group of young men who were going out into the world as doctors. "A library of books written in your honour", he said, "would not do what this picture has done and will do for the medical profession in making the hearts of our fellow men warm to us with confidence and affection. . . . Above everything, whatever may be the rank in your profession to which you may attain, remember always to hold before you the ideal figure of Luke Fildes' picture, and be at once gentle men and gentle doctors."

I have said that the idea of *The Doctor* had been in my father's mind ever since Dr. Murray had watched over Philip. He must have thought a great deal on the subject for when after thirteen years he came to paint *The Doctor*, it was the easiest and quickest painted of all his "big" pictures. He had few studies to make, though for the principal figure, the Doctor himself, he acted the part and was photographed in the pose for the guidance of future models. Particularly was it important that the doctors hands be right. Hands, for my father, were as expressive as a face. He made a feature of hands in his portraits. He and Woods spent a week at Hope Cove in Devon sketching fisherman's cottages, and from these sketches a full-size interior of a cottage was built in a corner of the studio in Melbury Road, with rafters and walls and a window—this last part of one of the studio windows—through which the light of dawn would come, for he had set himself an "artistic exercise", which was to record how dawn and lamplight would mingle.

With Woods back in Venice correspondence was normal. Woods was writing a series of letters from Venice for William

Thomas' new venture, *The Daily Graphic*, and was sending
the manuscript to my father to edit and pass on. He had
news to give of the Prinseps. "We were at Padua the other
day—We had just entered the carriage after visiting the
Giotto Chapel when Val commenced a story—'King
Robert of Naples was very intimate with Giotto and upon
one occasion said—'How is it, Giotto, that you paint such
beautiful children when your own are so ugly?' Quoth
Giotto: 'My Liege, the reason may be that I paint my
pictures by day, and make my children by night'. Mrs. Val
who was sitting alongside me, broke out: 'Look here, you
had better stop!' There was something so comic in her
indignation that it made me burst out laughing. Val,
delighted with the success of his story, puffed at his cigar,
filling the opposite seat. She let fly at him again, calling him
'an old booby'!"
In another letter, Woods wrote:

A most intelligent, amiable and cheery-countenanced
sister artist was in my studio this morning who talked
enthusiastically about painting and pictures, and besides
putting me up to a thing or two on the former, gave me
two very good subjects for the latter.
I could scarcely realise the fact, as I looked into her
face, that she was the Empress Frederick. . . . "Italy,
after all, is the best country to paint in," she said, "but
I have seen Devonshire, Wales and Scotland at a time
when I should have liked to stay and work there also, but
I could not." Then she said, "When I was in this studio
last I saw Mr. Luke Fildes working on a single figure—
How interesting his work is! He is a fine artist. Does he
come to Venice every year? And tell me what he is doing
now?" . . . She had heard of the Tate business . . . and
when I told her that you were painting a picture on the
lines of your early pictures, she said: "I am so glad." Her
next proceeding was what my mother would have called
"rummaging". . . . "You must finish this", she said,
holding out the Piazza at Serra Valle. "I intend working
there a whole summer if I live." She also told me to finish
one or two more. I intend to.

Altogether her visit, and praise, was a great pleasure to me, and one I shall never forget.

That winter *The Graphic* came of age and William Thomas was given a public dinner, at which my father had to respond to the toast of Art. I think the occasion must have been the one I remember when he spent days at his desk in the studio, composing a speech and learning it by heart, and then pacing up and down as he declaimed it to my Mother. At all events, I have found amongst his papers the draft of that speech he delivered at *The Graphic* dinner. After some opening play with his drawing *Houseless and Hungry* being the first which Thomas had commissioned for *The Graphic*, and Thomas, when he heard the price, saying that if that was the kind of price it would have to pay, the paper had better be abandoned, my father took as his theme the influence of the Art of the Illustrator upon the Art of the Painter in this country. "Should the time come . . . when our younger artists neglect the study that would qualify them to excel as Designers and Illustrators it will not be a good day for English Art." Illustration, he went on, was a Branch of Art singularly and peculiarly English in which our supremacy was unquestioned from Hogarth, "the great Father of the English Illustrators", down to the present time. After digressing to warn young artists in this country not to neglect the "opportunities of study and training at their own doors to seek abroad the mannerisms, taste and ideas of foreign countries", he continued: "It may be said, scoffingly, that the Art of the Illustrator is but the Art of the Multitude. Be it so! But he who by earnest and sincere efforts arrests, stirs, or gives pleasure to the many does good work, perhaps great work."

The speech was a great success and memory could not have failed him! He always thought he could not make a speech unless he committed it to memory. On the only two occasions, both of them many years later; on which I heard him speak in public, he spoke impromptu and with admirable effect.

The Doctor was to be accompanied to the Academy of 1891 by a second portrait of Mrs. Lockett Agnew. But it was to the "big picture" itself that Fildes was giving all his attention that winter and the early weeks of the New Year. Rumour had got around that Fildes was coming out with something better than ever before—a noble tribute to a noble profession. His medical friends kept asking him if they might be allowed to sit for the chief figure. They wanted to say in after years: "I sat for *The Doctor*". On Sunday mornings they came down to Melbury Road in relays. The one who came most often was my parents' friend Thomas Buzzard, an eminent consultant of his time. But the figure in the picture was not a portrait of any one individual; it was a composite out of the painter's imagination. The doctor in the picture wears a beard, the model who sat most, a professional, was cleanshaven. He used to say to my father: "You will let me know, Mr. Fildes, when you want the expression." My recollection is that he had been on the stage.

On the 23rd of March, less than a fortnight before Show Sunday, Fildes wrote to Woods a curiously subdued letter.

The picture promises well. Of course it is far short of what it ought to be and what I know I could do—but there, it will have to go. . . . Mr. Tate saw it for the first time last week and I believe likes it. . . . I have seen nobody else's work this year, for I have no time. All accounts agree that it will be a poor R.A. this year—nearly every important picture has been given up through the perpetual darkness.

Woods, arriving in London straight from Venice the day before Show Sunday made this entry in his diary:

"I arrived at Melbury Road soon after six o'clock and in good time to see Luke's picture of *The Doctor* by daylight. I was greatly struck by the completeness of the picture in every way. The story is admirably told. I was prepared for this, but not for the consummate skill with which he has told it. I have never seen painting that pleased me better than the Doctor and the Child."

And on Show Sunday itself:

"Luke had a great number of visitors. They had a dinner party at night. Tom Angell, Schultz Wilson, David Murray the latest A.R.A., Val Prinsep and Mrs. Prinsep. I enjoyed it immensely of course. Excellent dinner and lots of champagne and fun."

Earlier in this chapter I called the appearance of *The Doctor* a triumph. One must have lived in times when Contemporary Art really was popular in order to understand how a new picture could make such an appeal. An experience of my father's brings out that sense of actuality. Years after *The Doctor*'s appearance my father was up in town one day and he hailed a taxi to take him home to Melbury Road. Arrived there, he was about to pay the fare when the driver, who had been looking up at the house, asked:
"Isn't this where Sir Luke Fildes lives?"
On being assured that it was, he continued:
"Then do you know him?"
"Well, yes I do," my father answered. "I happen to be Sir Luke Fildes."
"It was you who painted *The Doctor*?" came the reply. "Oh, sir, I don't think I want to charge you for driving you!"
The last time I saw *The Doctor* in the Tate it looked magnificent; well hung and well lit in the centre of a wall with some contemporaries near-by, amongst them Millais' *Boyhood of Raleigh*, though I felt surprise at the suggestion in the Official Guide that the picture had sentimentality and was painted—by my father of all people—under French influence! Sentiment yes, but not sentimentality. As sharp an eye as anyone's to detect false sentiment was W. S. Gilbert's, and what Gilbert thought of *The Doctor* was this:

Graeme's Dyke,
Harrow Weald,
2nd May, 1891.

My dear Fildes,
Pray let me join the chorus of congratulations which your noble picture has evoked. Nothing since *The*

Widower has hit me so full in the heart. And please convince me that this letter is not an intrusion by leaving it unanswered.

With kindest regards to Mrs. Fildes.

I am,

Very truly yours,

W. S. Gilbert.

Seeing on that visit of mine to the Tate three or four people looking at the picture sent my thoughts back. I had been at school when the Academy opened in 1891 and my mother had written me: "Dada's picture is a very great success. I went today to the Academy, but there were so many round it that I came away without seeing it."

An engraving of *The Doctor* was published in this country by Agnews, and had large sales. An engraving of it was published, too, in the United States by an American firm. This had even larger sales, supposedly at the time to be one million copies. This success in America, however, was for my father nothing more than a *succès d'estime*. There was no copyright in the United States then, and not a cent came to my father from those sales. *The Doctor* has never ceased to be popular in the United States. It has, since the last war, been reproduced as a postage stamp there, in commemoration of the centenary of their oldest Medical Society.

In the autumn after *The Doctor*'s appearance my parents went visiting in Scotland, thus beginning a practice they followed for several years. The first house-party was at Altyre, near Forres, which the Lockett Agnews used to take regularly from the Gordon-Cummings. Sir William Gordon-Cumming, the central figure in the sensational Baccarat Scandal, had brought an action earlier in the year to clear his name of an accusation of cheating at cards. Gordon-Cumming had lost his action. On one of those visits of my parents to Altyre, the Gordon-Cummings themselves were fellow-guests in their own house, and after a week spent in their company my mother was firmly convinced, as were many other people—for the case had aroused much public interest—that Gordon-Cumming was innocent. I asked her once why she was so positive of that, and her answer was,

"Simply because he is not the type who would cheat at anything".

In December 1891 came the introduction to Royal Portraiture. Prince Albert Victor of Wales and Princess Victoria Mary of Teck were betrothed, and permission was granted for *The Graphic* to present the Princess with her portrait. It was to be painted by Luke Fildes. Writing to my uncle on the 22nd of the month, my father told him:

> I have been to the White Lodge twice about the Princess's portrait. Yesterday I lunched there and it gave me a good opportunity of forming an opinion of her. . . . She comes with her mother tomorrow morning for her first sitting, and afterwards they will lunch with us, for they are going to London to shop.

London and Richmond were in different orbits!

My uncle made a prophetic comment: "I hope it will lead to something more important in the same line! *Chi sa*?"

Scarcely had the portrait taken shape when the country was plunged into mourning by the death of the Prince. More than a year would go by, and then the portrait would be resumed.

It was now two years since Henry Tate had given his collection of pictures to the nation, and there had been time for dissidence to be expressed in certain quarters. There had been delay, too, in finding the site which the Government was to provide for the Gallery. Millais wrote to my father at the end of March 1892.

> Dear Fildes,
>
> I heard you had written to the Council about the Tate affair and I should very much like to know what you have done in the matter which I regard as a most serious concern to all artists of the day. I have only just returned to Town and have been out of all current news and have only just learned there has been strong opposition to the gift. . . . There is a mischievous insolence abroad which is very difficult to meet, as one man's opinion, if cunningly expressed, is regarded as worthy of acceptance as any other's, especially in such an obscure subject as Art. Amongst ourselves, we are not always unanimous, and

there is nothing to *prove* a picture is first rate. The condemnation, therefore, of Tate's Gallery will be accepted by thousands of ignorant people as a correct valuation.

Ever yours,

J. E. Millais.

Three days later, he wrote again:

2 Palace Gate,
Kensington
28 March '92.

Dear Fildes,

. . . I should tell you Mr. and Mrs. Tate dined with me when he first expressed his intention of giving his Gallery to the Nation, and to forward his wishes I got Leighton, Lord Carlisle and Burton to meet them, but after being first in the field to help, what was my surprise to see a large Committee formed without even the grace of asking whether I would act on it.

Too many cooks spoil the broth and directly I saw who had been chosen I foresaw trouble, and I suspect the failure does not altogether rest with the Artists, whose mouths are to a great extent closed, as it is their work which is offered as a gift, and there would be a kind of indecency in their taking an active part in the matter; at the same time there will doubtless be some vigorous expression of our feeling by the President at the Dinner. . . .

Ever yours,

J. E. Millais.

My father was now engaged on the painting of portraits almost exclusively. He had five in the 1892 Academy— two of them, *James J. Bibby*, the head of the Bibby Line of shipping, and his wife, were amongst the best he ever painted. He had more commissions on his hands than he could cope with. He had not abandoned the idea of another "big picture"; he had the subject for one in his mind, but matters did not turn out that way and every year he became more deeply involved in his second career as a portrait painter. In all, one hundred and nineteen portraits of his were exhibited at the Royal Academy, and there were a quantity that he never exhibited. In their quality they were enough for fame in any representative collection of English Portraiture. I make this point because the Royal Academy had a Winter Exhibition of British Portraits a few years ago without a Luke Fildes in it.

I have spoken of my father's liking for the theatre. In the Easter holidays of 1892, Beerbohm Tree lent him the Royal Box at the Haymarket, a kindness Beerbohm Tree had a way of showing, and my parents, my uncle, my brother Paul and I went to see Beerbohm Tree as Hamlet. Between the Acts, Tree came up to the ante-room behind the Royal Box to see how we were liking it, and on one of these visits, placing his hands on my head and my brother's he thus addressed us: "Me boys, when you are men, you will be able to say 'I saw Tree as Hamlet'." This made a great impression on me, and although I knew that the dying Hamlet was only my father's friend, Mr. Beerbohm Tree, when the end of the play came, and with it Horatio's "Good night, sweet prince", I felt quite upset.

My mother had been one of the sufferers of the big influenza epidemic at the beginning of the year, and she had never really recovered. Mountain air was recommended by my parents' old friend, Dr. Buzzard, who besides his other attributes, had a discriminating taste in Swiss holiday resorts. Saas Fée, at a height of 6,000 feet, and very remote to get at in those days, was the place chosen and because "the boys", if left behind, would see scarcely anything of their parents in those summer holidays, I and Paul were to be taken along. Having heard all this in letter from my father, my uncle in Venice looked at a map and discovered that "Saas is not twenty miles in a direct line from Domodossola, but I imagine the country to be pretty high and rough between the two places".

In due course my uncle arrived at the village of Macugnaga at the foot of the Monte Moro Pass, a track which led on foot into Switzerland and the Saas Valley. He had luggage for several weeks' holiday, which would have to be carried up 5,000 feet by hand and down the other side. He set off at five o'clock the next morning, with two guides, and after an injudicious lunch at the top of the Pass, when he slaked his thirst, and his guides', on iced red wine, he arrived with his luggage at the inn at Mattmark where my father and I had gone with a mule to meet him. There was still some little distance to go before Saas Fée, which my Uncle, who was stout and out of training, was in no shape to tackle. We hoisted him and his luggage on the back of the mule, and his diary tells the end of the adventure: "Fanny met us with Paul in the meadow near the Hotel, looking wonderfully well. . . . I was ready at 7 o'clock for dinner. . . . I drank a bottle of champagne which pulled me through."

After a week more at Saas Fée, and a week at Berisal half way up Napoleon's road over the Simplon, my uncle left us in the horse diligence for Domodossola on his way back to Venice.

Gradually the "Tate affair" was being solved. "I think I shall have to accept the Millbank site for the National Gallery of British Art", Tate wrote my father in November. "It has many advantages, a central situation, good approaches by road and river, a fine frontage, $2\frac{1}{2}$ acres of land which means room for future extension. . . . Can you tell me of any other site where I can have $2\frac{1}{2}$ acres of land?"

My father was pessimistic. He wrote my uncle: "Tate has arranged to take a part of the site of Millbank Prison for his Gallery. A woefully out of the way place. Nobody will go."

Two letters from the President of the Royal Academy at the end of the year touched up a difficulty my father was constantly up against.

22.12.92

Dear Fildes,

I shall be grievously disappointed if we don't get you represented at Chicago. *Do* help us—and if you can't (but I hope you can) get us a Venetian picture, let us have *The Casuals, the Americans have not seen it*—and it is a very fine one representing at all events one side of you.

In haste,
Yours very sincerely,
Fred Leighton.

29.12.92

Dear Fildes,

Alas! Tate is absolutely obdurate (or *she* is). I should like to have the *Return of the Penitent and* some Venetian work—is that unget-at-able? I should much rather you sent Venetians than nothing. They represent a distinct phase of your career and a much admired one; then there is Mrs. Fildes' portrait, which is excellent. What I don't want is the absence of your handiwork from the show.

Very sincerely yours,

Fred. Leighton.

The root of the difficulty was that whilst my father was willing to be represented in International Exhibitions—on the understanding that he would be *hors concours*—his important works were in public or private collections the owners of which were chary about lending them. It generally, was, therefore, that he could only be represented by the loan of his own property, and the only important work he had unsold was his portrait of my mother. That much travelled painting was never hung on a wall at Melbury Road during all the forty years it belonged there; it used to stand on an easel in the Studio, waiting for its next journey.

Thus it happened that my father's work never became well known abroad.

❧ XIII ❧

THE FIRST ROYAL PORTRAITS
1893-1896

My father was concerned about my uncle's chances of becoming a Royal Academician. His work was sufficiently well regarded and there were only two Associates senior to him—Val Prinsep and the landscape painter John MacWhirter. But the fact that he lived abroad might be an obstacle. Would he be able to carry out an Academician's duties? Whenever my father heard that question asked, he said that Woods would find a way should the case arise, and he was now writing Woods to look ahead and provide himself with a *pied à terre* in London.

Some vacancies were falling in. The large-hearted Val Prinsep, who had already been passed over more than once was in Paris hoping to finish a "big" picture for the next Academy.

He wrote to my father: "I rejoice to hear that Harry Woods has acquired a domicile in London and he has a very good chance of election. The wily one of Melbury Road [Marcus Stone] will no doubt infinitely prefer him to me—and I shall be glad to congratulate him if he succeeds and back him up if his election is deferred to another time. If I don't succeed this time I shall take myself out of opposition for I am rather tired of it."

The election was on the 4th May, and Woods, MacWhirter, and Henry Moore, the marine painter, became Royal Academicians—"I am sorry indeed about Prinsep", Woods put in his diary, "as I looked forward to him as a colleague".

Two days previously Princess Victoria Mary of Teck and Prince George of Wales, Duke of York, had become engaged to be married. The project of her portrait was immediately revived and what was more, the Duke of York's portrait was to be painted too. Some entries in my uncle's diary bear on this:

> *May 9th*: Luke has just been to Marlborough House and had an interview with H.R.H. Duke of York. . . . He said that the Duke was a most pleasant chatty fellow, altogether as nice as could be.
>
> *May 19th*: Luke has been at Marlborough House all day, having had a long and successful sitting from the Duke of York. Wedding presents were arriving during the day, greatly interesting the Duke. Luke feels sure that he will make highly successful portraits of the Duke and Princess Mary, who he says is perfectly charming.
>
> *May 21st*: The Prince of Wales saw [the portrait of the Duke] yesterday. After looking at it for some time he asked the Duke, "Has your Ma seen this?"

The final sittings were early in June. My father took my autograph album with him to Marlborough House, and on a page of it, in a rather school-boy hand, is "George, Marlborough House, June 6th 1893", and in a superb sweep of calligraphy "Victoria Mary of Teck". There used to be a coloured smudge on the page. This was the result of the Duke's fondness for unscrewing the caps of my father's tubes of paint. But the action of time has been at work, and I cannot any longer claim to own a fingerprint of an heir to the Throne of England.

A few days later my mother wrote to my uncle, who by that time had returned to Venice: "The Princess of Wales is delighted with her son's portrait and wishes Luke to paint her. . . . It will be a good thing for Luke if he does it, although it will quite upset our visit to Switzerland."

My father's method with the Duke of York had intrigued the Princess of Wales. He had let any member of the Royal Family or of the Household who came into the room at Marlborough House when he was painting, watch what he was doing. The Princess's experience of painters up to then had been that they were mysterious and only willing to show their work when it was finished.

A beginning with the Princess's portrait was made immediately whilst some of the London Season still remained, and so well did matters go that a letter to Venice a month later ran:

> 12th June, 1893.
>
> General Ellis had a talk with me, and it was arranged I should begin at once while she was in a consenting humour . . . I got on very well *every day* without any drawbacks . . . and I believe, though she is quite ready to sit to me again, that I can now finish without her. They are all, without exception, extremely pleased with what I have done, though in a sense there is everything yet to be done *pictorially*. It is just an ordinary homely portrait, not of the "Court" style, in a very plain black dress, and she is nursing a dog in her lap. . . .
>
> Remember me to all old friends,
>
> Affectionately Yrs,
>
> L. F.

The dog in her lap was Facey, the Princess's pet pekinese. On one of the days at Marlborough House, when it was not Facey's turn to sit, a scratching came at the door as my father was painting. The handle turned and in pranced Facey followed by the Prince of Wales. Facey made a bee-line for a paint-rag my father had dropped on the carpet, and began tossing it in the air and gambolling round the room.

"Bad dog! Drop it at once, Sir! Drop it, I say!" the Prince ejaculated, making ineffectual grabs to get hold of the rag.

"Please, Sir, it's of no consequence," said my father, "I have plenty of others."

The Prince looked up with a flushed countenance: "It's not your damned rag I'm bothering about. It's the *dog*! Why! he may *poison* himself!"

In the 'nineties that very popular monthly magazine, the *Strand*, ran a feature of "Illustrated Interviews" with people

who were in the news, and one of the series was due to appear
in the August number about my father. There would be
illustrations of his principal works, views of the house and
garden, and photographs of my mother and the children—
"the usual sickening rot" my father described it to my uncle
"which the 'literary man' regales us with, be his subject a
music-hall artiste or a divine". He prayed my uncle would
not see it.

But the warning came too late. "I had not been at the
hotel two hours", my uncle wrote back—he was on a holiday
in Switzerland—"before the parson put it into my hands.
Certainly every person in the hotel had read it. It is true that
some parts have a sickly flavour, perhaps only to us! I heard
many remarks such as, 'Oh! how interesting!' The rapture
was general concerning your house. Such a place could
scarcely have been imagined in London."

Shortly afterwards the house was in danger of near
disaster. My father and mother were at breakfast one morning when—to quote from a letter my mother wrote me at
school—"Frederick rushed in"—Frederick Spikesman, I
must explain, was the studio-hand, gardener and general
factotum, an important person in the No. 11 household—
"Frederick rushed in to say the studio was on fire. Dada and
I flew upstairs. The four curtains [separating the glass
studio and the main studio], the wall and floor were in
flames. I flew to the pictures to take them out of the room,
and everybody in the house carried water for Dada." (I
learned in the next holidays, that the receptacles which were
handed up to my father on the top of a ladder were mostly
the "commodes" from the nearest bedrooms—and none the
worse for that.)

To resume my mother's narrative: "The room was so
full of smoke we couldn't see each other. . . . The firemen
waited about for some time and they helped to clear away
some of the dirt. The children were quite excited to see the
firemen and engines; they brought two escapes also, because
I suppose they never know how bad a fire may be. Dada is
quite well after his hard work, but I feel a little upset today."

Woods, before beginning his duties on the Academy
Council on the 1st January 1894, had provided himself with

a *pied à terre* at the home of his friend William Lomas in Victoria Road, Kensington. This was an attractive Regency villa—no longer in existence—with a large studio in part of the garden at the back. Included in the "let" were Lomas' "married couple", Shaw and Mrs. Shaw. So my uncle was able to set about some entertaining, and one of his first dinners was for Val Prinsep, Marcus Stone, Frederick Eaton, the Secretary of the Royal Academy, William Thomas and my father. During the evening Eaton told my uncle that one of the elder Academicians, had resigned. "Prinsep would have been interested to hear this", my uncle put in his diary, "but of course until tomorrow's Council meeting it had to be kept secret." The following evening he dined at the Arts Club and came down to Melbury Road, "with Prinsep who is excited about the vacancy". The end of that story was that Prinsep was elected.

My father had felt impelled early in the year, before the Christmas holidays were ended, to give up the studio for a short time to the inauguration of "The Theatre Royal, Melbury Road". This was a venture by myself, my brother Paul, and my sister Kitty for the production of plays in rhymed couplets of my own composition. The venture which lasted for several years, met—as I sensed at the time—with success. The glass studio was all one could wish for as a stage; the arch and the curtains between the two studios were an ideal proscenium. Audiences might consist of as many as a dozen. In addition to the "Little Hunters" from across the road and our parents, our chief supporters were Uncle Harry, Gordon Thomson, H. T. Wells and my godfather Val Prinsep.

Not long after the Theatre Royal's reversion to its functional use as the Studio, the Empress Frederick, the Princess of Wales, and the Duke and Duchess of York, came to see the portrait of the Princess before it went to the Academy for the 1894 Exhibition. The Empress suggested several alterations to my father, but as my uncle's diary records "the Princess signed to him not to make them, and left word also to the same effect by General Ellis".

Remembering how joyous and energetic a person our mother was I find it difficult to think of her as ever being an invalid. And yet she was always being ordered away by doctors to the seaside. Whether my father thought that a house of her own would be more comfortable for her than a series of lodging-houses, or the glass-studio at Melbury Road had not solved the problem of foggy winters, or both influences were at play, he suddenly bought—and it came upon us all suddenly—a seaside house.

By a freak of coincidences the house—Holland House, Kingsgate, in the Isle of Thanet—had been built by Henry Fox, the first Lord Holland, the owner of the famous Holland House in Kensington, where Melbury Road was. The Kingsgate Holland House stood on the coast half way between Broadstairs and Margate. "Gate" in that part of the country has the meaning of a cutting in chalk cliffs leading down to the shore. There was such a cutting at Kingsgate.

The spot—the house was built in the 1760's—had sufficient interest to have attracted the notice of Thomas Gray, who wrote these lines:

> Old and abandoned by each Venal friend
> Here Holland formed the pious resolution
> To smuggle a few years, and strive to mend
> A broken character and constitution.
> On this congenial spot he fixed his choice,
> Earl Godwin troubled for his neighbouring sand,
> Here seagulls scream and cormorants rejoice
> And mariners, though shipwrecked, dread to land.
> Here reign the blistering North and blighting East,
> No tree is heard to whisper, bird to sing
> Yet Nature could not furnish out the feast;
> Art he invokes new horrors still to bring.

The "new horrors" which Lord Holland had invoked were sham ruins dotted about the landscape after the fashion of the time. Some of the deficiencies Thomas Gray had observed had by the year 1894 been made good; trees had grown up and there were birds which sang. But the place was still pretty bleak. "Blistering North and blighting East" were recognizable.

Lord Holland's "pious resolution to smuggle a few years" was facilitated by the neighbourhood which was riddled with galleries and caves in the chalk cliffs, and great was our excitement when unsuspected cellars were discovered underneath the basement of Holland House. But there was no treasure hidden there, and as my father wanted the workpeople out as soon as possible, he had the cellars filled up with rubble, and have done with it.

It was not a stately home my father had bought. Sometime at the beginning of the nineteenth century the "mansion" which Lord Holland had designed as a reproduction of Tully's Formian Villa, had been cut up into five separate dwellings and a coastguard station. It was the central portion that had kept the name of Holland House, and it was that which my father had bought.

There were omens, though not recognized as such, which could bear upon my father's future. My mother had two notes from Millais. One in May 1894: "I suppose I am getting better, but it is slow work". The other, in June: "You know how I was looking forward to dining with you, but my *voice* has completely failed. . . . I cannot say how it distresses me to give up dining with you."

Millais had two half-finished pictures in his studio which he was painting for the next Academy. One was *Speak! Speak!*, an exercise in mingled dawn and artificial light. "I should never have attempted it if the 'Doctor' hadn't shown the way," he told my father. The other was *Saint Stephen*. This latter gave my father the opportunity of being some service to Millais. He called Henry Tate's attention to it, who bought it while still in its half-finished state.

When the time came for the first summer holiday at Holland House, Kingsgate, my father was doing a "cure" at Kissingen. "I left Fanny very busy making preparations for the new house", he wrote somewhat light-heartedly to his brother-in-law early in August, "with the hope she may get into it about a fortnight from now. . . . I quite expect them to be installed by my return."

This looks like "escapism", but my father knew perfectly well that nothing could have given my mother more pleasure than carrying out a move of that kind all by herself. As he expected, he was able to have his after-cure at Kingsgate.

I have said of my father that he was a type who might have

been "good at games" had he been born into different surroundings. He and my mother were staying that autumn at Hardwick Grange in Shropshire, with the Bibbys—two of his early "portraits". There was a meet of hounds nearby which he went to see, mounted upon a quiet old fox-hunter in retirement. My father was not an entire novice on horseback. Some years before, on medical advice, he had taken up riding. He had bought a horse—a handsome one, which he called Caramel from its colouring, and stabled at a riding school round the corner near the Prinseps—and he used to ride Caramel in Rotten Row. But that morning at Hardwick he had no thought beyond being a spectator at the meet. However, the quiet old fox-hunter became very restless when hounds moved off and my father let him have his head. Before my father quite knew what was happening he was in full chase. With the help of a groom who rode ahead and opened the stiffer gates—and the merciful intervention of Providence—my father was in at the "kill".

The episode gave rise to some talk and in due course my father had this letter from the Master:

Cloverley,
Whitchurch,
Salop.
Dec. 11, 94

My dear Mr. Fildes,

When I had the pleasure of meeting you at Hardwick and you saw the fox killed, you may remember that I offered you the brush as a memento of the day. You however declined it on the ground that you "knew enough about brushes and they were no novelty to you". Notwithstanding this I venture to send you the brush made up to represent more or less one of your own as remembrance of our meeting and your first day's fox-hunting, which I hope you will now accept.

It goes by parcel post today. . . .

Yrs. vy. truly
A. P. Heywood-Lonsdale.

To which my father answered:

Dear Mr. Lonsdale,

I had no idea my jocular observation about the fox's brush . . . would result in such a delightful souvenir of that very pleasant day.

My pleasure this morning was as great as my surprise when I received your very handsome gift. It is very tastefully mounted, and it will always be a remembrance of my first day with any hounds and my most agreeable association with yourself. That the matter may not entirely pass from your mind I venture to ask your acceptance of a proof engraving of one of my pictures. It will serve to show in some degree I reciprocate your kind recollection of the 8th of November.

As further evidence of my father's "gift for games", my uncle, who was at Kingsgate for Christmas, recorded that my father was playing golf at Sandwich!

I have mentioned that Wells, the arch-contriver, had marked down my father for high office in the Academy. The high office was the Presidency. Events now began to take a turn. There are these entries in my uncle's diary, he serving a turn on Council:

"*March* 3, 1895: I called at Perugini's this afternoon. Millais was there playing Bezique. His voice is very weak."

"*March* 26, 1895: At the Council Meeting tonight Sir Fred Leighton spoke of his health and told us (reading letter) that it was the opinion of the most eminent specialists that anything like excitement might have serious consequences, and that as soon as possible he must go away. . . . It was very disturbing to hear this. . . . We endeavoured to persuade him to absent himself from the General Assembly tomorrow, but he insisted on attending."

"*March* 27, 1895: At the General Assembly tonight Leighton repeated the account of himself. Afterwards Millais spoke very feelingly, hoping that the President would not stint his rest".

On that same night Wells wrote:

My dear Fildes,

Just to say that I think you managed that little bit of business at the Assembly exactly rightly and have made good standing ground for the future.

In Leighton's absence the chair at the banquet on the opening of the Summer Exhibition was to be taken by Millais. But Millais might not be up to it. My uncle proposed at a Council Meeting that an understudy should be ready. Millais, however, saw the evening through. "Millais did admirably in the Chair", was my uncle's comment. "It was difficult to hear him at first, but with the great silence kept it was easy afterwards. His simple speech, mostly about himself, told very well."

Outside the Academy, too, there had been some mention of Fildes as a possible President one day. The Christmas number of the Art Journal that year was to be given up to the "Life and Work of Luke Fildes, R.A.", and my father was in correspondence with the Editor, Croal Thomson, about the proofs. "The allusion to the Presidency some time", my father wrote, "is so marked that I personally would be much pleased if you would not refer to it. You have done it as delicately as it is possible to do it I know, but it is not possible to refer to it at all without some susceptibilities being touched. It would not be agreeable to Sir Frederick I am sure; it would not be agreeable to me, though it is complimentary. Moreover, it is very questionable if I should consent to accept that very exacting and irksome position, however others might think I should."

In the summer of that year, 1895, my father had paid a second visit to Kissingen and in his absence the Annual General Meeting of *The Graphic* had been held. He had been elected to the Board. New interests were opened up which would absorb much of his time—possibly too much— as the years went by.

Wells and my father were busy in September and October writing each other about the Constitution of the Academy, but with no reference, it would seem, to any possible change of President. Meanwhile Leighton, in search of health,

arrived in Venice. Unlike his usual habit he had not let my
uncle know, and it was by the merest chance they met.

Nov. 1st, 1895.

My dear Luke,
. . . I have seen Leighton here. I was up for the day from
Serra Valle and met him in the Piazza. He complained of
his attacks being worse. . . . I told him Poynter was here
and lunching with me on that day. I asked Leighton to
join. He declined, saying that he had much to do, and
asked me "to give his kind regards to Poynter and beg
him not to call upon him". Poynter and myself agreed
that Leighton was in a most unsatisfactory state, travelling
quite alone and consequently from his state of health
most miserable.

My father replied:

Leighton has come back. I haven't seen him, but I am
told he isn't a bit better, worse if anything, This is very
bad news, for it means great difficulties for the Academy.

The difficulties came of both Millais and Leighton being
ill. It was typical of Millais, in the midst of his own troubles,
that he should write my father:

Bowerswell,
Perth.
19 Novr. 1895.

Dear Fildes,
I heard from Calderon that your wife was in trouble,
and I am extremely anxious to hear better accounts of her
state. I know how anxiety destroys all the joy of life, and
how working under such circumstances is not possible.
Give her my love and tell her she is not forgotten by
Yrs sincerely,
J. E. Millais.
I am better, but voiceless.

At the end of 1895 my uncle went off the Council, and
my father came on for a second round of duty. This
synchronized with Leighton's elevation to the Peerage.

"Leighton's honours", my father wrote to my uncle, "have given us a topic of interest, and by the way, I am sorry to say on calling tonight to enquire, having heard he was not at all well, I was told he was very ill indeed: as bad as could be. So write to him."

Two days afterwards my father wrote:

Dear Harry,
   Leighton's dead! A few hours ago.
   What a disaster this is to us!
                              In haste
                                    affectionately yrs
                                              Luke

Wells, Norman Shaw, my father and Val Prinsep were appointed a committee to make the arrangements for the funeral. It was a public funeral at St Paul's, preceded by a Lying-in-State at the Academy. Great crowds assembled along the route and at the cathedral. It would become an historic event was the opinion of *The Times*.

I, at school, heard from my mother: "I went to Lord Leighton's funeral last Monday. It was very grand, and nearly everybody shed a tear. Sir John Millais is going to be asked to be President and I believe he will be."

So ill was Millais that he had thought of going into retirement, but at the funeral at St Paul's the whole Academic Body had been swept by emotion for him, and at a General Assembly, with Calderon in the Chair, he was elected unanimously to the Presidency.

Millais was able to be at the Academy to receive the Prince of Wales before the exhibition of 1896 was opened. One of the exhibits was a portrait by my father of the eminent surgeon, Frederick Treves. Shortly afterwards my father has this note from Treves:

                                    6 Wimpole Street,
                                              W.1.
                                         Sunday.
Dear Fildes,
   You may be interested (and sorry) to hear that I

performed tracheotomy on Sir J. Millais at 2 a.m. this
morning. Although in terrible distress he whispered in
my ear before the operation, 'My old friend Fildes
painted your portrait', He was very comfortable when I
left him, and I hope he will do well.

Yours sincerely,

Frederick Treves.

Lady Millais used to call with news at Melbury Road,
and my parents for news at Palace Gate. A strange air of
optimism prevailed. Millais might be recovering. Early in
July a note came for my father from Mary Millais that her
father wanted to see him. Millais died on the 13th of August.
My father travelled backwards and forwards to the Academy
each day from Kingsgate. Millais was to be buried at St
Paul's but, as my father wrote my uncle, "As everybody is
out of town, the funeral will be enormously shorn of the
importance and impressiveness of the late Presidents. The
election of the new President will be in November."

There was a strong feeling amongst the older
Academicians that the new President must not be a foreigner.
Whom they had in mind to debar does not appear, several
members of the body could have been in their minds. Apart
from that, the Presidency was very open. Seeing how close
was the interest my father and my uncle always took in the
filling of vacancies amongst the Academicians, I am struck
by the absence of any speculation in their correspondence
over the next few months on the question of who the next
President should be.

Calderon, the Keeper and therefore the senior official in
the Academy when there was no President, was holidaying
that summer at Broadstairs, and he and Mrs. Calderon were
often over at Kingsgate. I remember him and my father
being in close confabulation. One evening, after such a
confabulation, my father asked me to go out for a stroll
before dinner. He told me that Mr. Calderon had been asking
him to accept the Presidency of the Royal Academy,
supposing he was elected, and many members wanted to
vote for him. It would be a great honour for him, and it
might be of help to us children in after years. But he saw

difficulties. He did not think he could afford it. He would have to live more expensively ("Your mother would have to have her brougham"—sticks in my memory). And the duties of President would prevent him painting as much, and earning as much, as he wanted to. He was anxious above all not to have to stint the education he wanted his children to have.

All this was said in a manner of thinking aloud, and I gained the impression that he was not so much repeating what he had already said to Calderon, as rehearsing what he intended to say.

On the 26th of October Woods wrote about the election, announcing his intention of coming over for it, and saying: "Our choice must be made amongst five it seems to me—yourself, Stone, Prinsep, Rivière and Poynter."

My father replied from Kingsgate by return of post: "I have not written you about the R.A. for the reason that I have nothing to say. You know I have been from town since Millais' funeral and have seen no one. . . . No one has spoken or written to me on the subject, with one exception—Calderon. I saw him down here during August and September, and he told me Wells is interesting himself very much in Rivière, having dropped me who at one time was his favourite. . . . Even now, were I by some miracle elected, I am in much doubt if I should accept it. . . . Of the candidates you mention I think Poynter would be the best to elect for the Academy's interest."

This might seem to be defection on the part of Wells, but it was not. There was no break in their friendship. In my father's quandary Wells, a realist, had switched to Briton Rivière, having found out he was willing to serve. The election, when it was reached, was a close run thing between Poynter and Rivière, and Poynter won. He was to remain President for twenty-three years during the whole of which period he and my father were the best of friends.

The year ended with Calderon at Burlington House writing to my father at Kingsgate:

We get up by gaslight, breakfast by gaslight, lunch by ditto, and live (if it can be called "living") in a stinking yellow pea-soup atmosphere. The only change is in our Galleries where "Val" and "Marcus" hang the Leightons by electric light. It is an extraordinary exhibition of industry and ability, a wonderful instance of a man sticking to his Art principles from youth to age.

❧ XIV ❧

THE CLOSE OF AN ERA
1897-1900

During the next four years Fildes exhibited fifteen portraits at the Royal Academy. These were not the whole of his output; some "sitters" wanted their portraits home without being sent to an exhibition. He was being offered more work than he could do and the highest prices of the time. A letter from Lockett Agnew throws some light:

39B Old Bond St.,
London W.
March 16th 1897.

My dear Fildes,
    I have at last come to the conclusion that your charm of manner completely eclipses your artistic talent, and you know the high opinion we all have of the latter. It is a fatal charm and promises in the future to make your life unbearable in your studio. Only yesterday, for instance, a client of ours told Morey [Lockett's cousin Morland Agnew] that he wanted his portrait painted, and you had been so consistently nice, so warmly appreciative of his wife's character, and *so* painstaking that really he must offer you the commission. Now when I tell you that the client whom you have charmed is one Lever of Soap fame you will clearly understand the rocks ahead.

Yours ever,
Lockett A.

My father and Sargent, the two leading portrait painters of their time, used to be spoken of as rivals. They were not. Nobody who had a mind to be painted by one of them would have been likely to think of the other, so dissimilar were their styles. Sargent, I suspect, cared less for my father's work than my father cared for Sargent's, and yet he set great store by my father's opinion:

Monday night,
33, Tite Street,
Chelsea, S.W.

My dear Fildes,

I am delighted that you have had such a good report of my picture from Mrs. Fildes, and that you will come to see it. But I have a scruple about letting you come tomorrow as there is a bare possibility of my not being able to show it to you properly, for tomorrow a lot of furniture and tapestry belonging to some people I have been painting is to be packed and removed. I will send you a wire tomorrow afternoon early to let you know how things are going on, and if you come another day, please let me know in the morning which day it would be.

I am sorry for this complication.

Yours sincerely,
John S. Sargent.

My father by now was in his middle fifties. He had become one of the leading personalities in the Academy and was looked upon by the younger men as a "friend of reform". When, a "ginger group" of these latter which included Arthur Hacker, Abbey, Sargent, Frampton, Clausen, Swan, Shannon, Parsons, La Thangue and Solomon, were wanting changes made in the Academy Schools my father offered them his studio at Melbury Road for their first discussions.

My father took as keen an interest in the Academy's affairs when he was off the Council as when he was on it. Frederick Eaton, the Secretary, who was a close friend of my parents, once said to my mother, when he was staying at Kingsgate: "Can't you do anything with that husband of yours? He gets so carried away when he speaks in General Assembly that the men think he is angry! They don't understand why, and they don't like it."

One of the most interesting of the portraits my father did not exhibit was one of Cecil Rhodes, painted in 1899. It was before the days of telephones, and Rhodes was under the impression that without any prearrangement he could send telegrams announcing his arrival at Melbury Road at an hour's notice. Cecil Rhodes might be an Empire Colossus, but my father was an eminent portrait-painter, and once upon a time an Emperor had been known to stoop and pick up a painter's brush. The arrival of a telegram one evening when dusk was drawing in: "Am just leaving for your studio; Rhodes", brought matters to a head. Something bordering on a slanging match ensued in which Rhodes called my father "A hot-headed Lancashireman", and my father told Rhodes not to come for a sitting smelling of brandy.

Eventually the portrait, though it was never finished by Fildes' standards, after years in the studio with its face to the wall like a naughty child, came to rest in a board room in the City.

Considerable changes had been coming over my parents' domestic background. For months on end, Melbury Road and Holland House, Kingsgate, were denuded of children. All six of us were at boarding schools or university. In a letter from my father to my uncle one autumn, he said: "I got through a good deal of work last month for, of course, I could not do much until the children had left for school at the end of September. Up to then it was desirable I should be with them a good deal, for it is the only time in the year I really see anything of them, and it is not good to cut one's self entirely away from their sports and amusements for they would get into the way of doing without one which would be a very undesirable state of affairs".

Without yielding any affection for my father's memory, I cannot help thinking that in that letter, and in others he wrote my uncle in the same strain, he was indulging himself in a bit of self-persuasion.

By writing what I have, I must not suggest that my father lacked a sense of humour. No man, could lack a

H.R.H. The Princess of Wales
1894

H.M. King Edward VII. State Portrait
1902

sense of humour who on happening to notice, through the
window an unwonted incident in Melbury Road, burst
into *vers libres* on the spur of the moment:

> *"I wish I may choke*
> *If there isn't a bloke*
> *On a moke*
> *With a sack of our coke "*

This is not to say that his sense of humour was at its strongest
when he thought his professional status was in danger. A
classic instance of this was when my mother rummaged in
my father's wardrobe one morning and found a yachting
cap he wore on "P. & O. occasions", and the riding boots
he wore when exercising himself and Caramel in Rotten
Row. No sooner seen than acted upon. She climbed into
the riding boots, tucked up her petticoats into the top of them,
balanced the yachting cap on her mass of Titian hair and
walked upstairs to the Studio. But it happened that my
father had an important visitor that morning whom she had
forgotten. On throwing open the door and striking an
attitude, she found herself confronted by a total stranger
and a mounting expression of displeasure on my father's
face. With a wail of horror, she turned about and shot downstairs.

My father saw nothing amusing in the incident. Not
even when the important visitor (as my father unguardedly
let out) had said "Was that Mrs. Fildes? I thought she was
charming, if I may say so."

A minor lack of humour—minor because no reprimand
this time came of it—was an occasion when my father and
mother were in a corner of the garden at Melbury Road,
some fifty paces from the house, and the parlourmaid
came out to say that an unexpected visitor had called. With
a deep sigh, my father remarked: "I don't know why it is
Fanny but I can never be left in peace, even in a remote
part of my own garden". My mother seized on the expression
with joy, and for ever afterwards that particular corner was
known as The Remote Part.

I have already referred to my father's tendency to drama-
tize his affairs. My mother in a letter to me at Cambridge

F

says: "Day [a contraction of Dada] thinks he will have to give up portrait painting, it worries him so and makes his life unbearable. Although he would not make so much money I am sure it would be better; at least I am sure he will live longer not doing them. Don't mention this to anyone."

But he went on painting portraits for another twenty-five years without the consequences foreshadowed.

A great event in the year 1897 had been Queen Victoria's Diamond Jubilee. My father, Paul and I saw the procession from *The Graphic* office opposite the Law Courts. My mother and the younger children were on a balcony in Pall Mall. The following eye-witness account is from a letter she wrote to Uncle Harry:

> We had a wonderful day on Jubilee Day. We all got up at 5 o'clock and started out at 6.30, I going with Kitty, Geoffrey, Denis and Dorothy to a balcony in Pall Mall near the Reform Club. Mr. Lever asked us to it. We had a wonderful view . . . the carriages, horses and dresses of the Indian Princes; our Princes and all the soldiers were beyond description. I never felt so excited as when the Queen passed, looking such a nice old woman . . . quite touched at all she saw. . . . Everybody dressed in their best, and everybody in a good humour. The children and I went in a cab to Pall Mall and much to their joy we got mixed up with some of the troops.

That was a year when home photography—hand-cameras and photographers doing their own developing and printing in their bathrooms—was almost a social craze; as also was bicycling. Uncle Harry, on his arrival at Victoria Road, had taken up both. My father, my mother, Paul, Kitty and myself were already bicyclists, but the pedestrian to Padua, cricketer on the *Campo di Marte*, long distance swimmer and rescuer of many a child from drowning in Venetian canals, never succeeded in mounting and dismounting a bicycle with any confidence. His diary over the next few years was a tale of contused shoulders and sprained knees. Photography was easier. Encouraged by my brother Paul, who already had a scientific mind, my father became adept and was showing the way for my uncle to become a

better photographer than cyclist. I think it was mostly to
look into some new thing that my father took up photography. He had no ideological objection to using it in
portraiture. Why not, when the Old Masters used the *Camera
Obscura*? But it was not of much help to him. My uncle, on
the other hand, found a camera a great saving of time. He
could dispense with the tedium of having to make notes
of relative proportions of foregrounds and backgrounds,
and continue in his technique of painting the latter first.

Easter holidays in those years were always spent at
Kingsgate. We all, my mother included, cycled about the
unfrequented roads of Thanet and penetrated as far as
Canterbury, while my uncle went by carriage or by train.
At the end of the holidays we returned to London, and after
the Varnishing Days, there came the Academy Banquet.
For the second year running my uncle noted, in 1898,
"Poynter did admirably". But a gloom was cast over the day
by the death that morning of Calderon, the Keeper.

Kingsgate, as I have said, was "pretty bleak", as well it
might be, exposed to the North Pole without any inter-
vening land. The fertility of the garden in trees—notably a
mulberry and a medlar as old as Lord Holland—was
explained by Lewis, our ex-sailor gardener, by the sousing
the garden used to get when the winter nor-easters sent the
spray scudding over the house-top. In summer the place
was a suntrap, and the house having been furnished by my
parents in a lighter vein than Melbury Road, was easily
lettable. After spending four summer holidays there my
mother and the children wanted a change. They wished to
go abroad. The first tenants in that summer of 1898—and
when naming them I must emphasize again that Holland
House was not a stately home—were the Duke and Duchess
of Fife. "Luke and Fanny will be having the Princess of
Wales there next" was my uncle's comment, a not unnatural
thought seeing that the Duchess was the Princess's daughter.
Writing me when he and my mother were down there
tidying-up, my father told me: "The Fifes left the place
terribly topsy-turvy, and that you can readily imagine with
19 servants sleeping on the premises, inclusive of two in
the harness room."

A reference to the summer holiday that year was contained in a letter my father wrote to my uncle in October: "Fanny decided to go with the family and governess to France. . . . I elected to stay in London and go on with my work. . . . She went to a place called Paris Plage, a hell-hole—a kind of watering place—which they left after a dreadful experience and made their way inland to Montreuil, an old fortified town, ramparted completely, quaint and delightful as could be imagined. I went over at the end of their stay for 3 days to bring them back and I was charmed. . . . We stayed at the old coaching Inn where Sterne put up during his *Sentimental Journey*."

Though Paris-Plage—Le Touquet in future years—was then only in its infancy, my memory of it is more favourable than my father's description.

My uncle came over for a week to spend Christmas of 1898 at Kingsgate. I fear, although none of us children had any inkling of it, that the week could not have been entirely happy for him, notwithstanding the entry in his diary: "I was never so sorry to leave them." He had been taken seriously to task by my father, who set it all out again in a letter to Venice.

New Year's Day '99.

My dear Harry,

I am afraid you left on Friday feeling rather sore at what I, rightly or wrongly, felt impelled to say.

It is perhaps, no part of my duty to make reference to such matters but I want to disabuse your mind, if any such thought exists, that I trouble you, and myself, with my views out of pure cussedness and a delight to say unpleasant things.

I fear I am much too serious for ordinary companionship and that I preach a deal too much, but I want you to understand that when I spoke I was sincerely anxious and that I had the greatest difficulty in bringing myself to the scratch to speak at all. It has been on my mind for a long time that your life in Venice is not at all conducive to your physical and artistic development.

I sincerely believe it would be good for you in every

way to consider, most seriously, if you cannot arrange your time and affairs to permit more association with people who have some sympathy with your welfare, artistic and otherwise. You appear to have none in Venice; at least I don't think so. I am sure such isolation is not good, and tends to degeneration. . . . I firmly believe you would benefit greatly with your work if you would only give one the opportunity of being assistance to you, by being with you in the early stages of a picture, while designing and scheming out ideas. I am egotistic enough to think you would derive great benefit from my assistance. I say "my assistance" but any one who has sympathy with your work and confidence in what you can carry out, would be equally advantageous to you.

I don't counsel leaving Venice—not at all—but six selected months there a year is more than sufficient for all your needs with the enormous knowledge and experience you possess of the place. . . . You will do unquestionably better work and do twice as much, vastly improve your chances of health and add to your prospects of a pleasant old age. . . . We send our love and all good wishes for the new year.

Yours affectionately,
Luke.

To which my uncle replied:

Venice
January 6, 1899.

My dear Luke,

I was very glad to get your letter of New Year's Day. I agree with every word, and feel grateful for it.

I left Kingsgate with no feeling of soreness I assure you. I knew that you had only said what you sincerely felt, and was already glad that you had spoken. At the last moment I was about to tell you so; but I was suddenly overcome at leaving you all, and could not speak.

Truly, I have long disliked living here during so much of the year, and at the finish of my present work, shall begin to make new arrangements. . . .

Very sincerely,
H. Woods.

Despite the meekness and submissiveness of this reply—
for after all he was well into middle-age by then, and had
achieved no small success in his profession—my uncle did
not finish his work for that coming Academy and did not
set about making the "new arrangements" of which he had
written. A visit to England a few months later lasted no
longer than his visits normally did, and though he went for
a couple of days to Winchester, where Paul was at school,
the entry he made in his diary after walking round the
Cathedral Close was, "undoubtedly a lot to paint about here,
but what to do in the way of figures would puzzle me".

The storm my father had raised was blowing itself out. In
a letter from Holland House towards the end of the year,
there was only a momentary gust:

1 Nov. '99.

My dear Harry,

Fanny and I have only just come here for a sort of
working rest if I can so call it. . . . It does Fanny and me
good; it shortens the winter and I can manage very well
to do a lot of work one way or the other. . . . I hope you are
trying your best to carry out the programme we talked
over of not staying so long in Venice. I have not changed
my mind in the least on that point.

We are quite alone here. Dorothy having gone to
school now, where Kitty is.

What shocking blundering our Generals are committing
in South Africa. . . .

Affectionately yours,
Luke Fildes.

The momentary gust was ignored in my uncle's reply:

2727 San Maurizio,
Venice.
Nov. 15th 1899.

My dear Luke,

I was very glad to hear from you that you are both
well, doing Darby and Joan, and getting on with the
work as well, and above all that you are at Kingsgate
storing up health for the winter.

I think there has been some blundering in Natal. . . .
Where is your portrait of Rhodes? He is doing all he can
to make it valuable to you. . . .

> Yours very truly,
> Henry Woods.

As an old Volunteer with memories of "sham fights" on
Wimbledon Common, Woods was following closely all the
war news. In his next letter he "had been delighted all day
at reading of General Warren capturing a hill that overlooks
the Boer Guns south of Ladysmith. This means everything."

Woods stayed at Melbury Road on his next visit to
England and on the 18th of May, 1900, "towards midnight
Luke and I, sitting in the Studio, heard distant shouting
and guessed that the news of the relief of Mafeking had
come at last!"

I was surprised by a letter my mother wrote me later in
that year when she and my father were on a visit to my uncle,
after my brother Paul and I had been spending a very
agreeable and comfortable holiday with him.

From her letter it seemed that my parents' stay had not
been at all comfortable and she went on to say "I am going
about this next week hunting for lodgings for Uncle Harry.
I would so much like to get him out of here."

This second storm, like the first, blew itself out. I never
seriously thought my mother would turn her unfortunate
brother out of the only home he had and move him back
into lodgings.

Anyway, my parents could not put up with Anna's cook-
ing, and they treated themselves to dinner at Quadri's every
night where, too, they did their entertaining.

In another letter my mother wrote: "I am in a state of
excitement. Lady Layard has been telling Day that she
knows of a place here where good pearls can be bought for
much less than in England, and Day is going to buy me a
necklace!! Lady Layard is going with us to help us to buy
them. I shall not know where I am, shall I?"

My father's main purpose in going to Venice that autumn
had been to paint a Venetian single-figure subject. It was
intended to be the first of a series he had agreed with Agnews

to paint for them over a period of years, though as events turned out, it was the only one he did paint.

My parents were back at Melbury Road in time for the last Christmas of the Century and the last weeks, as they proved to be, of the Victorian Era.

INTERMISSION

Twenty-seven years had gone by since Fildes made his name by painting *The Casuals*, and he would be in the public eye for as many years more. The close of the Victorian era with the death of the Queen did not put an end to pictures being painted in the way the Victorian public had liked them—Victorian painters remained Victorian painters in style and outlook, and the changes of fashion that lay ahead would not come so soon that most of those painters would have to witness the decline of their reputations. In that respect Fildes, who was the one of them who would live the longest, was particularly fortunate.

The proverbial difficulty of accounting for changes of taste applies, perhaps, less to Victorian Painting's eventual fall from public grace than it generally does. It will be recalled that the *cause célèbre* of *Whistler* v. *Ruskin* in the late eighteen-seventies had lent authority to the notion that a picture could not be "good art" if it were not "finished". Since then French Impressionism had arrived, and the notion had become less firmly established. I do not recollect my father and his friends ever having much to say about French Impressionism; very likely they did not regard it as the novelty it was subsequently proclaimed to have been— painting in the open-air, catching the fugitive interplay of light and shadow, noting how atmosphere changes the look of things, was what every artist did on a day in the country with paint-box and brushes. It was "sketching".

There is a sheet of sketches by my father inscribed "May Day 1868"—before ever "Impressionism" had been heard of—on which are studies of branches of trees and of shadows cast by a hedge, and of children and haystacks in different lights. Another sheet of the same year has a field with sheep and on the back of the sheet is the same subject against which he has written "the scene as sketched on the other side, only ¼ hour later". Yet another sheet bears this note: "Bright light on leaves lighter than field beyond"—there had just been a shower of rain. All that is of the quintessence of Impressionism. I have spoken earlier of some watercolour sketches he did at Hurley on his honeymoon; to them, I would now add one he did of my mother at the same time, which with her glorious Titian head of hair out-Renoirs Renoir. Victorian sketch-books and portfolios must be full of Impressionism, and so little was Impressionism a break-away from Traditionalism that Van Gogh was an admirer of the work of my father, of Millais, of Frank Holland of Frederick Walker. Van Gogh in the 1880's was collecting old numbers of *The Graphic* and in letters of his of that time he mentions "a couple of beautiful pages by Fildes" and "a figure such as one finds in the work of Holl and Fildes". He regrets having missed buying a copy of Fildes' *Graphic* drawing of *The Empty Chair*.

The lesson of Impressionism was that the vigour and freshness of sketching could be used with a sense of finality; vigour and freshness could be more than a means to an end and could have attractions which in a "finished" picture might be lacking. Neither ideologically nor aesthetically therefore, would there seem to have been any reason why a taste for Victorian Painting should not have combined with a taste for the new-found Impressionism—I use the word to include Neo-Impressionism and Post-Impression, and all their derivatives—and public interest in Art today would have been greater had that happened. But there were to be reasons of another kind that would stand in the way. The first consignments of Impressionist pictures to be exhibited in this country were arranged by Roger Fry, the leading art critic of his time. A state of co-existence between Victorian Painting and Impressionism would not have suited him, and in his capacity as the leading art critic, he proceeded to lambast all Victorian painters and their works. (I believe he fell foul of *The Doctor*, though I have been unable to trace the passage.) "England in the Nineteenth Century", he summed up, "had enjoyed a veritable debauch of trivial anecdotic picture-making such as the world has never seen before." That, and much else, in language of a persuasive virulence, spread over a period of years, would have its effect, and the last two generations of British public have been brought up to think there is little in Victorian painting to be taken seriously.

It was to be against a background of changing taste that the rest of my father's career was to be spent, without however any loss of his reputation in his lifetime.

XV

STATE PORTRAITS

1901-1904

On the first day of the new century Fildes received the first
payment from Agnews under the contract I mentioned his
having made with them. He was already regretting having
bound himself to produce work to a timetable, and he wrote
to Woods towards the end of the month in a very unsettled
frame of mind: "I have been quite unwell since I came back,
and what with that and the incessant dark and gloomy
weather I have done little or nothing. There is no doubt it
would be worse than useless for you to winter here and
anything I may have said to induce you to do so, I retract."
At that stage my mother stepped in with this result:

> 39B Old Bond Street,
> London, W.1.
> Feb. 22nd 1901.

My dear Fildes,
　　A little bird has suggested to me that your nerves are
on the stretch because you are not progressing with the
work for me as quickly as you would like. Will you please
bear in mind that I do not care a two-penny d—n when
you send me your pictures. I made the arrangement with
you as a relief of your mind, not to harass it, and if you
go worrying over a bit of a wretched clause in that agreement which may bind you to time, you will upset both
yourself and me. So treat our arrangement as one between

Pals, and if the time limits are not carried out they can be jolly well extended.

My love to you and yours,

Ever,

Lockett A.

In any case, as events turned out, my father could not have carried out the agreement. Within a few days of Lockett Agnew's letter my father's affairs took a new turn. One morning, quite unexpectedly, Sir Edward Poynter drove up in his brougham to see my father. After he had gone this was what my father had to tell us. Sir Edward had come straight from the King who had sent for him, as the official head of British Art, to advise who should paint the State Portrait which His Majesty understood had to be painted on his Accession. Poynter, it must here be interposed, had painted portraits but was not regarded as a specialist in that line. My father had been greatly impressed by the simplicity, and the dignity, with which Poynter continued his story. On hearing the reason why he had been summoned he had, as President of the Royal Academy, deemed it his duty to offer his services to the King. Whereupon there had been a pause. At the end of the pause the King had said:

"Supposing, Sir Edward, it is not you who paint the portrait, whom would you advise me to choose?"

To which Poynter had replied:

"There can be no doubt as to that, Sire; it should be Mr. Luke Fildes." A look of pleasure had passed over the King's face, and he said.

"I should like Mr. Luke Fildes to see me as soon as possible."

My father had to get rid of two pages of minor gossip in his next letter to my uncle, before coming out with:

"The chief thing I want to tell you is that the King has commanded me to paint his life-size, full-length, Court portrait.

I had an audience with him this morning and it is all settled. It is to be the swagger portrait in crimson velvet and ermine mantle that all Monarchs have, and which is copied to send to Embassies and presents to other Kings.

He told me this morning that probably about 30

would be required for India, Canada, Australia, South
Africa and all over the World. Of course I'll have nothing
to do with them but I shall be expected to superintend
and pass them—and probably I shall have something
satisfactory out of doing any for such places as the Cities
of the Empire who may commission me if the King turns
out well as it must."

My uncle replied, "You take rank now with Reynolds
and Lawrence".

The King preferred Melbury Road to Buckingham
Palace for his sittings. "The King came and sat to Luke in
his studio last Tuesday morning", my mother wrote to my
uncle in the middle of June. "He sat very well and Luke did
a lot from him. He took an interest in the house, admired
the staircase, went into the Drawing Room and looked
round. Mary [the parlourmaid] of course was very excited
because he bowed and smiled when he passed her in the hall.
I did not see him at all, but heard his voice; it sounded all
over the house."

When giving "sittings" the King never assumed the
posture of the portrait. He sat in an arm chair raised up on
the platform, or "throne", which is a feature of an artist's
studio. The strong north-light could be trying to anybody
unaccustomed to it, a circumstance which, combined with
the tendency inherited from the Royal House of Hanover
for the King's eyelids to droop, led my father into a trap
from which, as I shall tell later, he was most fortunately
rescued by Queen Alexandra.

It was at that first sitting that the King, on entering the
studio, made the observation, "One of the finest rooms in
London". My father wrote an account to Henry Woods:
"He was most chatty and affable . . . looked into the Garden
('Quite like a country garden'), and generally admired the
house and thought I had a great many pretty things. Sir
Arthur Ellis came with him. . . . I had no red carpet nor
anything in the least different than usual. No one saw his
arrival or departure and that is, I am sure, what he would
wish. . . . He sent for me to see him at Marlborough House
last week, and asked me to meet him another day at

Buckingham Palace to select where the picture should go. He decided on a place to the right of a door, the other side being, I understand, for the Queen's picture whoever may paint it."

One of the King's uniforms had been lent to my father, who did not like the idea of its being worn by a professional model, and it was Gordon Thomson who used to come down to Melbury Road and don it. One day Gording was in a hurry to get back to Town. Having changed back into his clothes, he was walking up Kensington High Street to the Underground Station when he became aware of a certain constriction round his waist. Making such investigation as he could in public, he discovered he had pulled his own trousers over the King's riding breeches. There was nothing to be done but return sheepishly to No. 11 and confess, to my mother's immense joy.

In the portrait the King is standing upon marble steps. My father had no marble steps. My mother, the thoroughly practical-minded woman she was, went up Kensington High Street and bought a roll of American cloth. This she spread out, and my father painted it. He received particular congratulations on his marble steps—"as good as anything Tadema has ever done"—Tadema being the Academy specialist in marble.

Writing on the 4th November to Woods my father said:

> The King came yesterday to see his portrait and gave me a sitting, but it was so foggy and dark I didn't attempt to do anything. . . . I shall not see him again until January when he returns to town from Sandringham. . . . He liked what I had done—it was light enough to see the picture—and took considerable interest in it. He stayed quite an hour—made several suggestions which were good and which I shall carry out in his absence.

The King's next visit was early the following March. Half an hour after his arrival the front-door bell rang, and on Mary, the parlourmaid, answering the door there were a lady and gentleman on the door step to whom Mary said, "Mr. Fildes cannot see anybody". They were, in fact, the Princess Louise, and her husband the Duke of Argyll.

"Oh! but I am the Princess Louise, and the King expects me," said the Princess.

Not quite knowing where she was, Mary showed them into the drawing room. She was then told to bring them to the studio, but half-way up the stairs the Princess turned to the Duke and said, "You had better wait below until the King sends for you".

The Duke went back to the drawing room and opened a book he had brought with him. Mary returned and began lighting the fire because the drawing room being a ceremonial apartment, not used in the morning, did not normally have its fire lit until after lunch.

"Don't light it on my account!" the Duke exclaimed. But at that moment he was sent for to go up to the Studio.

The King and the Princess Louise both approved the portrait. The King went poking into corners of the studio and calling out to the Princess to come and look at things.

A week later the King came again. This time he was in a less approving mood. He felt that the outstretched arm was too outstretched. He would send Sir Arthur Ellis to have a look at it. The King was in a state of deep depression that morning. There was bad news in *The Times*, and it was being read aloud to him as he sat. Lord Methuen had been defeated and made prisoner by the Boers, and my father said afterwards that the King broke into groans.

The outstretched arm was nothing to what was to follow. My father was now considered to have made the King look too short, although having studied State Portraiture from Hyacinthe Rigaud and Louis Quatorze onwards he had made the King two inches taller than he really was. A remark the King had made when dining at the house of friends was reported to my father—the conversation had turned to the subject of the strange obsessions from which people can suffer—"Take Mr. Fildes for instance", the King had said, "to whom I am sitting for my portrait—He is under the impression that I am a short, stout man."

These eleventh-hour criticisms, coming within a couple of weeks of "sending-in day", upset all rules and regulations. After the picture had been "hung" so that various schemes of wall-decoration might be tried round it, it had to be taken back to Melbury Road for my father to complete the alterations.

One of the most helpful suggestions, though an unintentional one, had come from Queen Alexandra. She had paid a private visit to see the portrait in the studio and had stood looking at it for a long time, a smile playing over her lips. The pomp and circumstance of Majesty would seem to have interested her less than some thoughts of her own.

"I like it *very* much," she said at last. "I think it is *very* good. I know that expression *so* well. It is *just* like him when he begins to feel drowsy."

Fortunately, to modify the Hanoverian droop of eyelids which had become too emphasized under the strong north-light of the studio, was an alteration my father could quickly make after the Queen's departure.

In his speech at the Academy Banquet that year, 1902, the Prince of Wales paid a compliment to the "King's Portrait by my friend Luke Fildes". On my father thanking him later in the evening, and particularly for having referred to him as the Prince's friend, the Prince had retorted—"Well, you are my friend, aren't you?" which foretells the sort of terms upon which King George V would treat my father in later years.

On the opening of the Academy the normal uncertainty of art criticism was intensified by doubts, after more than sixty years since Queen Victoria's accession, as to quite what a State Portrait ought to be. Was the convention of the Grand Manner still to apply? One writer, after remarking that "The King's head is not even a good likeness", committed himself to the assertion that "Mr. Fildes has not risen to the scale of his great canvas". Against that, another writer, after testifying that the portrait was a perfect likeness, asserted that "Mr. Luke Fildes has risen to the occasion, and displays something like genius". The general opinion was that he had performed a very difficult task with skill and tact.

Personal contacts with the Royal Family ended for the time being with a letter from Queen Alexandra. My father had sent the Queen a study he had made some years previously for a posthumous portrait of the Duke of Clarence

painted for the Duke's regiment. Down came an orderly in
uniform from Buckingham Palace pedalling a push-bike. In
the letter, after expressions such as a mother would use of
a "speaking likeness" of a well loved son now dead, the
Queen wrote, "No words can adequately express my
gratitude to you for a gift more precious to me than anything
else in the world, which I shall value as long as I live.
Thank you a thousand times over and over again and believe
me.

Yours very truly,
Alexandra.

The date of the Coronation was approaching. Up and
down the country preparations were being made for celebrating it.

I have mentioned how my father and W. H. Lever
became acquainted. He had painted Lever's and Mrs.
Lever's portraits, and the acquaintance had ripened into a
friendship—all the more so because my mother was a very
appreciative listener to Lancashire stories of which Lever
had an inexhaustible fund. William Lever, the founder of
Port Sunlight, 1st Viscount Leverhulme, and one of the
great industrialists of his time, was still a plain Mister in
1902, but already an outstanding figure in his part of the
country, and he was intending that the Coronation should
be celebrated in the Wirral with all suitableness. Being a
great Art collector he was having an Art Exhibition in the
village of Port Sunlight as one of the features of the celebrations, and he asked my father to persuade the President of
the Royal Academy to perform the opening ceremony.
Poynter was at Bath, "doing a cure", from where he wrote
my father:

I have been thinking over Mr. Lever's proposal and
I am convinced that it will not be possible for me to
undertake what he wants, for the simple reason that with
all the duties which I *must* perform I can hardly find
time to get to my studio, and I cannot make up my mind
to give up painting altogether. . . . For this reason I have
consistently for many years declined to give lectures,

distribute prizes, open exhibitions or perform any of the numerous functions which are passed on me. . . . Please do not think I am not in full sympathy with what Mr. Lever has done and is doing to promote a happy and healthy state of things in the district he has under his care. In providing a picture-gallery he is affording a great opportunity for a whole some form of enjoyment (all the more enjoyable if there is no pretence of education about it, for that is all nonsense—pictures are to give pleasure, not to teach). Also I am very sorry to be obliged to refuse you anything, and I hope that not only you will not think me disobliging, but that you feel that I really have reason for not complying with Mr. Lever's request. I am sure he would entertain me most kindly.

The upshot was that my father performed the opening ceremony himself. This took place on the 21st of June 1902, five days before the day appointed for the Coronation, and it was out of that exhibition that there grew the collection of pictures, furniture, porcelain and tapestries which the 1st Viscount presented to the nation twenty years later, with a Gallery to house them—the Lady Lever Art Gallery at Port Sunlight.

The subject of my father's address at the opening ceremony was "The Mission of Art Collectors". The use that was made of a work of Art was a higher consideration than its mere possession. Suiting himself to the majority of his audience, who were workers in the factory at Port Sunlight, he stressed the relief and elevation afforded by works of art to those whose occupations were mechanical. His address was one more variation on his theme of "Art for the Multitude".

It is a matter of history that the Coronation did not take place on the day originally appointed. The King was stricken with appendicitis on the eve of it, and it was postponed until August.

In the autumn Fildes had to begin the copying of the King's State Portrait. The King's own estimate of thirty official copies was below the mark. Every Embassy and Legation abroad must have its copy. Government establish-

ments at home and throughout the Empire likewise. Nor
was that the end.

Side by side with the official copies there would be private
copies which my father would be at liberty to supply, for his
own benefit, to City Companies, big West-end clubs and
other like buyers. These private copies may seem to be a
lucrative source of income to the artist. They were meant to
be. Unless the copyright of the State Portrait had been
transferred to the artist, a worthy State Portrait could not
have been painted. The fee available for the painting of it
fell short of compensating an established artist for the
anxiety involved and for the interference with his other
work. And there was the copyright in black-and-white.
The sum my father was paid by Agnews for the right to make
an engraving of the Portrait was three times the sum he
received for painting the Portrait itself.

The actual copying was done by a team of artists under
the painter's supervision, and a situation was revived like
those in the studios of the Old Masters where assistants
did the painting under the Master's eye. The *atelier* used
for the purpose was one of the galleries in St James's Palace,
and the work, with that of copying the Queen's portrait
subsequently, lasted to the end of the reign. From time to
time strange and unpredictable problems would arise as
when Sir Arthur Ellis wrote: "I send you the accompanying
case containing the copy of your Portrait of the King which
fell from the back of a camel in transit to Teheran and was
damaged. I daresay it can be doctored up and made good,
but you will be the best judge of this. Kindly advise."

Inevitable preoccupations with the business side of State
Portraiture did not lessen the sense of honour and glory. A
letter from my father to Woods, refers to his painting the
King as an event "which with most people would be deemed
more important than painting my finest picture".

Fildes found the responsibility of all the copying an
ordeal, but having got it started in the autumn of 1902, he
retired to Bath. He had been advised by his doctors to take
up horse-riding again, which he had been neglecting.
Woods was opposed to the idea. "This horse riding: I do not
like the idea of your taking it up again in these days of motor

cars." My uncle had made acquaintance with motoring the previous May when staying with friends in the country. ("Sometimes I had to insist upon a modification of speed" was an entry he had made in his diary.) He now wrote my father: "I have had experience of their effect upon horses. . . . I was much concerned about a lady on horseback we met, I thought the horse would have fallen backwards with her. There must be a lot of these machines in your neighbourhood. . . . One day a week at the golf links, and the Bike generally, ought to do you."

And that would seem to have been my father's opinion, too.

So far there had been only desultory talks about a companion State Portrait of Queen Alexandra. The Queen did not want to sit. Sir Arthur Ellis, who had negotiated the painting of her as Princess of Wales with "Facey", now told my father it would be helpful if he would make a sketch of what a State Portrait of the Queen might look like. Armed with this, Sir Arthur Ellis then asked the Queen if she would care to see a sketch. "Whom is it by?" the Queen enquired. "Mr. Fildes". "Well, I should never sit to anyone else."

Sir Arthur Ellis then produced the sketch. "She expressed her great pleasure. The King was asked to come and see it. He also was very pleased."

And so by May of 1903 the first sittings began. By June difficulties were already arising. The Queen's personal sittings were being given at Buckingham Palace, but my father wanted to have the robes in his own studio. The robes, however, must not leave the Palace. And then the Queen, for a time, thought of being painted in profile, not full face. The problem of the robes was not settled until my mother, who could turn her hand to anything, went to the Palace, took notes (having "a long chat with the Queen" meanwhile), and made a set of robes for studio use.

The painting of the Queen's State Portrait was to prove a long affair and it would not be until the Academy of 1905 that a portrait was ready to be exhibited.

In the meantime, my father had only one portrait for the Academy of 1903, but it was one of the best he ever did— *Mrs. James Reynolds and her daughter Leila* was, to borrow a standard of comparison from my Uncle, in my father's "Thomas Lawrence" style.

Woods was one of the "hangers" that April. My parents were at Kingsgate throughout the month and he used to come down at week-ends. On one of them Alma Tadema came with him, and my uncle noted in his diary that "last night and most of the day Tadema asked riddles and told stories". Alma Tadema, by that time well on in his sixties, was remarkable for his atrocious puns and juvenile sense of humour. At the stage in the Boer War when General De Wet's forces were at last being rounded-up and the final defeat of the Boers was imminent, Tadema had happened to catch sight of me at an Academy Private View. "Ah, my deal Wowl" (his pronunciation of my name, Val). "Vy does Kruger vear galoshes?" he exclaimed. "I see you do not know! I vill tell you. Kruger vears galoshes to keep de vet from de feet!" emphasizing the point by stamping his feet on the floor and going off into peals of laughter.

Occasionally people would go out of their way to explain why some well-known artist had never been elected to the Academy, and that he never would have accepted even if he had been. It was now Whistler's turn to be thus discussed. My father had a letter from Marion Spielmann, the well-known writer on Art.

21 Cadogan Gardens,
S.W.
20 Aug: 03.

My dear Fildes,

As you perhaps have seen, they are denying that Whistler could ever have been willing to enter the Royal Academy—as he told you in Venice. Would you object to my naming you as the Academician whom he sounded upon the subject? Of course I have given no hint as to who my informant was, nor should I without your consent; but I should be glad to be able to accept the challenge and disperse the doubt that has been cast . . .

Yours sincerely,
M. H. Spielmann.

11 Melbury Road.
Kensington, W,
21 August 1903.

Dear Spielmann,

Redounding as it does to his credit you are quite at liberty to quote me as an authority for the statement that Mr. Whistler at one time, was not averse to the idea of being a member of the Royal Academy.

Meeting at the house of a mutual friend he had a conversation with me on the possibilities of such an election.

It was not crudely put, but he without any doubt "sounded" me on the subject, and left me with the distinct impression that, could it be arranged, election into the Royal Academy would be most acceptable to him. He, moreover, did not in the least convey that feeling of antagonism to the R.A. I understand his "friends" say he entertained.

The conversation was in London some 12 or more years ago. I never saw him in Venice.

Sincerely yours,
Luke Fildes.

The Magazine of Art,
La Belle Sauvage,
Ludgate Hill,
E.C.
September 3rd 1903.

Dear Fildes,

I am greatly obliged for your letter to me, and still more so for the clear and emphatic letter in *The Times*. These wretched people, Quilter, Pennell, McColl and the rest, are always snarling and misleading the public on matters of fact with their quibbles and innuendos. . . . Of course the matter is not of great importance, but it *is* of importance for me to prove the facts I produced. As to their attempts at mischief-making by setting me up as the "apologist", the "champion", or the "lackey" of the Academy, which has been said over and over again, all this is simply intended to sow discord. I suppose that

nobody will be misled by it. With many thanks, I remain,
Yours sincerely,
M. H. Spielmann.

For several years my father had not been living up to his
protestations that he must give part of the summer holidays
to being with his children. Holland House had been let
each summer, and my mother had taken the younger
children away on holiday whilst the elder ones followed
their own devices. Except for a week or two at Altyre with
the Lockett Agnews, my father had been spending the months
of August and September at Melbury Road by himself,
working. The light was good, and there were no social
distractions. But he was taxing himself too much, and by the
middle of January, 1904, he went to see Sir Thomas Barlow
and came home very depressed. Sir Thomas Barlow had
told him he must drop his work and go away as soon as
possible. He was doing himself serious harm by trying to
finish the Queen's portrait.... At the end of the consultation,
Sir Thomas Barlow, who was the King's physician, told
Fildes that he would take all responsibility with the King
about the Queen's State Portrait not being ready for that
Year's Academy.

Within a fortnight my parents were on their way to
Egypt for a voyage up the Nile. Their travels were smoothed
by John Aird, the builder of the Assouan Dam and by that
time a baronet, whose word went a long way in Egypt.
They were on holiday all February and March. "Venice
isn't in it", was an excited comment in one letter from my
mother, and in another "Never had such a time".

I have mentioned that throughout the many years they
knew each other Gilbert and my father never quarrelled.
Neither my parents nor any of us children ever saw Gilbert
cantankerous, nor as the *raconteur* of "funny stories" which
he has been made out to have been. His wit was entirely
different from that. It was not his way to hold a luncheon-
party hanging on some drawn-out anecdote—as I have
read in one book of memoirs. His way was to sit listening
to other people's talk, and suddenly rap out a remark—
sardonic admittedly—which was witty for its aptness and

timing, but not "funny" in the abstract. It was a very fugitive wit.

The first occasion I met W. S. Gilbert was soon after I left school. My mother had taken me to some social function, and a tall, ramrod, military-looking man came up and spoke to her.

"I should like to introduce my son to you," she said (and turning to me), "This is Mr. Gilbert. *The* Mr. Gilbert."

"One of the *many* Mr. Gilberts, I'm afraid," he shot out.

Something in the way he said it, and my mother's laugh, showed me that there was more in his remark than I understood. Coming away from the function, I asked my mother.

"Oh, you see," she answered, "Mr. Gilbert feels it very much that he was not made a knight when Sir Arthur Sullivan was, and all his friends feel the same."

When the Savoy operas were revived early in the century, around the time of which I am now writing, I became a fervid Gilbert and Sullivan "fan". One Sunday afternoon the Gilberts were having tea at Melbury Road, and I in my unguarded enthusiasm said to him how much I was enjoying the revivals and admiring the performances, in particular that of Walter Passmore as "Bunthorne" in *Patience*. A frozen look came over Gilbert's face—"He does what he's told," was his comment.

A benign memory of Grim's Dyke is of a week-end with my parents, Cyril Maude, Winifred Emery, and my sister Kitty. After dinner one evening we listened to Gilbert, seated on a sofa, his pet lemur balanced on his shoulder, and Nancy MacIntosth—who was the adopted daughter of the Gilberts—seated by his side. She with the voice of a Savoyard and he with a one-note croak, sang Sea Shanties together, whilst Mrs. Gilbert smiled approvingly. It is a wonder that anybody with so little ear for music as Gilbert could write lyrics with so musical a lilt for Sullivan to work upon.

H. T. Wells was dead. My father, as though Wells must have a successor in keeping the Academy up to the mark was calling the President's attention to a non-observance of the Laws: for a good many years there had been no engravers elected to the Academy despite the Laws and Constitution laying down very clearly that there should be a class of Engravers. The President replied that as he read the Laws, the class of engravers should not exceed four in number "but it may at the discretion of the Academy consist of a less number, a discretion which the Academy has exercised by letting the number diminish until no members of the class remained". This was more than my father could stomach. "The discretion of the Academy," he answered, "applies to the election of a less number than 4 but not to the total abolition of the class altogether." The end of that matter was that the Academy proceeded to elect some engravers.

And now a sad thing happened. Val Prinsep died. The warmth of his and my parents' long friendship and, indeed, of his friendship with all his brother artists, had been slowly cooling off. His wife had not taken to them. My uncle, on the Prinseps' various stays in Venice, had been one exception. Val Prinsep was due to go into a nursing home for an operation which held out no difficulties. On the previous Sunday he had called unexpectedly at Melbury Road and, to quote my father to Woods, "had tea with us and was something like his old self. He did not, nor anyone else, anticipate any danger and was quite jolly about getting over a miserable nuisance which I am sure greatly affected his spirits the last year or more." But he did not come round from the operation.

In that same letter my father said: "I am still at work on the Queen's portrait. It is difficult to finish, particularly so now with dark short days, but it is going on all right."

Agnews were to publish an engraving of the Queen's portrait as a companion to their engraving of the King's. But a rival firm of Fine Art publishers had been clever. Taking advantage of the delays in my father's completing the official portrait they had jumped in and commissioned somebody to paint an unofficial one, and announced an engraving of it ahead of Agnews. Acrimonious correspondence ensued. My father's and Agnew's case was hampered by the clever publishers having gone behind everybody's back and obtained the Queen's approval, in some sense, of the "fake" portrait, for which, incidentally, she had not sat. Sir Arthur Ellis gave good advice. He was sure that, if my father and Agnews took steps to expose the "fake" portrait, "you will simply get into hot water with the Queen. . . . No one appreciates more than I do the difficulties you have had with the Q's State Portrait."

But those anxieties which Queen Alexandra caused my father must have a charming incident put in the balance against them. He was painting one day on the big canvas at Buckingham Palace, and wanting to do something at the foot of it, he dropped down on his knees.

"Mr. Fildes," the Queen reproved him, "you musn't do that. You will get housemaid's knee."

"What do you know, Ma'am, about housemaid's knee?" my father asked.

"Much more than you might think," the Queen answered.

And so it was. King Christian IX, before he came to the throne of Denmark, had lived in circumstances which were modest. He and his family had occupied a palace, but had few servants to attend on them. Young Princesses had taken turns at household chores, and Her Majesty Queen Alexandra was speaking to my father out of actual experience.

❦ XVI ❦

KNIGHTHOOD

1905-1909

The Queen's State Portrait was a success in the Academy of 1905. If it attracted less popular notice than the King's had done, the explanation was that a State Portrait in 1902 had been a novelty. My father's own opinion was that the Queen's was an improvement on the King's as a work of art. What chiefly mattered was that it was liked by the Royal Family. The Prince and Princess of Wales had been to see it at Melbury Road and "had stayed chatting for an hour and ten minutes, praising the portrait highly". This my uncle noted in his diary, adding a Pepysian touch, "I was glad to hear that the Prince asked after me".

There was a quiet time at Melbury Road that season of 1905. My mother, taking my sister Dorothy with her, was away most of it doing a cure at Aix-les-Bains and an after-cure at Chamonix, and soon after their return they and my father went down to Dartmoor to stay with the Strubens at Spitchwick. My father had exhibited a portrait of Mrs. Struben in that year's Academy, and now was to paint the husband.

Frederick Struben's career had been a romantic one. He was one of the early gold prospectors on the Rand, and at this time, 1905, he was deeply engaged—unsuccessfully as events turned out—in financing a scheme for re-opening disused gold diggings in the interior of South America. He had settled down in England and bought an estate near Ashburton. His choice of my father to paint a portrait of

174

his wife was the beginning of a very happy and lasting friendship between the two families.

The Spitchwick estate included a reach of the River Dart, and my father decided to paint Struben seated on the bank and selecting a fly for his cast. On hearing that news, my uncle aptly observed that my father was "getting back to outdoor nature". He had not painted outdoor nature since the eighties.

One week in October, 1905, the *Times Literary Supplement* reviewed two books, one by Andrew Lang, the *Puzzle of Dickens' Last Plot*, and the other by J. Cuming Walters, *Clues to Dickens' Mystery of Edwin Drood*. Charles Dickens' explanation to my father of the development of the plot of *Edwin Drood* had been long on record, but Andrew Lang brushes all that aside, maintaining that Dickens, for security's sake, had deliberately misled my father. Beside the waters, not of Babylon but of Harrogate, my father was deeply aggrieved, and wrote to the *Literary Supplement* to say so, but Andrew Lang would not recant and a stalemate resulted. My father was always being dogged by *Edwin Drood*.

Towards the end of the year my father was at Kingsgate suffering from a painful form of blood-poisoning. Writing about it to my uncle he said, "Fanny has been most devoted and kind". To which my uncle could not resist replying: "Fanny is the most devoted wife I ever knew or heard of."

At that time my brother Paul was a pupil, at the London Hospital, of William Bulloch, F.R.S., the Professor of Bacteriology there. Paul persuaded my father to come up to London and have a course of inoculations from Bulloch. The result was, in the state of knowledge at the time, miraculous. In 1905 the wonders of bacteriology were little known to the public. William Bulloch became a close friend of the family. My mother brought him under her cloak of kindliness, and with Gording, he became a regular Sunday supper-taker at Melbury Road. I can recall now the click of the wooden spoon and fork on the glass bowl as my mother mixed the salad, for Sunday was a day when the cook and the parlourmaid had their "evening out".

The time would come when Paul, Bulloch's favourite pupil, became qualified to practise as a doctor, but his interest lay in research. Thereupon my father gave an example of his creed that never must anything, if he could prevent it, stand in the way of his children's education. He told my brother that he need not take up medical practice in order to earn money; my father would see him through the lean years of research.

In 1906, my father was created a Knight Bachelor. The honour was generally thought to have come tardily. At the beginning of the year the Conservative Party had lost a General Election. For years its leaders had been notoriously uninterested in Art, and now it took a Liberal Prime Minister, Campbell-Bannerman, to make good an oversight. "Radical Knights, Baronets and Peers; Luke perhaps the only Conservative amongst them", was my uncle's comment on the Honours List.

My uncle was over in England at the time in order to attend my sister Kitty's wedding. She was marrying Whittaker Ellis, Sir John Aird's eldest grandson. The wedding took place on the 3rd of July, at St. Mary Abbot's, Kensington, and my parents' friend, the Bishop of Peterborough, conducted the service. I fill out my own memories of a glorious summer's day, crowds in the studio, crowds up the Triumphal stairway and in the garden, by a detail out of my uncle's diary of a circumstance which I had forgotten: "The refreshment tables were to the right under the trees." And he jotted down the names of Royal Academicians present, and added "I liked to see so many members of the Academy". He and Gording stayed to dinner.

My parents had a new neighbour, at 70 Addison Road, not ten minutes' walk away. The President of the Royal Academy had bought the house because of its garden in which he had hoped that Lady Poynter in her latest illness, would sit and enjoy it. She never was able to. After her death, Poynter used to call at Melbury Road and talk about her to my mother, whom he found always ready to be sympathetic. He liked sending notes round on Sunday mornings, when the weather was fine, asking my parents to tea in his garden.

In October my parents and Dorothy, with Gording, went to Venice; they to Uncle Harry's, Gording to Ruskin's old haunt, the "Calcina" on the Zattere. Five years had gone by since my parents had been in Venice. It was not only for a holiday they now went. On finishing the Queen's portrait the previous year, my father had made up his mind— erroneously—that he would have no more portraits of "interesting sitters" to paint. He had decided that he must introduce some diversity of subject into an output of portraits, and this visit to Venice in the Autumn of 1906 was the beginning of a second Venetian Period. If less ambitious than the first, it produced painting better in some people's opinion than the works which had made his reputation as a painter of Venetians back in the 'eighties.

For the present, however, he was feeling his way, and the first result, *La Giardiniera*, did not appear until the Academy of two years later. They went to Serra Valle, and into the mountains to Ponte nelle Alpi. A new experience was beach picnicking at the Montalbas' hut on the Lido. I should have said more of the Montalbas before this. Old Mrs. Montalba, now ninety years old, and her daughters and her son, August, had been friends in Venice of my uncle and parents for many years. The daughters were artists, the best known being Clara the eldest, a contemporary of my father's as an Academy Exhibitor. My mother wrote home about wonderful luncheons cooked by August Montalba at the hut.

But August Montalba was being useful in a more serious purpose. It was evident, and even my uncle now agreed, that 2727 San Maurizio was no longer large enough, or comfortable enough, to put up my parents, particularly now that Dorothy was likely to be travelling with them, and if my father's plan of a second Venetian Period, entailing annual visits, was to be carried out, other quarters would have to be found. There was a house of two floors in a garden on the Zattere where the Rio di San Vio joined the Giudecca Canal. The owner of the house, the Cavaliere Rocca, lived on the ground floor, and the upper floor, known as *Casetta Rocca*, with a separate entrance of its own, was to let. There was no access to the garden, but the garden lay there, beneath the windows, to be looked at, a rarity in Venice. And there was room in the *Casetta* for my uncle, my parents, members of the family and guests.

So Woods was to give up 2727 San Maurizio at last, and my father and he were to take the *Casetta Rocca* jointly, if it could be had at a reasonable rent. When the time came for my parents to return home that year, August Montalba, who knew the Cavaliere, was busy carrying on negotiations. In the end a lease was obtained for 1500 lire a year—£60— with possession the following summer.

During his stay in Venice my father had been bothered with correspondence from England about the affairs of *The Graphic*. Since his election as a director eleven years previously, he had been in the uneasy position of being the only member of the Board who was not a member of the Thomas family. On William Thomas' death his eldest son, Carmichael Thomas, had succeeded to the chairmanship. From his boyhood, when *The Graphic* had been founded, Car Thomas had grown up to look upon my father with a reverence which had never wavered. After he became chairman over a board composed of his younger brothers and my father, Car Thomas, a less strong personality than at least one of the brothers, received my father's whole-hearted support in various differences which arose, Car and my father wishing to continue the policy which William Thomas has so successfully laid down and the Thomas brothers taking the line that attempts at Art in illustrated journalism was old-fashioned and that "one must march with the times". What should have been nothing more than a business disagreement appeared to my father as a plot to oust Car Thomas from the chairmanship. Matters came to such a pass on *The Graphic* Board that it was obvious the shareholders would have to be called in to decide between the two factions, and soon after my father's return from Venice in that autumn of 1906 an Extraordinary General Meeting of the company was convened, of which, Lord Northcliffe got wind. The *Daily Mail* sailed into action, and gleefully my mother wrote to her brother, "The *Daily Mail* has taken up the matter *on our side*. I will never abuse the paper again." Midnight conferences were held at Melbury Road between my father, Car Thomas, Gordon Thomson (whom

H.M. King George V. State Portrait

1912

No. 11 Melbury Road in Luke Fildes' time: The front

The back

somehow they had co-opted on to the Board), and eminent City solicitors. By day, typists were at work copying piles of documents, and *The Graphic* affair became the absorbing interest in my father's life.

Little wonder that the shareholders appointed a committee of their number to enquire into the whole matter, and that the end of it was that all the directors were voted off the Board—all, that is, other than Car Thomas. Thus the cause into which my father had thrown his energies won the day, though he himself was a casualty. The shareholders, like his Academy colleagues on occasions, were frightened of his vehemence.

The struggle had not been without some lighter moments. Marie Corelli, by that time settled in Stratford-on-Avon, had written my father to know what it was all about. Not receiving an answer by return of post she had accused him of discourtesy, only to turn to effusiveness on the arrival of a belated letter from him.

Amidst those buffetings my father could derive some comfort from a sale at Christies. Albeit the price a work of art fetches in the sale room may bear little relation to its intrinsic merit, yet if in the lifetime of its creator a work goes substantially up or down in price from what its creator originally received for it, this is a matter which concerns him closely. When, therefore, the Lewis-Hill Collection came up at Christies in April, 1907, and my father's *Flower Girl* of 1884 had to pass the "ordeal of auction", he had the satisfaction of the picture being received with a round of applause on the start of the bidding and of its fetching twice the sum he had received for it twenty three years before.

The taking of possession of the *Casetta Rocca*, 583 San Vio, began in May. First of all, Woods moved in and was soon "breakfasting on the terrace every morning, where it is perfectly delightful". The next stage was my mother's and my sister Dorothy's arrival some months later to find there was a great deal to be done. As furnishing was one of the joys of my mother's life she was quickly on to it. The *Casetta* was to be a corner of England: Chintz curtains and loose-covers on the chairs. It had been my mother's ill-luck

G

to find her brother without a cook after weeks of fruitless searching with Clara Montalba's help. My mother found one within forty-eight hours, and the *Casetta Rocca* was ready for my father's arrival the following month.

There was an expression of my mother's that somebody was "speaking about it". Whether it was an importation from the North Country or an invention of her own, I am unable to say. To "speak about it" was to express opinions one had no intention to implement, which everybody knew you had no intention to implement; but nobody must show he had that knowledge. Here is an example. My father soon after his arrival in Venice that autumn wrote to me that the difficulties of finding suitable models was so great that it was not worth a painter's trouble coming to Venice any more. I—my mother's son—knew that he was "speaking about it", and would continue going to Venice. And yet there was something in what he was saying. Not only were there changes in the way the people lived, but in the physical look of the place. The Lido, so long a rustic retreat from Venice in the heat-waves was being spoilt by the building of big hotels. The old timber *Stabilimento di Bagni* was being replaced by something more up-to-date in concrete. Old-time residents—and my parents saw the situation from that angle—were finding Venice was "not what it had been". However, in his very next letter my father's mood had vanished. "The model difficulty will always exist but, notwithstanding, Venice with all its changes for the worst exercises a wonderful attraction. It, and the people, are so picturesque and to me artistically fascinating."

When my mother and Dorothy returned to London in the middle of December my father stayed behind to finish *La Giardiniera*. She had written me: "I have had no time for painting I am sorry to say. I have felt at times I could do wonders." Two days before Christmas she wrote to my father: "I am very sorry that you have been in such a difficulty over the picture. I feel being away from you at those times, because up to now we have always pulled a thing together, however lost it has been."

As for my mother's helping him to "pull a thing together", my father thought more of her criticism than of anybody else's, even his brother-in-law's. If she did not actually work on my father's pictures—as sometimes she did on Uncle Harry's—she might well have done so and nobody been the wiser. There was an occasion at a friend's house when a small sketch hanging on the wall caught my father's eye. Adjusting his glasses he examined it more closely.

"Charming! Charming! I remember doing that so well. I wish I could paint like that now!"

"But, Luke," said my mother quietly, "you *didn't* paint it. That is one of *mine*!"

The year 1908 was domestically much like the two previous ones except for the return of my brother Denis' ship, H.M.S. *King Alfred* from the China Station and his welcome home in March after two years away. There was a visit to the Strubens at Spitchwick in August; agitation at the *Casetta Rocca* in September to find another new cook before my parents' arrival; my parents' and Dorothy's arrival without a cook having been found; and my mother's finding one again within forty-eight hours.

One of the Venetian subjects my father had been painting was called *The Devotee*. He had arranged with the Berlin Photographic Company to publish a photogravure of it. He had now this letter from them:

14 October 1908.

Dear Sir Luke,

I hope I will not shock you by making the proposition that you should allow us to call your picture *A Lancashire Lassie*. . . . We already talked of the similarity of the custom in Venice and Manchester in wearing of shawls over the head. Our Travellers think with me that if we gave the picture an English interest . . . it might sell better. So if you have no objection to the new title I would be glad to adopt it.

My father's reply was:

Dear Mr. Levi,

Your proposition certainly does startle me. The idea, type and conduct of the head of this picture is so founded on a Venetian motive that I cannot understand where Lancashire can possibly come in. It is true factory girls in Lancashire do wear shawls over their heads but so do some Irish, Scotch and Spanish girls, as they do shoes on their feet, but the type of the head in my picture, the expression and sentiment of it is as opposed to a Lancashire Lassie as anything I could imagine.

In Venice, the pattern of the previous year was being repeated, and this time he was "speaking about it" with a vengeance. "I have extreme difficulty in finding any one to sit", he wrote me, "and I fear very much it is one that will not be got over, and it will greatly interfere, if not entirely stop me, coming to Venice any more. . . . The whole Venetian life is changed, and the artistic side of it is played out. There is little difference in the people now to those you would see in Milan, or Florence or Soho".

Nevertheless he continued going to Venice and working there.

Before going to Venice that year, he had received a commission out of the ordinary run of portrait painting. It was to paint Lloyd George for the Law Society. Lloyd George had become the first member of the Law Society to be Chancellor of the Exchequer. The commission had given an opportunity of painting a striking personality in a picturesque set of robes. On his return to London from Venice my father had to administer a reproof to the Chancellor:

> 11 Melbury Road,
> Kensington, W.
> 23 Decr. 1908.

Dear Mr. Lloyd-George,

I fear you must have overlooked your engagement with me for this morning. I ought, perhaps, to have written to remind you.

I am getting very anxious as to the fulfilment of my promise to have the picture ready by the 29th of January. . . . I hope nothing will interfere with your coming to-morrow morning as so much depends on it, and I must ask you to arrange for good solid sitting of an hour and a half at least—snatchy ones of $\frac{1}{2}$ or $\frac{3}{4}$ an hour are of no real use for serious work. . . .

I hope you will excuse my insistence, but as your holiday I understand, will last until almost the date of presentation, it practically only leaves me tomorrow for the final sitting.

Sincerely yours,
Luke Fildes.

The Chancellor was in the throes of preparing the famous "Peoples' Budget", nevertheless the portrait was sufficiently finished for a formal ceremony of presentation and its exhibition in the 1909 Academy. Half the critics thought it was all "Chancellor's Robes"; half thought it was memorable for the artist's insight into the sitter's personality. It was one of my father's best portraits, and was praised by the Prime Minister, Asquith, at the Academy Banquet.

At the beginning of that year, 1909, my father had come out as the champion of contemporary British art. For a number of years the Royal Academy had been devoting its Winter Exhibitions to showing the works of Old Masters. These were selected out of the big private collections throughout the country, and the picture-loving public had been able to see masterpieces of the Past which otherwise they would not have seen. It happened, however, that George McCulloch, an important collector of modern pictures, had recently died, and the notion had come to the Academy that instead of the usual exhibition of Old Masters, the Winter Exhibition of 1908–1909 should be the McCulloch Collection *en bloc*. Mrs. McCulloch agreed and the notion was acted upon. One of those situations now developed when the Press sometimes goes wrong. This move on the Academy's part was not well received and, encouraged by the adverse Press criticism, Sir Henry Howarth, a well known figure in political and Antiquarian circles, wrote a letter to *The Times* which appeared on the 5th of January 1909. After deploring the interruption of "the very acceptable practice of the Royal Academy to hold in the winter an exhibition of the works of deceased master of all schools", he stigmatized the McCulloch show as "a means and mode of advertisement of their own wares by the Academicians themselves which is not very seemly". He suggested—quite erroneously—that the Collection was going to be sold; "hence the exhibition is really on a par with similar exhibitions in the galleries of the great dealers, of Christies, etc."

Correspondence in *The Times* followed; a not convincing letter from Poynter, an injudicious intervention by Croal Thomson of *The Art Journal*, a weaker second effort by Howarth sticking to his point that the Academicians were advertising their own wares.

Fildes could stand it no longer. He wrote to *The Times* a letter which appeared, on the 11th of January 1909, in type—a significant detail—of a larger size than that accorded Sir Henry Howarth. Really the letter is so good that I must set it out in full:

The Editor of *The Times*.

Sir,—Sir Henry Howarth, after criticising the Royal Academy's decision to exhibit the McCulloch collection *en bloc*—a decision with which, as you have heard from the President, many members of that body did not agree —has allowed himself to be carried away into expressing views betraying such indifference to modern art that, if they came to be shared generally by the public and art patrons of the present day, the progress and continued existence of a living art in this country would be seriously menaced.

Sir Henry Howarth's observations upon the McCulloch collection inevitably lead to the conclusion that the Academy must not (except at the annual Summer Exhibition) show any collection of pictures which includes works by its members still living; for to do so is to 'advertise the members and their works'. Evidently, then, a picture by a member of the Academy is to be condemned, after its initial exhibition at Burlington House, never to appear there again during the artist's lifetime!

This view seems to me to be unjust. It is an absurd and unnecessary limitation of the rights of both artist and public. It denies to generations of people who could not, or did not, attend the Academy the year the picture was originally exhibited all participation in the pleasure it may give thereafter; and the artist and the public have to trust to the vague chance of, say, some international exhibition for the picture ever to be seen again publicly until the author has passed away!

The remarkable collection brought together at the Franco-British Exhibition was a revelation to the present generation of the high position to which modern British art attains when judged by the standard of properly selected examples.

Such an art is worth encouragement at some one's hands!

The opportunities of renewing acquaintance with the works of the Old Masters are numerous; on the other hand, in the case of works of living artists, when once they have been exhibited, these opportunities are very few; and in these days when (if Sir Henry Howarth is right) there is grave danger of the English becoming a nation of antiquaries, it behoves those who have at heart the maintenance of modern painting and sculpture from time to time to rescue representative modern works from the oblivion of private galleries and houses. What organization is better fitted to undertake this duty, with a proper degree of authority, than the Royal Academy? And what is more reasonable and necessary than that the works of living members of the Academy should be eligible for exhibition equally with the works of other men?

One other *dictum* is to be gathered from Sir Henry Howarth's letters. The Royal Academy must not exhibit any picture which may eventually come into the sale-room; for by so doing the Academy is conferring upon the picture an enhanced value that will be turned to profit by the owner. If there is anything in this contention it applies as well to 'Old Masters' as to modern works, and if acted upon it would land the Academy in the obvious dilemma of having to cease its exhibitions altogether, or of being branded as an 'appurtenance to the auction-room'! It is generally understood that some lenders of 'Old Masters' have not been above taking advantage of this prestige and enhancement of value arising from the exhibition of the Works of the Academy. Frequently the Winter Exhibition is not the 'appurtenance' alone, but the actual sale-room itself. The Academy has wished it otherwise; and nobody as yet has accused the Academy of being a party to the deal. Why, then, should the accusation be brought as soon as the Winter Exhibition happens to be of modern works and not of 'Old Masters'?

Sir Henry Howarth also finds fault with the Royal Academy for not holding its usual Winter Exhibition of Old Masters this year. I hope I do not run the risk of having improper motives imputed to me when I point out that the 'cult of the Old Masters' has been very well looked after by the Government, the Press, the picture-dealers, and the Academy itself for the last 40 years.

And now Sir Henry Howarth comes to cap us all. With the exception of the Academy, few, if any of these influences have been brought to the aid of modern art— at any rate, the modern art of this country. And yet I cannot imagine why a proper appreciation of the styles and schools of art of the past should deny its proper place to the national art of the present.

With regard to the particular charges made against the Academy in connexion with its present exhibition, I will only say that there are not any grounds for imputing to the Academy any motives beyond the legitimate desire to benefit modern British art in its catholic aspect. Is it not conceivable that the body could be actuated by other than the sordid reasons that Sir Henry Howarth so readily attributes to its members?

Personally, I think it is regrettable that Sir Henry Howarth has taken a part in the popular and easy game of baiting the Royal Academy, which hitherto has been confined to players of a less liberal order of mind.

Apologizing for the length of my letter,

I beg to remain, your obedient servant,

Luke Fildes.

11, Melbury-Road, Kensington, S.W., Jan 9.

A flood of congratulatory telegrams and letters poured in. Nothing more remained to be said; though a few more letters appeared in *The Times*. By the middle of February Howarth had got so far away from his starting point that all interest had evaporated. Woods, back in England for another turn of duty on the Council, characterized Howarth, after a visit to the Winter Exhibition as a "mischievous old scoundrel".

Fildes had five works in that year's Academy. Besides two Venetian subjects, *Lloyd George* and *Sir William Allchin*, M.D., F.R.C.P., he had a head-and-shoulders of Henry Woods which George Alexander liked so much that he commissioned his own portrait from Fildes for the Academy next year.

> 57 Pont Street,
> S.W.
> 7 June 1909.

My dear Fildes,

I am "devilishly" busy during the next few weeks. What would suit me best would be to give time to you on return from my tour in October when I hope the Pinero play will be running successfully without me. I think, and my wife thinks so too, that the Woods type of portrait is delightful in size and everything, though we should both like you to do what you would wish to do. . . .

> Yours sincerely,
> George Alexander.

My parents had not been at Holland House lately. It had been let for some time. The tenant had a prize Persian cat which she allowed to keep its claws sharpened on a Chinese needlework screen of which my mother was very fond. Whether by the cat or by other agency, a good deal of furniture got broken as well. In fact on going down for a day that summer to inspect after the tenant's departure my parents were so appalled that the only thing to do, so my father said, would be to sell the place lock, stock and barrel. Woods, unversed in "speaking-about-it", but with happy recollections of stays at Holland House, was much upset at that prospect. However, a month later the house was reprieved, and my mother was installed there with Dorothy and Denis, the latter on leave, tidying up the mess.

At the beginning of September, my father was sent off for another cure to Kissingen. It was on that stay at Kissingen that he and Philip de Laszlò first met. I doubt if they knew much about each other up to that time, my father not having cultivated a reputation abroad and Laszlò, though one of the leading portrait painters on the Continent, being not yet known in England. They immediately struck up a friendship which was to have some interesting moments as time went on. From Kissingen they went to Munich so that Laszlò might show my father the works of the German portrait-painter Lenbach, with which my father was not familiar. From there my father joined my mother, my sister Dorothy, and my uncle at Cortina in the Dolomites whence they soon moved on to Venice.

Whilst at Kissingen my father had been doing a little sketching to keep Laszlò company, and he had done a little at Cortina. It may be that two very "impressionist" sketches I have of his, done on the Lido also date from that same holiday. Otherwise, he was not working in Venice that year. He wrote to Laszlò telling him about the usual autumn exhibition there, in which was some of Laszlò's work, Laszlò replied:

3 Palace Gate, W.
28 Oct. 09.

Dear Sir Luke Fildes,
I was very pleased to receive your kind letter. . . . It is very interesting to read your account of the exhibition. It seems that it grows more extensive every year. A 'one man' show of Zorn would be good to see; just now in Budapest I saw a fine collection of his etchings. I look forward to hear more from you personally about the exhibition. I am glad you like my pictures. After a day or so more at Munich after you left us, we went to Vienna for two days and then to Budapest.

My dear mother returned with us here to London, where we found our family all well. . . . My wife, who begs to be remembered to you, and I have both the pleasantest souvenir of Kissingen and our agreeable walks and talks together with you. . . . With our best greetings, believe me,

Your truly,

P. A. Laszlò.

My parents were home again by early November. My father had not, himself, been satisfied with the *Lloyd George* and he had been promised a sitting or two on his return to London. But this sort of thing happened:

Whitehall,
O.H.M.S.
11.42 a.m.

Regret detained will try and be with you by twelve o'clock.

Lloyd George.

Even George Alexander was trying to one's patience:

57 Pont Street,
S.W.
29 Dec. 09.

Jerome K. Jerome comes to read his play tomorrow, so I shall not be with you until Friday at 11.

G.A.

❧ XVII ❧

DIVERSIONS AND DISTRACTIONS

1910-1914

Before the Academy Council began its work of "selecting" for the Summer Exhibition of 1910 my father wrote them with some proposals for improving the procedure. The procedure had been that after selecting a few obviously excellent works and rejecting a number of obviously bad ones, the Council had marked the rest as "doubtful", and left the members of the Hanging Committee to do their best with them. The "doubtfuls" were far more numerous than there was room for on the walls; thus the "hangers" had far more to do than they could cope with and aspiring exhibitors were often not having their works properly judged.

Fildes' remedy had the great merit of simplicity. It was merely that the full Council should continue the winnowing of the "doubtfuls" until these were reduced to approximately the number there was space for. Woods, who was on the Council that year but had not seen the letter which Fildes had written, immediately after the Council meeting at which the latter was considered, went round to the Arts Club and wrote:

My dear Luke,
    Your letter made a great impression on the Council. Eaton read it well, and every member at the finish expressed his approval, beginning with Clausen. There

was a general feeling that you had put the case well, and
a wish to carry out your plan.

Yours,

Harry.

George Clausen was one of the younger Academicians
and he was held in some suspicion by my father as a near-
anarchist. The following morning he wrote to my father
enthusiastically, as might one revolutionary to another, and
when the work of selection began Uncle Harry entered in his
diary, "Luke's proposals were acted upon and we made a
large number of accepts".

My father had a full complement in the Academy of 1910,
five portraits and a Venetian subject. Royal Day was on the
28th of April, and the King was received by the Council.
"He shook hands cordially with us as we were introduced",
my uncle recorded, and exactly one week later—"Rumours
today that the King is ill. There is a Bulletin saying that
symptoms give cause for anxiety. This is taken as very
serious."

That was a Thursday. On Friday evening Woods,
returning to town after dining at Melbury Road, was told
by the bus conductor that the "Flag was still up all right"
on Buckingham Palace. He called at the Arts Club, and
when he left to go to his rooms in Bury Street, "the streets
were ringing with boys shouting 'Death of the King'. It is
all very sudden", he put in his diary that night, "and one
shudders at the consequences".

Two days afterwards *The Graphic* was given permission
to publish a drawing of King Edward on his death bed. It
was a condition that the drawing would be done by my
father. He had not done any black-and-white work for many
years and was very uncertain of himself. However the
condition was almost a command.

He spent the morning of Sunday at Buckingham Palace,
and was received by Queen Alexandra and the new King
and Queen. Things were made as easy as possible. At the
head of the bedstead on which the dead King lay was a
festoon of Keepsakes, each one—my father supposed—
being a memento of some occasion of congenial entertain-

ment, and put there by the King himself. As my father was at work there was a tap on the door and Princess Victoria came in. She watched my father at work and noticing he kept glancing at the head of the bedstead, she suddenly said, "I see you keep looking at those mascots of his. The Old Dear used to think they brought him luck."

The drawing was returned from the Palace next day with a note from Lord Knollys telling how much the Royal Family liked it. My father however never cared for it, and he had been disconcerted at finding how difficult black-and-white had become for him.

He now was taken ill himself. Pains in the back, of which he had complained for some time, were diagnosed as appendicitis, and he went into a nursing home and was operated on. My father made a good recovery, and by August he and my mother were staying with the Strubens at Spitchwick. Later they were in Switzerland at St Beatenberg with Dorothy, Geoffrey and Gordon Thomson. There was no Venice that year.

My father was in a prodding mood again at the Academy towards the end of the year. Against the wishes of the officers he persuaded a General Assembly to decide on having professional auditors for the accounts. "Eaton vexed with Luke after the meeting", was Woods' note of it.

The Graphic intruded once again. A letter came from Car Thomas. A new director had to be appointed. Although one or two members of the new Board had been consulting my father surreptitiously from time to time about artistic standards, there was no question of the Board as a whole wishing him to fill the vacancy, nor would he have wanted it himself. But what did my father think Car Thomas asked, of Harold Cox? To which my father replied:

Dear Car,
My knowledge of Mr. Cox does not go beyond the information that he is a political journalist of Radical views . . . and an exceedingly clever man. . . . At all events Mr. Cox has brains, which may be useful.

In the middle of March, 1911, my father wrote my uncle: "Rather to my surprise, for I had given up the idea that I

should be asked—in fact I had secretly hoped would not be—
I today have been commanded to paint the State Portrait of
The King. Sir Douglas Dawson this morning told me of the
King's wishes, and said the King hoped I would undertake
it. . . . The King said 'I liked very much what Sir Luke did
of my father, and I have known him a long time and I like
Sir Luke personally, and we get on very well together, and
I would like him to do it if he will'."

On the 4th of April the King received my father and spent
an hour and a half showing him over the private part of
Buckingham Palace. "The King's own room was hung
almost entirely with Luke's portraits" (according to my
uncle's diary). "Amongst them was the one of Queen
Alexandra as Princess of Wales with Facey". The King told
my father that another painter was to do the State Portrait
of Queen Mary so that both State Portraits should be
exhibited in the same Academy. This piece of information
lifted a weight off my father's mind. He had been feeling
unequal to repeating the experience of two State Portraits.

The choice of the artist for the Queen's portrait was
William Llewellyn, an unexpected choice, for he was
comparatively little known at that time, but a success. In a
sense my father and Llewellyn had to be collaborators. The
two portraits had to be a pair. It would not have done if the
measurement of tops of heads and bottoms of feet from the
edges of the canvases had been dissimilar. The two painters
got on very well together.

That year my father had a big success in the Academy—
a full-length group of "the two little Scotch girls", as Uncle
Harry called them, *Ailsa and Dorothy, daughters of P. M.
Inglis, Esq.*—as good a portrait group as my father ever did.
The picture was given the place of honour in the centre of
the west wall in the Big Room.

With the opening of the Academy my father would have
liked to begin the King's portrait. The official intention was
that the two portraits would be in next year's Academy.
Whatever experience Llewellyn was having with the Queen,
my father's with the King was entirely frustrating. It was a
time of great political stress and the King was not able to
give any sittings. Moreover, unlike the case with Edward

VII, a uniform and medals were not forthcoming, and to make matters worse, His Majesty was due to leave for India in the autumn and be away for several months. My father had other work he must get on with, and he put aside the State Portrait for the time being.

In October he and my mother were on holiday at the Villa d'Este near Como, and from there they went on to the *Casetta Rocca.* They had been in Venice a bare week when a telegram came from the Lord Chamberlain informing my father that the King would give him a sitting before sailing for India.

My parents returned to London, post-haste, and my father had a successful sitting from the King in the first week of November. He could now get started on the big canvas. Relying on an uninterrupted run of time up to 'Sending-in' day, my father was hoping to finish the State Portrait from the King himself after His Majesty's return from India. But, unexpectedly, Marcus Stone, because of increasing deafness, thought it better not to take his turn on the Academy Council of 1912, and this brought in my father. His painting time would thus be shortened, and yet he did not wish to miss his turn on the Council.

On the King's return from India, Sir Douglas Dawson, began enquiring how the portrait was getting on. "Perhaps you will let me know at once".

My father replied that he was sorry to say it was not getting on at all. He had not been able to have any of the "robes and paraphernalia". This drew from Sir Douglas Dawson a private hint that it would be advisable for my father to "try for a sitting of the King in the near future". My father wrote back that "now the light has come after the dark and gloomy winter we have had, and also I have the material waited for so long, I am at work. I will go on from day to day . . . to the finish, but I cannot do it in time for the R.A."

All that he had hoped for came about. Within a fortnight it was settled that the portrait of the King should be sent to the Academy a month late, and that during that month the King would give my father more sittings, and this time at Melbury Road instead of at Buckingham Palace.

My father remained in London, working, over Easter,

The Staircase

The Drawing Room

No. 11 Melbury Road

The Studio, dubbed by
King Edward VII 'one of
the finest rooms in London'

Luke Fildes standing at the
French windows of his studio

whilst the family were at Kingsgate. A week at Easter was about all the use we still made of Holland House. The place was usually let for the summer, my parents preferred Venice in the autumn and nobody wanted to be away from Melbury Road at Christmas time.

On the opening of the Academy my father had another success with a full-length portrait of a child—*Herman, the son of Lord Michelham*—another exercise in his Thomas Lawrence manner. It was one of his few pictures he ever thought not well treated by the "hangers", and he wrote complaining to the President. Poynter replied that when the "King" was placed my father would have two works already in the Big Room, and a third would be unfair on other members. "I am sure that your portrait will be a success." And so it proved, for on the Members' Varnishing Day the general opinion, as noted by my uncle, was that "Luke's portrait of the boy in black looked very fine indeed".

The King now gave my father his promised sittings. Like King Edward VII, King George V had the morning papers read to him whilst he sat for his portrait. The Home Rule Bill was being debated in the Commons, and public life was greatly embittered. The King had no hesitation in expressing in front of my father exactly what he thought of the crisis. He was not complimentary to any political party.

"Spoke very straight as usual about persons and matters generally", was what my uncle gathered from my father's account—"a real common-sense Monarch".

The Pepysian touch came out again. "I was very gratified to hear (the King) asked about me. 'Ah!, that is by Mr. Woods isn't it? He is your brother-in-law isn't he? I have two pictures of his.'"

King George V always treated my father very easily. On one occasion he told him this story about an Eastern potentate who had been staying at Buckingham Palace, and whom the King had been showing round. Noticing some of Nash's marble-ized pilasters the visitor had gone up to one of them and given it a rap with his knuckles, whereupon a hollow sound had rung out.

"Aha!" the potentate had exclaimed, "*Cela, c'est bois?*"

"I don't know," the King said to my father, "what *you'd*

call it, but I call it damned cheek. Fancy having that said to you in your own house."

After his last sitting at Melbury Road the King brought the Queen to see the portrait. It was a Sunday, the 2nd of June. "They expressed themselves very pleased with the picture", my uncle's diary records, "and spent some time looking about the Drawing Room and Dining Room, frequently expressing their pleasure in everything, particularly the well-polished furniture."

The picture was in its place in the Academy by 9.30 the following morning, the King's Birthday. It was well received by the Press and attendance at the exhibition went up.

But Fildes felt he still had things to do to it:

> Buckingham Palace,
> 11th June 1912.
>
> Dear Sir Luke,
>
> The King has read your letter to me of the 7th June.
>
> Certainly your Picture of His Majesty shall be returned to you at the end of the Royal Academy Exhibition.
>
> The King and Queen are delighted with it.
>
> If I may say so it is excellent and this seems to be also the general opinion.
>
> Yours very truly,
> Stamfordham.

My mother now went for a cure to Harrogate. Where upon "Letter from Luke", my uncle put in his diary on the 22nd of August, "who is alone in London, and has got moping and soliloquizing, instead of taking half a day off and thinking matters over at Hampton Court, Zoological Gardens, etc. But he will not go anywhere alone. I am glad to hear that he will be here [Venice] in October".

In September my parents went to Salsomaggiore and thence to Venice. My brother Geoffrey and Philip Webb, Sir Aston Webb's son, both of them young architects in Sir Aston Webb's office were also there, and for a time there was a full house at the *Casetta Rocca*.

It was only a few days after the party dispersed that the Venetian Scene was greatly changed. Lady Layard died. The City Authorities gave her a Public Funeral. "The break-

up of the *Ca Capello*" was all that my uncle could bring
himself to say.

On and off for the last two years my father had been
painting a posthumous portrait of the late King Edward. It
had been commissioned privately by Queen Alexandra and
it was to be like the State Portrait in size but more intimate
in character. Having the studies he had made from life for
the State Portrait, my father had not felt the inhibitions he
usually did with posthumous portraits. The portrait was now
ready, and one day in November, Queen Alexandra, Queen
Maud of Norway and Princess Victoria came to see it at
Melbury Road. They greatly liked it. It was then sent to
Marlborough House. The Queen's intention had been that
the portrait should not be exhibited, but later she changed
her mind and arrangements were made for it to be shown
at next year's Academy, but not as part of the summer
exhibition; it was to be separately shown in the vestibule.

The new year opened in discord on the Academy Council:

> 11 Melbury Road,
> 13 Jany. 1913.

My dear Harry,

... There was quite a tiff on the Council between me
and the Sec. and President. *The Graphic* wished to bring
out a special supplement on the opening of the Tadema
Exn. and wanted the R.A. to let them have a list of the
works intended for exn. so that *The Graphic* would put
in hand only those that would be shown. Eaton inter-
fered, with the upshot that the R.A. declined to give the
information. Car wrote a few straightforward truths in
reply. Poynter and Eaton said Car's letters were grossly
improper and insolent. I said I thought they were fully
justified; that Thomas only said very mildly what everyone out, and most in, the R.A. said strongly that the
Institution was run in a stupid manner".

My uncle replied: "You were right to justify what Car
said. Although your qualification of the conduct of business
at the R.A. was strong for the Council table, there is no
question but that you were quite right."

In the middle of February it was my mother's turn to be operated on for appendicitis. She made a perfect recovery, and a use was found for Holland House as a place in which to convalesce.

At the end of March, Woods arrived in London on his customary spring-time visit, and within a few hours he was at Melbury Road. "Luke has two fine ladies' portraits. One a full-length, very beautiful." Those jottings in my uncle's diary of the effect my father's work made on him each year, coming straight to it with a fresh eye, fill a number of gaps in my own recollections. I have no recollection at all of the "full lengths" but it would seem to have been an outstanding success, as I mention in a moment.

In April he began helping with the selection for that year's exhibition. He caught cold in the galleries and had to stay in bed a few days. Feeling better on the fourth day he got up and went to the Academy in the afternoon. The cold came back, and he was in bed again. Two more days, and pneumonia had set in. That was the first of the Varnishing Days. My uncle had been at the Academy all day and in the evening he came down to Melbury Road to tell my father that the "full-length" was in the centre of the south wall of the Big Room and was generally thought by the members to be almost the most beautiful thing he had done. He was worrying about the varnishing of his two pictures, and to calm him my uncle told him he would carry out his instructions.

A period of great trial now began when the doctors were unable to say whether he would live through it. He had to undergo two operations to relieve abscesses on the lung. All this was happening at Melbury Road, for it had not been possible to move him into a nursing home.

Early in June my uncle was able to write in his diary: "I went to Melbury Road where I found Luke seated in a chair by the window. . . . I stayed on. Gordon Thomson came. Prof. Bulloch stayed to dinner."

The former nursery, with its large bay-window looking on to the lawn had been turned into a bedroom where a few friends began calling to see him—from the Academy there were Poynter, Marcus Stone, David Murray and Dicksee.

My parents' old friend, the Bishop of Peterborough, brought bad news one day which distressed them both: Eaton was very ill, and could not recover.

By the beginning of July my father was well enough to go to Worthing where my mother had taken rooms. They stayed there for two months, and my father grew very bored. The family grew very bored. The family took it in turns to go down from London to infuse some variety into events. By the end of September he was able to travel abroad. The wound from the last operation was still open, but my practical-minded mother saw no reason why they should take a nurse with them and she made the nurse show her how to do the dressing. "I might have done it this last month", she wrote home, "Bulloch suggested a sleeping draught for Day; the result was that he slept all night and was really none the worse for the journey".

They had gone to Lenno on the Lake of Como, a place to which they would become very attached. "We are more and more in love with Lenno", my mother wrote, "Day has had an hour's rowing on the Lake the last two days, and it has not done him the least harm, in fact it seems to have done him good". And that was a man in his seventieth year who a few months previously had been at death's door.

After three weeks at Lenno they moved on to Venice, but in a fortnight were home again at Melbury Road. My father had lost two-thirds of the year and was chafing to get at work again.

There is an entry in my uncle's diary towards the end of the year 1913: "A letter from Lockett Agnew. He says that he had just had a long chat with Luke and does not like his account of Fanny: 'She doesn't get back her old spirits'". Was it to be wondered after all she had been through that year? As for my father, he had been proved to have a constitution of iron but he had been left with a badly impaired lung which would need more care as every winter came along.

That winter of 1913, after twenty years of ownership, my parents sold Holland House, Kingsgate. The puchaser was Charles Lawrence. Afterwards when he was raised to the Peerage, we were not certain whether we were sorry or glad that he took for his title the appellation of Lord Lawrence of Kingsgate.

Understandably my father had little work for the 1914 Academy—a woman's portrait, and two "heads" of doctors who had looked after him in his illness, E. A. Barton and William Bulloch.

My parents decided to spend Easter at Lenno, their previous autumn's discovery, and they asked me to go with them. It happened, and it was the merest chance, that an Academy colleague of my father's, the sculptor, Goscombe John, R.A., and his wife and daughter were to be in the same hotel. Muriel Goscombe John and I thus met. Eighteen months afterwards we were married, but that is another story all of its own.

That summer my father made a pact with Laszlò. They were to paint each other's portraits, and Laszlò said he would start straightaway. Laszlò's studio was on Campden Hill, in G. H. Boughton's former house, and my father walked round there on Sunday mornings to sit. I think two sittings were all Laszlò needed. On the first one I walked round with my father, and Laszlò asked me if I would like to stay and watch. He sat me in an armchair behind him, and began. Sometimes I had seen my father begin a portrait, and I was interested to see how Laszlò set about a clean canvas. He attacked with even greater assurance than my father, in the sense that he seemed to get his effect at the first attempt— *alla prima*—or, putting it the other way round, the effect he got at the first attempt seemed to be what he wanted. He made an admirable likeness of my father, if one concedes a bit more twist to the moustache and a bit more sparkle in the eye than were true to life.

My father's half of the pact was never performed. It was to have been after the summer holidays, but the outbreak of War stopped it, and by the time the First World War was over I knew not what impediment stood in the way.

On that baking-hot afternoon of August Bank Holiday, 1914, my father and I stood in the crowd that filled Parliament Square. Every few minutes newsboys came running along with new editions of the evening papers, and we could read in the stop press what Sir Edward Grey was saying inside the House of Commons. When the speech came to the ultimatum the Cabinet had sent to Germany, to withdraw from Belgium, everybody knew it was war. I do not pretend to recall our conversation as my father and I walked away from Parliament Square. I am certain, however, that neither he nor I had the slightest inkling of the demands of modern war. As the months went by my father would find, at first with great reluctance because of the inter- ference with our professions, that having begun the war with one son in uniform he was to have four, He, and they, were fortunate in that all came through.

The day following that August Bank Holiday my parents and Gording went down to Devonshire on a visit which had already been arranged. "We are very anxious about Denis", my mother wrote me. "I am trying hard to look on the bright side of things but it is difficult. Of course I know it is a splendid thing to 'go' for Germany". And a few days later: "Just a line to say that we are returning on Tuesday. The fact that we only get news once a day is a great strain to us both and we prefer to be in London."

The other chief anxiety my parents had during those first weeks was to know what might be happening to my uncle in Venice. Italy was the third partner in the Triple Alliance. However, it soon became apparent that Italy was not coming into the war on the side of Germany and Austria. Much- delayed letters from him told of difficulties in getting cheques cashed. The situation was put right, but not before my uncle's available resources were reduced to thirty francs.

In the middle of October my father heard from my uncle that their old friend Van Haanen had died three weeks before in Vienna. None of Van Haanen's relatives in Vienna had thought of informing my uncle, and it was only a chance remark by a waiter in a restaurant which had caused him to make enquiries.

At the end of November another one of their old set died—Laura Stone, Marcus' wife. She had been very ill and unhappy since the summer. Two such mercurial husbands as theirs had at times been an obstacle to my mother and Laura Stone seeing as much of each other as once upon a time. As the years went on, the neighbour from No. 8 across the road had become a less frequent visitor at No. 11. Latterly they had come together again, and my mother had been able to be attentive to her in her last illness. My father's and my uncle's thought now was what would happen to Marcus.

❧ XVIII ❧

WARTIME
1915-1918

The war had little bearing on my father's artistic life. He had as much work to do as he could manage, and although it was not ambitious, being mostly "heads and shoulders", its quality was equal to anything he had ever done. His health remained good and he never had fewer than five exhibits in any war-time Academy. The war made a greater artistic impact upon my mother; it decided her to try to become an Academy exhibitor again after an interval of thirty years. She had three still-life works accepted and she sold them for the benefit of the Red Cross.

There was plenty in Academy politics to engage my father's interest. An early problem was that of male students joining the Forces. He wrote to the Council suggesting that for the period of their absence awards of all sizes in the Schools should be suspended. "The girls may feel they have a grievance, but it would be a slight one. They could not feel much satisfaction in winning prizes in such circumstances."

Then there was the decision, of which my father strongly disapproved, that for the period of the war no work should be exhibited in the Academy which had been done by a native of an enemy country, whether a naturalized British subject or not. To treat naturalized British subjects no better than alien enemies was to run counter, he maintained, to the terms of Letters of Naturalization; but what had troubled him most was that his friend Laszlò, Hungarian born and

British by adoption, came under the ban. He disavowed the Academy's action in a letter to Laszlò, and heard in reply that he was the only British artist who had written to him.

He could not help however worrying about things in general. The war was yet young when my uncle remarked in his diary: "Letter from Fanny, I very much regret to hear Luke is very down in the mouth. . . . He will make himself ill I am afraid. Of course the anxieties are terrible, but they are not for him alone."

The relaxation of holidays abroad was missing, though when I come to my uncle's war-time journeys it will be seen that travelling between England and Italy was always possible. But the journey was likely to be long and tiring and my parents did not feel up to it. Instead there were annual "cures" at Harrogate and stays with the Strubens at Spitchwick.

But there was one respect in which the war did strongly influence my father. His letters to us on active service took on a new warmth, for us in the front line the best of all perhaps would be such news from my mother as that Struben had caught a ten-pound salmon in the Dart and that one's father was going to try for his first salmon next day. From my mother I heard that Cook was going to send me another juicy cake; that Uncle Harry had only got his pictures into the Academy in the nick of time by taking them himself in a taxi; that Day had been so busy with his pictures up to the very last second that he could attend to nothing else. "Oh, these artists!!!! The battles of Verdun are nothing to what they think they go through!!" And then again, "Day and Mr. Struben are talk, talk, talk and settling all matters".

Zeppelins had been over the British Isles quite early in the war. The first to reach London was in the summer of 1915. I remember being somewhat flabbergasted when on one of my leaves my father blandly remarked that he supposed we had nothing in Flanders to come up to what London had been experiencing.

The first time my father felt the war really close to him had been on the last day of the year 1915. A telegram came from Denis: "Safe and well." My father took it as a thought-

ful seasonable greeting. My mother sensed there was more
in it. She was right. H.M.S. *Natal* had blown up in harbour
with the loss of the greater part of the ship's company. My
brother owed his life to the fact that as officer of the watch
he was on the bridge at the time; all other officers on board
were below and were killed. The cause was never discovered.
Apart from the formal enquiry which was held, various
senior officers wished to have my brother's account of it,
and one of his letters was seen by the King, who sent
congratulations to my father on my brother's escape.

Some months afterwards came the Battle of Jutland. In a
letter to my mother at that time Lady Jellicoe mentioned
that she saw the wreck of *Natal* every day and it always made
her sad. She hoped that Denis' luck would hold good. It is
a matter of history that the first news of Jutland gave the
public the impression that the Grand Fleet had been defeated
and Britannia no longer ruled the waves. The beginning of
Lady Jellicoe's letter therefore is interesting: "Ever so many
thanks for your most kind congrats: I feel when you read his
despatch you will think they are well earned. The despatch
went a fortnight ago to the Admiralty, so it rests with them
when it is published. . . . My husband is as fit as can be after
the fight."

An incident of that year 1916, though unimportant in
itself, throws light upon a side of my father's nature. He
gave up the chairmanship of the Arts Club. Nobody was
more esteemed and admired than he in his professional life,
but in his private life he never achieved popularity in the
sense that Millais, for example, or my god-father Val
Prinsep achieved it. He was too self-centred ever to think of
popularity. His resignation of the post of chairman of the
Arts Club after filling it to everybody's satisfaction for
twelve years, was almost a gesture of indifference. Virtually
it meant his giving up the Club altogether after being a
member of it for more than half his life. But old acquaintance
was not enough to hold him. The Athenaeum could give
him all he needed.

In one of his relaxed moods he sent me this piece of
war-time news: "We, Mama, Dorothy and I are going for a
week to Goring-on-Thames. . . . I am very well indeed, and

greatly enjoying the annual miracle of Spring in London. Though I have seen many, each recurring one astonishes me with its beauty—the magical change in a few days from grim sordid ugliness to everything that is exquisite and hopeful."

My mother, with Dorothy, had gone ahead the week before, and indulging her memories of old times had written him: "We had such a lovely walk this morning to South Stoke; it is very little changed. . . . I found my little cottage I painted and several of Harry's pictures. It was perfectly lovely walking back over the Downs. The "Leather Bottle" is nearly the same . . . we went in the sitting room that we used to have and also down at the front where the ferry was. . . . Be sure you arrange to come here next Monday."

The first time my uncle had made a war-time journey between Venice and London had been in March of 1915 for his customary spring-time visit. The journey had taken no longer than the usual two days of peace-time. Uncertainty as to Italy's political intentions had kept him in London until September. News had come from him after his return of how Venice had changed. A strict blackout, with the Austrian frontier so near, had turned a city of canals into a most hazardous area, and he had ventured out after dark only twice in two months. Therefore it was with a feeling of relief that at 4 o'clock one April morning of 1916 he found himself back at Victoria Station after a journey on this occasion, of eight days.

The problem of my uncle's residence in Venice became an increasingly difficult one as the war continued. My parents would have like him to stay in England, but he had a living to earn, and try as he would the inspiration for subject he could find over here did not extend beyond the gardens of Hampton Court, the Serpentine in Hyde Park, the Green Park and the Welsh Harp at Hendon. At all four of which he would spend much time, but with small result. Seeing that from time to time he brought over quantities of old sketches and studies he had accumulated in Venice, and out of them was able to produce as many pictures for war-time Academy Exhibitions as his output in time of peace, he could very well have remained in London. But the trouble really lay in the fact that he was sick of Club life and was always hankering after his own house and books.

Thus, by October of 1916 Woods was again in Venice, blackouts and fuel shortage notwithstanding. He had not been two months there when he decided to give up the *Casetta Rocca*. The Commendatore was "an unprincipled landlord" who would not carry out repairs and proposed to put up the rent for a renewal of the lease. Before his next visit to London in early 1917—a journey which this time took nine days—my uncle had arranged for everything being removed and stored in the Studio during his absence. "I doubt", my father wrote to me at the Front, "if your uncle would ever screw up his energy to look for and arrange another abode." My father's doubts were to be justified.

My father was on the Academy Council again in 1917 and was soon immersed in two matters which attracted some public interest. One was the long-standing dispute over the Chantrey Bequest. Under the will of the eminent sculptor, Sir Francis Chantrey, R.A., the Academy held a considerable fund upon trust to use the income for buying works of painting and sculpture so as to form a national collection of British Art, an anticipation, as it might be, of the Tate Collection. During the course of years the Academy had come in for some criticism of the way it had administered the trust, the chief complaint being that too many works had been bought out of the Academy's own Summer Exhibitions. Whilst accepting that the complaint might have some substance, Fildes was strongly opposed to all suggestions that the administration of the Fund should be taken out of the hands of the Academy in flat violation of the testator's declared intentions, and now, when the dispute was still unsettled after many years of wrangling, he was putting some stiffening into Poynter whom he regarded as showing too much appeasement, as President, toward the Academy's critics.

The other matter was the affair of his friend Laszlò, who had been imprisoned for communicating with the enemy. Laszlò was devoted to his old mother, who lived in a country with which England was at war. He used the diplomatic bag of a Neutral State to get in touch with her, was discovered, was arrested and was lodged in gaol. Whereupon my father wrote to Mrs Laszlò:

> I am very deeply grieved to read last night of the arrest of your husband, and I send you my sincere sympathy, as I do to Laszlò. I trust this is but a temporary embarrassment to you both, arising from extreme precautions in these times and that all will come right again soon.
> My wife joins me in all good wishes for your husband's speedy return to you and the boys.

But it was not so simple as that. Public opinion was far more disturbable in the First War than in the Second. Forgiveable as his motives might be, Laszlò had committed a flagrant breach of the law, and on the grounds of policy his case could not be treated lightly by the Government. Therefore when a group of Laszlò's influential friends approached my father with the idea that the Artist Community might be organized to join in a petition for the Royal Clemency, my father felt obliged to point out that any such move would be very ill-advised and might do Laszlò's cause more harm than good. This advice was not palatable, and my father found himself in the position of having to defend the Artist Community against a suggestion of professional jealousy.

But Laszlò saw the point, and when finally all the trouble was over he wrote to my father:

> My dear Fildes,
> Let me thank you most heartily for your warm-felt sympathy in the happy termination of my unfortunate affair. . . .
> I feel greatly blessed to have such friends who stand by me.
> With kindest regards from us both to you and Lady Fildes.
>
> Cordially yours,
P. A. de Laszlò.

A letter from my father to me in June of 1917 was one of the most relaxed I had from him.

I suppose you followed the Romney Case as well as you could. It was very interesting. I have no doubt it was a fraud or as near as could be got, and very successful as far as it went. The picture's authenticity was vouched for by a cloud of art experts, but I do not think the Judge (Darling) would have given his verdict for it (he said he would not have done) even if the Ozias Humphrey sketch had not been so dramatically discovered. So the Art Experts got it in the neck very badly—only as most of them are connected with the Press, the Press has carefully closed the matter up and burked all comment. It was a vile case, and it seemed to me very thoroughly engineered. However, it failed.

This needs some clarification. It was a strong belief my father held that the opinion of a practising artist as to a picture's authenticity was worth quite as much as one based on theoretical *expertise*. Lockett Agnew held the same opinion and he often asked my father for his advice in such matters. A case now came into court in which the authenticity of a supposed Romney was in issue. Against the weight of "expert" witnesses on the other side, my father gave evidence against the portrait being a Romney. When pressed in cross-examination, he had gone to the length of comparing the portrait with the work of Ozias Humphrey who was painting about Romney's time but was not Romney's equal. Between the rising of the court that afternoon and its sitting again next morning, someone had the idea of going to the Library at the Royal Academy and asking if they had any sketchbooks of Ozias Humphrey's. Some were produced and in one of them was found a sketch which obviously was for the picture in dispute. That had ended the matter.

Lockett Agnew had been trying to persuade my father to paint another Venetian "subject picture". Quite how, with travelling as it was, I do not know. My father must have turned down the idea rather peremptorily for there is this letter (undated) from Lockett:

My dear old Boy,

Right oh! and I am glad to get your letter. I thought you were cross and I could not get at the reason. But why chuck a commission. . . . You remember my letter recommending a scene from Venice (Alas, poor Venice), and supposing Crosfields agree would you still say no? As for "Aloes, Myrrh and Cassia" Oh Lor: not much in your line nor mine.

Always yours

Lockett A.

At the foot of the letter is this note in my father's hand-writing: "Lockett's last letter to me. L.F. Novr. 1917."

I do not know when it was in those disrupted times that I heard of Lockett Agnew's death, but I do remember how surprised and touched and grateful my mother was at learning that Lockett had made her one of the beneficiaries under his will. There was a group of friends who were to receive considerable legacies after Mrs. Lockett's death, and he left a letter for my mother—a very typical touch of his—that as she had more children than the others he had given her the biggest share.

As the war went on, Woods' stays in London meant that my father and he were seeing more of each other than they had done for years. Waves of nostalgia broke over them. As two young artists on the staff of *The Graphic* during the Franco-Prussian War, they had worked up into finished drawings the sketches which "special artists" sent home from the Front. Now, in 1917, *The Graphic* was not to their minds as good as when Prussia last invaded France. This trend of thought started other memories and they began dining together and spending evenings at the theatre. Generally Uncle Harry's comments in his diary were caustic, out of which he got fun, but on seeing Martin Harvey as Hamlet, "I was agreeably surprised to find him very good . . . more intelligible than Irving, and very much better than Tree. Occasionally I thought him fine." My father wrote Martin Harvey and received this reply.

30 Avenue Road
Regent's Park, N.W,
June 20th, 1916.

Dear Sir Luke Fildes,

Your kind and generous words have given me the utmost pleasure and pride, coming from so distinguished an artist as yourself.

You could not give me greater praise than to say I had made Hamlet 'sane and natural'.

I thank you with all my heart.

I am, dear Sir Luke Fildes,

Sincerely yours,
J. Martin Harvey.

But nothing could compensate Woods for his dislike of air-raids and the separation from his belongings in Venice. Air-raids, though far fewer and incomparably less intense than those of the Second War, were enough to send people down into the Tube stations. My Uncle used the one in Dover Street—no longer in use—which was handy from either the Arts Club or his rooms in Bury Street. If a raid was on when he was dining at Melbury Road, he stayed there for the night.

In April 1918 Fildes was asked to take part in making the national film for demonstrating the country's war aims, an enterprise which the Government thought "very important at the present great and perilous moment". The Germans had broken through the Western Front a month before, and Haig was telling the British Army that they had "their backs to the wall". The scenario had been written by Hall Caine; Herbert Brenan, one of the leading "cinema producers"—to use the expression of the time—was on his way over from the United States to direct the production. Fildes was to design a cottage interior, on the lines presumably of *The Widower* and *The Doctor*, which, as Hall Caine put it would be "full of atmosphere and carry conviction to the audiences". The set would be constructed by a scenic artist from my father's design—Joseph Harker, one of the best of them, was suggested for this work.

H

In less than three weeks Herbert Brenan wrote my father from the Ministry of Information:

30th April 1918.

My dear Sir Luke,
    I must sincerely thank you for your wonderful kindness which I assure you through all my life shall be an inspiration . . .
    We in the art of the Motion Picture have not yet come into our own. I doubt if we will in my lifetime, although I have seen many absurd prejudices overcome.
    I have learned much from the painter, and I shall continue to study your art at every opportunity I have. It is impossible for me to express properly my gratitude for the picture, which is already hanging in my studio.
    I am not going to bother you to come and see us at work until I am doing an interesting scene, which may be about a fortnight from now, and then I shall send a car for you in the hope that you may spend an hour or two with us.

Very gratefully yours,
Herbert Brenan

Towards the end of May my parents were bidden to dine at Buckingham Palace. After dinner, Queen Mary patted a cushion on the sofa beside her and said:
    "Come along and sit by me, Lady Fildes. Now tell me. You have sons. What are they doing?"
    And when my mother had told her, the Queen resumed: "That is very interesting. *My* sons are serving too!"
    As if there could be anybody who did not know that! thereupon Queen Mary and my mother fell a-talking together as any two mothers might.
    A few days later the Birthday Honours were published, and my father was in the list as a K.C.V.O. He had business to do at the Academy that morning and he called in there. Finding the President, who had appeared in the same Honours List as a G.C.V.O., my father offered him his good wishes. Poynter suggested they should walk down to the Athenaeum and lunch together. On the way they were

stopped several time by acquaintances who after congratulating the President turned to my father and congratulated him. After the third or fourth occasion Poynter, who generally had his head in the clouds and could not have read the morning's papers, asked my father with a puzzled look: "What do they keep congratulating *you* for, Fildes?"

Poynter by that time was eighty years old and had been President for more than twenty. The conviction had been growing throughout the Academy, even amongst members such as my father who were close personal friends of his, that the time was due for a change. But Poynter gave no sign of wishing to retire, nor was there anyone of a suitable age who was particularly marked out for the office, at any rate amongst the painters. Younger members were growing restless over the agitations outside the Academy at its supposed shortcomings.

One of the younger men, Dicksee, President himself in later years, came to see my father to ask his opinion about Sargent for the Presidency. Would my father be one of the sponsors? Fildes was not convinced of Sargent's suitability, but he could not think of any better candidate amongst the painters, and agreed to join with a few other senior men who were being asked to sign a letter to Sargent. But the letter was not sent. Doubts arose whether Sargent would accept. Sargent's interest had never been bound up with the Academy. Three months afterwards, the letter still being with Dicksee, my father wrote withdrawing his signature. By then he had made up his mind that the next President ought to be, not a painter, but the architect Aston Webb.

It will be remembered that Maurice Webb, Aston Webb's elder son, had been painted by my father early in the War. He had come through safely with a D.S.O. Philip, his brother, my brother Geoffrey's friend, had been killed on the Somme. When Armistice Day came my father wrote to Aston Webb. "Geoffrey tells me you are very wishful that I should paint a posthumous portrait of Phil as a companion to Maurice's, but only on my usual business terms. I will do it with very great pleasure and satisfaction, only you must permit me to strike out the business proviso for I should not like anything of that kind to come into my relations with

poor, dear Phil, nor would my family, under the circumstances of his friendship with us and his pathetic end. This
is 'Peace Day'. Let me mark it in my own way, as one of
deliverance from peril and disaster, by a thanks offering in
memory of Phil who did his best to help the Great Cause?"

A change in the Presidency and a more vigorous opposition to the Academy's would-be Chantrey Fund despoilers
were very much in Fildes' way of thought, but there was a
third proposal afoot to which he was very much opposed,
and the three were difficult to disentangle. In addition to
an eighty-years-old President there were a number of
Academicians of seventy-five years and upwards who were
blocking the way of promotion for the Associates, and the
proposal was that all Academicians, on reaching the age of
seventy-five, should automatically pass into a new grade of
Senior Academician and be lopped of some of their privi-
leges. Without this lopping, the mere creation of a new
grade would not have opened the door to promotion. My
father had reached the danger age, and the proposal filled
him with indignation. He could not see that the hastening
of promotion was desirable. Those of the elder members
who did see the desirability and were prepared to perform
hara-kiri by voting for the proposal were, in his opinion,
traitors to their class.

The whole unhappy situation unfolded itself in stages
after Armistice Day. Woods, who was on the Council at the
time, recorded on the 19th of November that "the President
made a painful scene by announcing that he would resign at
the General Assembly on the 26th. He spoke bitterly, that
he felt that he was not wanted here any more." At the General
Assembly Fildes spoke strongly against the Senior Academicians scheme. It was carried however. But though it was
carried there were some amendments and the loss of privi-
leges was modified. Fildes made a good point that if the
scheme were operated in the form as drafted some 20 to 25
new Academicians would have to be elected within the
next two years "which unprejudiced minds will think a
decided calamity". The Assembly saw the force of that, and
the scheme was amended to operate in stages whereby not
more than five Senior Academicians would be created in any

one year, and Fildes won three years' reprieve for himself on that amendment.

At the same General Assembly Poynter made his formal announcement of not standing again for the Presidency. The announcement took many members by surprise and it fell to my father, on the spur of the moment, to propose the Academy's thanks to him for his past services. "And he did it very well" was my uncle's comment.

There were several gatherings, informal and formal, during December to consider the question of the next President. At one meeting my father spoke against the next President being a painter and won approval of that. At the next meeting he formally proposed Aston Webb who was in the chair. To my father's surprise, Webb evinced hesitation, and the meeting decided to postpone the election.

XIX

THE END OF MANY THINGS

1919-1921

My father's views about the Presidency prevailed and Aston
Webb was chosen. He wrote my father on the 21st of
January 1919:

> My dear Fildes,
> I cannot hope in any way to express to you what I
> feel in respect of your action respecting a new President
> of the Royal Academy, I know the result is largely
> owing to you, and though, as you know, I am greatly
> doubtful as to my adequacy for so important a position,
> being in for it, however, I intend to do my best to justify
> the selection. I know that I may look to you for guidance
> and advice as difficulties arise, as they surely will, and I
> shall not fail to avail myself of it. When I think of my
> predecessors in the chair I am naturally overwhelmed,
> but I shall look forward to seeing you before long and
> talking over with you what sort of line I propose to take....
> Yours gratefully and sincerely,
> Aston Webb.

Poynter wanted to remain on the Council. He had been
discussing with my father some means of bringing that
about. Could he be given a permanent seat on it in recognition of his long service as President? My father had to
point to the recent decision about Academicians becoming
Senior Academicians and thus ineligible for any office, after

the age of seventy-five. Before any solution could be found, Poynter fell ill and in July died.

Woods could now return to Venice after an absence of two and a half years. My father had been right in predicting that he would never bring himself to make another home. It might have been different had there been a question of my parents joining with him as at the *Casetta Rocca*, but there was no such question; my father was unlikely to work any more in Venice, and as for Italian holidays both he and my mother were set upon Lenno. And so on his return to Venice my uncle went into furnished rooms on the Zattere, two doors away from the Calcina. There he settled down to a mode of living which was a Venetian equivalent of rooms in Bury Street, St. James's.

His letters told of great changes. The old circle of friends had almost disappeared; Horatio Brown, Mrs. Eden, the Montalbas ("getting very old now") and Blaas seemed to be all of those who remained. In order to start working again in the Studio, where all the furniture from the *Casetta Rocca* had been stored, there had to be clearances. He sold most of the *Casetta Rocca* furniture on quite good terms. Florian's, in the Piazza, and Bauer's had lost their attraction. He took his meals at the Calcina. There was running through the letters a feeling that he was not unhappy and not uncomfortable, which was the main thing my parents wanted to know.

With the sale of his furniture, and money from his shares in *The Graphic*, which had succumbed to a "take-over bid", and a windfall from some shipping shares, my uncle found himself with quite an amount of money lying idle until my father got on his tracks. "It is absurd", wrote my father, "that you should be keeping a 'rather large balance' in your current account earning nothing . . . you ought certainly to get some 7½% or 8% quite sound and safe thing. . . . Money is much wanted by Companies and they seem to be very anxious to get it even by paying high prices for it. . . . Have you conned over the new levy of Income Tax and how it affects you?—Is there any one in Venice who can explain the difference of the terms of levying, and the exemptions you are entitled to?"

This was too much for Uncle Harry, and he handed over the money to my father to invest for him.

Fildes had six works on show at the Academy in 1920. One of them was a portrait of his old friend, Henry Dickens, K.C., the Common Serjeant, as good a man's portrait as he ever painted.

Woods came over for the opening but soon returned. He now left his furnished rooms and moved into the Calcina permanently. "Life at the Calcina seems to suit me", he wrote. He had given up his gondola. "Ernesto was obliged to accept permanent service at our Consulate. The pay is good. He will still have time to attend to business for me. He lives close to the studio. I don't want a gondola for some time, and then I know a respectable man."

On hearing from my father that Marcus Stone was seriously ill, my uncle wrote "It must be a deal of comfort to have you so near, because after all, you have been his best friend". Marcus Stone rallied temporarily, and my father wrote back, "I saw Stone yesterday, who recognized me".

In the Academy of 1921 Fildes had been greatly struck by the work of one of the younger Associates—A. J. Munnings—and he wrote telling him so. Munnings replied:

May 4th, 1921.

Dear Sir Luke,

Many thanks for your very kind letter, and I am more than glad that you liked my pictures. I will remember what you tell me.

Masefield once wrote the following into one of his books which he gave to me—

> "Man with his burning soul
> Hath but an hour to breath
> To build a ship of Truth
> On which his soul may sail.
> Sail on the sea of Death,
> For Death takes toll
> of Beauty, Courage, Youth,
> Of all but Truth!"

Very beautiful this is, don't you think so?

With many thanks I am, dear Sir Luke,
Yours sincerely,
A. J. Munnings.

The time had come when new influences had been finding
a way into the Academy which to my father seemed to bear
not any truth to Nature, and they had made their presence
felt that year by a wholesale rejection of many of the best-
known Outsiders, men and women who had been before
the Public as artists for many years. Polemics over Art were
not yet the commonplace they have since become and this
outburst of "Modernism" on the Council's part created
something of a shock both within the Institution and outside.
An exhibition of the rejected works was organized to be held
in the Guildhall Art Gallery, and my father, whose sympathies with them were well known, was asked by the rejected
artists to be the chief "hanger". He accepted. Woods who
had again been in London for the opening of the Academy
was eager on his return to Venice to have the latest news
about this English version of the *Salon des Refusés*. My
father wrote him on the 25th of July, "I heard that David
Murray intended at a General Assembly raising the question
of the disloyalty of certain members to the Institution re the
Guildhall Exhibition, but I never heard anything further
of it. He perhaps thought better of it—to my disappointment. I believe the exhibition was a very considerable
success. Some 36,000 people visited it.... I never went again
after I had finished the hanging, but I was told it looked
first rate—as *The Times* said, jeeringly, 'like an ordinary
Academy Exhibition'. I got a letter signed by 36 of the
exhibitors on the varnishing day expressing their thanks
and gratification. As I have not seen any of the R.A.
members I do not know their opinion."

At the beginning of September my parents went to
Champex in Switzerland. My wife and I, and my father-in-
law, Goscombe John, R.A., were there, and, it was on that
holiday that the knowledge was borne in on me that my
father, whom I had been seeing only at intervals in recent
years, was physically ageing. He was a month off being
seventy-eight, and one day as we were walking up a

mountain path, I carrying his sketching materials, he told me that ever since his serious illness before the war he had only one really serviceable lung.

After a fortnight my parents moved on to Lenno, and at Lenno my father did more sketching. In a letter to Woods in Venice he wrote, "I am sure you would greatly enjoy this place and hotel. . . . There are most beautiful subjects for you if you cared to come here to work. I have never seen a more beautiful place, and there are no end of things to do almost at the door."

Five days later, on the 5th of October, Woods joined them—"I find Lenno full of beautiful subjects", he wrote in his diary, "that I should like to do". He was with them a week and then left them and went back to Venice, from where he wrote: "It was 1 o'c a.m. when I arrived at the Calcina in moonlight. The fair Fiorentina Emily had waited up for me. To-day I realize to the full the pleasure it has been to see you both so well at Lenno, and in such sympathetic company. I had never hoped to see the place, still less Bellagio etc. . . . Love to you both."

Two weeks later my parents, still at Lenno, received a telegram from Horatio Brown: "*Woods gravissimo prego venire subito Brown Hotel Calcina.*"

Some notes my father made at the time as closing entries in Uncle Harry's diary tell the rest:

October 28th. We hastily put a few things together, and in ½ an hour we were speeding to Como in a motor launch we had hired. . . . Brown met us at Venice and then told us Harry was dead and was when he telegraphed. He was then lying at the Hospital SS Giovanni e Paolo.

It seems that Woods went to the Ducal Palace and worked on his picture there during the morning the 27th, and at his usual lunch time he went to his studio for it and his gondolier left him there, instructed by Woods to call for him as usual about 4 to be taken in the gondola to the Calcina Hotel.

The gondolier did call and found Harry stretched on the floor on his back by his easel (where he apparently had been working) dead.

I heard afterwards that death must have come to him instantaneously, for he held his palette in one hand and in the other hand his paintbrush.

Today, Oct. 29th (a Saturday) was so bewilderingly occupied it is quite impossible to say in what order the different things occurred. And I may here say that but for Brown, or some other equally devoted and kind friend, what was done could not have been done at all. After innumerable visits to the different departments and officials, who ceased at noon until Monday, we succeeded in getting permission to bury, selected and purchased a grave in perpetuity, arranged for all funeral notices, subsequent interment and securing services of chaplain. In the afternoon the Consul broke the seals he had placed on the Studio and the room at the hotel Harry had occupied.

Monday, October 31. A Memorial Service was held in the English Church, San Vio, prior to the funeral in Cemetery. Archdeacon Sissons officiated. There was a very fair attendance considering the circumstances, the absence of so many of the English residents and the brief notice given of the Ceremony. The Accademia of Belle Arte—of which Woods was an Hon. Member—sent a representative. . . . The R.A. telegraphed that a wreath should be placed on the grave. He was buried in the Protestant Cemetery.

My parents were still in Venice, at the Hotel Regina, nine days later when my father wrote me a long letter:

It was our intention to leave here this morning. Everything packed, bills paid last night and good-bye said, but Mama developed so bad a cold, and she felt so unwell, we decided not to travel under those circumstances. . . . I hope we shall be able to make a start tomorrow morning for Como. Our programme is to sleep at Como . . . and the following day we shall take an early boat for Lenno. . . . We will pack and leave next morning for Como, catch the St. Gotthard train . . . on to Calais and London where we hope to arrive some time in the late evening of Sunday.

Let it be remembered at this point that my parents were seventy-eight and seventy years old and had been through a most harrowing experience without any support from any of us, and indeed had discouraged any of us going to help them. My father's letter went on:

I trust all will go well. At present we are pretty miserable having no clothes (and those summer ones) but those we stand up in. . . . We hadn't time to collect or pack anything when we rushed from Lenno! . . .

What has been done in Venice is a long story. . . . Everything worth taking to England has been packed, sealed by the authorities and delivered to the hands of Forwarding Agents, valued and insured. . . . There has been a tremendous lot of things to destroy and give away—8 easels, which I have presented to the Accademia Reale. And we have told Ernesto and Nina, his servants when he had a house, and old Pasca (probably five and twenty years younger than I), the caretaker of his Studio, that they will receive in time sums of money Uncle Harry wished them to have.

How it has all been got through nobody will ever know. I scarcely know, myself. The difficulties of not knowing the language (beyond asking for something to eat) have been enormous, and the going to and fro, trudging on my feet all day long—I am not so young as I was!—have completely tired me out. . . . I marvel how it is the authorities have permitted me to take possession of everything, not having a scrap to shew of any right. . . . It is better that no one came out but ourselves. You know all about poor Uncle Harry's end through your mother's letters.

Your affectionate

Day.

XX

"HORS CONCOURS"
1922-1927

My parents still kept in touch with Venice through a random correspondence with Horatio Brown, and when the latter came to England he called at Melbury Road and there were talks about old times. But my father always lived in the present and it was the gradual supplanting of Victorian Art by Modernism—the then Modernism of forty years ago—which was uppermost in his thoughts. He was quick to suspect any sign of it.

When, for example, he heard that *The Doctor* had been removed from the walls of the Tate and "stuck in a cellar", he was convinced that it was intended as an act of condemnation of the period in which the picture had been painted. He would not admit that possibly it was one of those situations when a Gallery, because it owns more works than it has room to show, has to keep them alternating between light and darkness. An explanation of that kind made things only worse. Collectors of works of art—and he drew no distinction between a public gallery and a private owner—ought not to hoard their possessions in cellars. If they could not let them be seen they had better part with them to people who could. I had long been aware of my father's views on that subject. Years before, I had gone with him and my mother to the house of a well-known collector of the Barbizon School. After tea the proud owner had taken us round the house, showing us masterpieces by Diaz, Rousseau, Corot, Daubigny and Harpignies, and then, remarking that those were not all, had led the way down the kitchen stairs to a storeroom. And in that storeroom, stacked on the floor four deep, their faces turned to the wall, were as many masterpieces as we had been admiring upstairs.

As we walked away from the house my father had exclaimed, "The man's a barbarian!"

After the affair of *The Doctor* came the case of Lady Butler. The help he had given to the Guildhall *Salon des Refusés* had shown my father's sympathies with old Academy exhibitors, and now in April, 1924, the case of Lady Butler called forth a formal—and even stern—letter to the President of the Royal Academy (no "My dear Webb"):

Dear Sir Aston,

Fifty years ago in 1874—Elizabeth Thompson—now Lady Butler—and myself contributed, she the *Roll Call* and I the *Casual Ward*, to the R.A.

With her it was the precursor of many notable works which achieved great fame for her, and, incidentally, great profit to the R.A.

We have felt a kind of artistic fellowship ever since, so that I could not help feeling grieved today to hear her contribution this year had not been hung. . . . It occurs to me that it would be gracious of the R.A. to give a compassionate consideration to old exhibitors who have done much for the Institution in the past and to be a little more human—I almost spelled it with an 'e'—in their relations with them.

However, my father's intervention was too late. Lady Butler wrote:

Dear Sir Luke Fildes,

I had no idea that our Royal Academy had laid aside its dignified conservatism to such an extent, or I would have been better prepared for such disregard for my work as it has shown. But, surely, it is not going to give in entirely to a passing phase like this? You will smile at my assurance that a few words from your President of sympathy and genuine regret for the "snub" that has hurt me so much would act as balm. As to sending any works in the future to my fondly remembered R.A.—well! we shall see.

With kind remembrances,
Sincerely yrs.
Elizth. Butler.

He replied that it was no "passing phase" which was affecting the Academy. The compulsory retirement of a batch of Senior Academicians [a step he never forgave!] had led to many vacancies being filled by young artists "who have different ideas on art matters to us. . . . I think all the present generation of artists will have to pass away, and probably the next, before any change of mind and of heart will again be restored."

Less than a week later the Academy Banquet took place. When the party broke up, Aston Webb offered my father, Llewellyn and another colleague, Melton Fisher, a lift home. At the top of Queen's Gate they were run into by another car, and all four of them and the chauffeur were badly hurt. My father and Aston Webb, who were seated together at the back of the car bore the chief brunt. They were knocked together so hard that each had his pelvis broken. Another member of the Academy, also making for Kensington from the Banquet—indeed he lived in Melbury Road—came upon the scene, waited until my father and the others were put safely in an ambulance, and then proceeded on his way, rang the bell of No. 11—midnight by now had struck—and told the family what had happened.

Six months previously, on the 18th of October, 1923, my father had celebrated his eightieth birthday. He was at Lenno at the time and he had written me "Curiously, since the 18th I have begun to fancy I must be getting aged. It did not occur to me before that I was!" "Getting aged" or not, he bore the shock of the car accident supremely well. In the shortest possible time he insisted on the hospital sending him home, and once again the nursery, with the big bay window opening over the garden, became his sickroom.

The time came when my father was well enough to go

out of doors, and the question was what form should the outing take. He decided he would like to be driven by my brother Denis round Richmond Park, just to see whether the accident had affected his nerve for motoring. He found it hadn't and he enjoyed the trip.

Among the letters he had received after the accident was one from Philip Connard. Though a younger member of the Academy, Connard was not an anti-Victorian. After condoling with my father on the accident he went on: "I tried to see you on Varnishing Day to tell you how much I admired your two portrait heads, but didn't get an opportunity to do so. Your period of painting is more lasting and better than ours I think is what I wanted to tell you."

At the end of that year, 1924, Aston Webb ceased to be President, having become a Senior Academician through age and therefore disqualified from holding office. He was succeeded by Frank Dicksee. My father happened to be at the Academy one evening with the new President when the Academy Club was due to be dining across the road at Prince's Restaurant with Dicksee in the Chair. My father had not intended going to the dinner, and he was not dressed for dining out, but Dicksee prevailed on him to go just as he was, his first appearance in public after recovering from his motor accident. I, who was the guest that evening of my father-in-law, Goscombe John, had not expected to see my father. I was surprised to find him seated at Dicksee's right hand. After dinner there were calls for him to speak, and that was one of the two occasions I ever heard him speak in public. Entirely impromptu he made exactly the kind of speech the occasion needed, and he was loudly applauded. I saw him that evening in the role of the Grand Old Man of the Royal Academy, and I sensed that everybody felt the same. Whatever thoughts still rankled in him over his enforced elevation as a Senior Academician, whatever clash of ideologies there were between him and the younger men in his audience, not a word was spoken about them.

He had three portraits in the 1925 Academy, of which the principal was L. S. Amery, the Colonial Secretary. In the 1926 Academy—the last he would live to see—he had five. It happened that his work that year received more notice in the Press than, with changing fashions it had lately been receiving. There is a story of him about that time cleaning his palette and brushes at the end of a day's work—the studio-man had not been replaced after Frederick Spikesman's death—and remarking "I have been painting for more than fifty years. If I had another fifty, I might do something worth looking at!" Remarks of that kind were not intended to be taken literally, but they did bear witness to his ever present seeking after self-improvement. There is —as I have said before—a "head" he had been working on within a fortnight of his death, which bear signs of a new technique.

He was greatly blessed in never losing his ability to express himself in paint, for had that ability left him there were no hobbies he could have fallen back upon. He had never, as I remember, been much of a reader except of *The Times* every evening and then by preference the reports of home and foreign politics. One of his sitters—of a somewhat "intense" cast of mind—once tried unsuccessfully to interest him in George Meredith. My mother tried him with *Bleak House* when he was recovering from one of his attacks of bronchitis—he startled her with this repudiation of the past, "Fanny, I have come to the conclusion that Dickens bores me". William de Morgan he liked and, in lighter vein, Henry Harland.

The family now was less scattered than at any time since the war. Denis, with a bride from Sydney, had returned after two years' attachment to the Australian Navy. Geoffrey, too, was married and in London. My wife and I were living in London after six years in the industrial north. Paul and Kitty had always been Londoners. But I cannot truthfully put forward my father as a patriarch, even with eight grand-children as by that time the number had become. At Melbury Road, where he and my mother and my sister Dorothy went on living, with five servants still to look after them, he led an increasingly quiet life. I recall this, not unhappily but rather the reverse, as showing that my father on his side was content.

In September of the previous year he and my mother had been to Lenno again. Now, in 1926, they did not go abroad. Geoffrey and his wife, Charity, had taken the Rectory at Buscot for the summer holiday—Buscot on the Upper River, close to William Morris' Kelmscott and to Fairford with its painted glass—and on a visit to them my father, within a month of becoming eighty-three years old, was out on the river doing things he used to do when he was fifty years younger. One morning he did not appear at breakfast. A search was made and he was seen coming down stream in a punt, having been for an early outing on the river by himself. There is some uncertainty whether it was a paddle or punt pole he was using; either way, it was a notable performance.

The New Year opened quietly. My father went to the Academy to hear the President give the customary Presidential lecture; and he wrote to him:

> My dear Dicksee,
>
> I had the pleasure last night to listen to your address on Flemish Art—re the R.A. Show—and it gratified me much to hear your opinion, not only admirably expressed but marked with an authority and assurance that should characterize the utterances of a President of the R.A. The address revived in me somewhat the memories and traditions of past times, and I congratulate you.

Dicksee wrote back:

> Jan. 5th 1927.
>
> My dear Fildes,
>
> Very many thanks for your kind words. I am very pleased that you liked my little address, and I think it good-natured of you to tell me so.
>
> It is not the first time that you have given me encouragement. I remember when I first found myself in the Chair of the R.A. Dinner, and after my first speech I caught your eye, and a little gesture of congratulation from you gave me confidence and helped me for the rest of the evening. Again my thanks.
>
> Yrs. always sincerely,
> Frank Dicksee.

It would be a lapse into sentimentality, for which there is no warrant, to wonder if my father ever regretted not having been President. He was too much of a realist.

Ever since his serious illness before the war he had been subject to attacks of bronchitis in winter time, and it was no surprise that he was now attacked again. This time, the attack was more than he could battle against. He died on Sunday, the 27th of February. My mother was not able to be with him in his last illness. By chance she had been taken ill on the same day as he. She knew when he died, but she was hardly well enough to grasp the full meaning of the knowledge. She survived him by six weeks almost to the hour, dying on Palm Sunday.

At the Academy that summer two portraits by him and a still-life by her, appeared posthumously. Exactly fifty years had gone by since my mother first exhibited at the Academy, and exactly sixty years since my father did.

It was a fitting curtain for the end of a great Victorian and of the wife to whom he owed more, perhaps, than he ever realized.

EPILOGUE

When my father, forty years ago, was deploring with his comrade-in art, Lady Butler, Victorian painting's decline in favour, he apparently looked for a change of mind and of heart, as he put it, just about this time when I am finishing my book. However, the signs of a revival of appreciation are not very apparent: occasionally a lecture at the V. and A.; an exhibition in Bond Street; an article in the Press— though writers tend to be non-commital ("Victorian Art enforces a grudging admiration", "it would be churlish to resist the call of Victorian Art", "Victorian Art is far from being contemptible").

As for what the public thinks, whose opinion is what really matters, all is confusion. The pre-eminently understandable Victorian painting has been held out to them as something not to be taken seriously, and nothing has been offered them that they can understand. Such encouragement as the sponsors of Modernism profess to draw from the large numbers of visitors who have flocked to exhibitions at the Tate, is illusory; even larger numbers have flocked to the National Gallery, so that one year Picasso is the public's man, and the next year Leonardo Da Vinci. But, of course, a turnstile criterion is not reliable; no account can be kept of those visitors who go out of a love of Art, and of those who go out of mere curiosity.

Many members of the public today would benefit from knowing more about Victorian painting. And so that they may rid their minds of prejudice against it, let them remember that the Victorians were a highly civilized people, who were endowed with much sense and sensibility, and who thought they were living in one of the great periods of British painting. The notion may then occur to the seeker after truth that the opinions of Victorians on matters of Art were just as likely to be as right as anybody's since. And on that notion I will end.

INDEX

240 A VICTORIAN PAINTER